D1758777

13 MAY 2025

WITHDRAWN

The Society for Asian and Comparative Philosophy
Monograph Series was started in 1974. Works are
published in the series that deal with any area of Asian
philosophy, or any other field of philosophy examined
from a comparative perspective. The aim of the series
is to make available scholarly works that exceed article
length, but may be too specialized for the general
reading public, and to make these works available
in inexpensive editions without sacrificing the
orthography of non-Western languages.

MONOGRAPH NO. 23 | Society for Asian and Comparative Philosophy

Compassion and Moral Guidance

Steve Bein

UNIVERSITY OF HAWAI'I PRESS | HONOLULU

© 2013 University of Hawai'i Press
All rights reserved
Printed in the United States of America
18 17 16 15 14 13   6 5 4 3 2 1

Library of Congress Cataloging-in-Publication Data
Bein, Steve, author.
Compassion and moral guidance / Steve Bein.
    pages cm — (Monograph series / Society for Asian
and Comparative Philosophy; no. 23)
Includes bibliographical references and index.
ISBN 978-0-8248-3641-2 (hardcover : alk. paper)
    1. Compassion. 2. Ethics, Comparative. 3. Self
(Philosophy) I. Title. II. Series: Monograph ... of the
Society for Asian and Comparative Philosophy; no. 23.
BJ1475.B45   2013
177'.7 — dc23   2012025445

University of Hawai'i Press books are printed on acid-
free paper and meet the guidelines for permanence
and durability of the Council on Library Resources.

Designed by April Leidig
Printed by Integrated Book Technology Inc.

To Donald and Dorothy Bein,
who taught me compassion by living it.

CONTENTS

Abbreviations of Works Cited ix

Introduction xi

CHAPTER ONE
What Is Compassion, and What Is It Not? 1

CHAPTER TWO
What Is the *Com-* of Compassion? 50

CHAPTER THREE
Defining Compassion 87

CHAPTER FOUR
Objections to an Ethic of Compassion 132

CHAPTER FIVE
Compassion in Action 151

Notes 183

Literature Cited 207

Index 219

ABBREVIATIONS OF WORKS CITED

AE   Nygren, *Agape and Eros*

Ak.   Kant, *Akademie-Ausgabe*

BCV   Śāntideva, *The Bodhicaryāvātāra*

DMW   Prejean, *Dead Man Walking*

DZZ   Dōgen, *Dōgen Zenji Zenshū*

E   Rousseau, *Emile*

LY   Confucius, *The Analects (Lun Yü)*, trans. D. C. Lau

MDS (1–4) Dōgen, *Master Dōgen's Shōbōgenzō* (vols. 1–4)

NE   Aristotle, *Nichomachean Ethics*

NS   Scheler, *The Nature of Sympathy*

R   Aristotle, *Rhetoric*

SZ   Ejō, *Shōbōgenzō Zuimonki*

TTC   Hall and Ames, *Thinking Through Confucius*

THN   Hume, *Treatise of Human Nature*

TSZ   Nietzsche, *Thus Spoke Zarathustra*

"COMPASSION" IS A WORD we use frequently in everyday conversation, but it is rarely used with anything close to philosophical precision. Indeed, one could go so far as to say we have lost the meaning of the word. As we generally use it, "compassion" appears in similar contexts with words such as "empathy," "sympathy," and "love" and may even be equated with one or more of these. *Roget's Thesaurus* lists "compassion" as having each of the following distinct connotations: "sensitivity," "philanthropy," "pity," "mercy," "forgivingness," "consideration," "leniency," "unselfishness," and "kindness." Other lexicons include "concern" and "care" as synonyms. Although at times compassion may closely resemble any one of these, it is not identical to any of them. A precise understanding of the word, if ever we had one, has faded into obscurity.

When I say "we," I include myself in two camps. One is the camp of philosophers; the other is that of North Americans, including everyone who is swayed by the cultural and linguistic influences that predominate here. I would not presume to suggest that the word is misused globally, but at least where I live, "compassion" is almost invariably used to mean "commiseration" (or else to mean nothing at all: The word is now used so loosely that a politician can describe his nakedly self-serving aggression as "compassionate conservatism" without being laughed out of office, and in fact without risk of being denied the highest political aspirations). I contend that it is a mistake to equate compassion with commiseration, and that one important difference between the two is that the former can serve as a foundation for ethical judgment, while the latter is not sufficiently sturdy to do so. This is admittedly an unorthodox usage of the word "compassion," but its unorthodoxy is the very point of this book. My goal here is to flesh out what compassion really means (as opposed to how we conventionally speak of it) and to show its application in moral reasoning.

I shall risk a short defense of my unorthodoxy before moving on. Imagine a brand of utilitarianism that expressed no concern for promoting overall happiness and instead focused solely on minimizing overall suffering. (In utilitarian terms, the concern would be only with reducing disutility and never with maximizing utility.) This theory guarantees happiness to no one; in fact, no one's happiness will even be a goal to strive for. The only goal is to alleviate suffering. Some may argue that a world without suffering is a happy world, and indeed such a world would surely be happier than this one, but a life without suffering is not yet a happy life. It is an apathetic life, neither miserable nor satisfied.

Given two versions of utilitarianism, one like I have just described and one that seeks not only to minimize suffering but also to actually promote our satisfaction (i.e., the traditional utilitarian method), the latter is arguably the stronger theory, for it promotes happy lives while the former only promotes apathetic ones. Analogously, commiseration concerns itself solely with the misery of the other, and as such the ethics of commiseration would ultimately prove to be insufficient. If compassion is understood to concern not only feelings of suffering but also of satisfaction, then the ethics of compassion will not fall short on this count. This is, as promised, only a brief defense of my unorthodox use of "compassion," but more shall be said in its defense as the book progresses.

One of the first observations to make in examining the moral role of compassion is its prevalence in the ethics of some cultures and its lack of prominence in others. Buddhism takes compassion—or, more precisely, wise compassion—as its ethical cornerstone, and as I will argue later, compassion is vitally important to Confucian and Daoist ethics as well. On the other hand, when we examine the ethics of Kant, Bentham, Mill, Aristotle, and most of their philosophical successors, we see that compassion plays almost no role at all. Indeed, Kant and Aristotle would arguably describe compassion as an impediment to good moral reasoning.

The observation here is not a reductionistic comparison of East and West, whatever those might mean; the matter is more complex than that. Indeed, "love thy neighbor as thyself" is about as succinct a mandate for compassion as one could ask for, and Christianity heavily influenced all of the so-called

Western philosophers mentioned before, with the lone exception of Aristotle. What is interesting to observe is that, *despite* his Christianity, Kant allowed compassion to play no role at all in his ethics. Despite the Christian culture in which they found themselves, neither Bentham nor Mill addressed compassion in any serious way, preferring impartiality instead (which is in many ways compassion's opposite). It is hardly original to point out the Old Testament's emphasis on justice, both mortal and divine, as opposed to the New Testament's emphasis on compassion. (I do not claim that compassion is absent from the Old Testament, nor that justice is absent from the New, but only that there is a difference in emphasis.) What is interesting is that, given the choice between justice and compassion, the most influential philosophers in so-called Western history preferred justice.

Aristotle, Kant, and the classical utilitarians have had the greatest influence on modern ethical theory, and those with less influence—though still luminary thinkers in the history of philosophy—have little more to add to the subject. David Hume and Adam Smith both wrote on sympathy, but sympathy is no more synonymous with compassion than pity is. Spinoza is in agreement with Kant regarding compassion's uselessness. Nietzsche, like Aristotle, writes on pity, but only vitriolically, and where he does describe compassion, it is scarcely recognizable as such. If compassion has not received the attention of those who serve as the pillars of the European and Anglo-American philosophical traditions, one might well expect that those who stand in their shadows would also pay it little heed.

And so we find that, as expected, analytic philosophers today tend not to use the word "compassion" with philosophical precision, for only the tiniest fraction of them pay it any attention at all. And, some may argue, they ought not to pay it much mind, for at least insofar as we commonly think of it, compassion seems given to imprecision. It seems to pull people in different directions and thus to lack the sort of consistency that so many philosophers prefer. For example, one might ask what guidance compassion can give on an ethical problem such as abortion. If I am opposed to legalized abortion, I might explain my position in terms of my compassion for the unborn and also my compassion for the women bearing them, since I do not want these potential mothers to have to live with the guilt of having brought about the death of an innocent fetus. This is likely to sound paternalistic to those who favor legalized abortion, but why should compassion not be paternalistic? Good fathers do have compassion for their children, after all.

On the other hand, if I am in favor of legalized abortion, I might also explain my position in terms of compassion for the unborn and for the women bearing them. Compassion for women faced with a difficult choice demands that I not seek to constrain their already limited options. Compassion for the unborn demands that I consider what it might be like to live as an unwanted child. The statistics concerning the incidence of psychological disorder and criminal recidivism among adopted children are well known; compassion will bid me to recognize the alternative of adoption as less than ideal. To my opponents, this too may well sound paternalistic, but again, what reason is there to believe that compassion is not paternalistic?

Compassion stands in no better stead with regard to many of the other perennial issues in ethics. For whom am I to show more compassion: the animals injected with experimental toxins or the human beings whose cancer goes into remission after the same toxins are administered as chemotherapy? The same question applies to two people applying to law school, one who gets in and one who does not, based in part on which boxes were checked under "race/ethnicity" on their applications. These cases are the easy ones. It is hard even to figure out what compassion means with regard to patients like Nancy Cruzan, Karen Ann Quinlan, or Terri Schiavo. Is it more compassionate to help them live or to help them die? Contemporary philosophers have written many pages on the issues of physician-assisted suicide, affirmative action, and the use of animals in medical research. If compassion cannot offer a definitive solution to problems like these, there seems to be little reason to take it seriously.

But all of this assumes that compassion is inherently vague. It might be noted that, at least in everyday conversation, "justice" is similarly vague, and that if we want to know whether extubating a patient in a persistent vegetative state is just or unjust, we need to have a more precise sense of what those words mean. Of course, the philosophers who have made the concept of justice their stock in trade are too many to list, and as a result we have any number of theories of justice to fall back on in determining the justice or injustice of physician-assisted suicide, affirmative action, and all the rest. I contend that compassion is worthy of the same attention.

In common parlance, compassion is roughly understood to be an awareness of the suffering of another coupled with the desire for that suffering's cessation. It is generally understood to be a commendable trait, Kant and Spinoza notwithstanding. But beyond this, the term "compassion" is largely lacking in philosophical precision. If it is a moral excellence, in what way does it excel? If it is nothing but sharing in suffering, does this not run against the basic utilitarian intuition that less suffering is better? (This is the thrust of both Spinoza's and Kant's objections.) We have an aphorism that suggests otherwise: "A sorrow shared is a sorrow halved; a joy shared is a joy doubled." But does such an intuition do any philosophical work for us? That is, is our intuitive sense of compassion capable of providing ethical guidance? If so, what sort of guidance can it provide? What would an ethic of compassion be like?

The following chapters constitute an attempt to answer these questions. Their purpose is to provide a precise and robust philosophical account of compassion, one that does ethical work for us, and to describe how compassion can provide moral guidance—how, in short, the ethics of compassion might work. In pursuit of this goal, I necessarily diverge from Kant and Spinoza, Hume and Smith, Aristotle and Scheler and look elsewhere for a robust account of compassion. Specifically, I examine the role compassion plays in the Buddhist, Confucian, and Daoist traditions. By comparing and combining these diverse approaches to compassion and to the many traits associated with it, I seek to flesh out an account of compassion that is capable of providing useful moral guidance and to give a sense of what form this guidance will take.

Chapter 1 is an analysis of pity, love, sympathy, and other traits associated with compassion as they appear in the works of Scheler, Aristotle, Aquinas and Augustine, Hume, Rousseau, and Nietzsche. I also take up analyses of compassion offered by several contemporary philosophers, including Robert Solomon and Martha Nussbaum. In each case I argue that compassion is not best thought of as the philosopher in question thinks of it, though in each case I seek to draw out some helpful insights on what compassion is and how it works.

In chapter 2, I examine compassion as developed by selected Buddhist thinkers, as well as the role of compassion in classical Confucianism and Lao-Zhuang Daoism. I argue that compassion is crucially important to all three of these traditions and that the compassion that appears in them is markedly different from everything that was explored in the first chapter. Though compassion receives little attention in contemporary literature on Confucianism and Daoism, I argue that these two traditions each convey a unique sense of compassion, distinct from each other and from the notions of compassion in Early Indian Buddhism and Zen Buddhism. Despite the differences between all of these views, I argue that each of them is grounded in a notion of relational existence that allows compassion to do real ethical work in those traditions.

In chapter 3, I draw upon the analyses of the first two chapters to describe a functional, philosophically precise account of compassion. This account runs against linguistic intuitions (at least in English), for the compassion I have in mind extends to sharing in happiness as well as sharing in suffering. I shall defend this interpretation more than once, but in these introductory pages, let me only point out that the "passion" of compassion finds its root in the Latin *pati* ("to suffer" or "to submit"), but this in turn finds its root in the Greek *paschein,* which is not "to suffer" but "to feel." The unorthodoxy of my account goes further than this, but I shall argue that it is justified.

Chapter 3 also describes compassion's application in moral theory, specifically compassionate virtue ethics, and shows how this theory would provide constructive moral guidance. In the fourth chapter, I address several potential problems with an ethic of compassion and offer solutions to those problems. Together, these two chapters are meant to serve as the theoretical basis for an ethic of compassion.

The fifth and final chapter shows how compassion can be applied to the problems of what contemporary ethicists call "applied ethics." Specifically, I will describe how an ethic of compassion will approach the issues of capital punishment and physician-assisted suicide. This approach can be extended to same-sex marriage, abortion, or any of the other traditional issues of "applied ethics," but in the end an ethic of compassion will move beyond what is typically meant by that term. Because compassion always seeks to be applied, the traditional distinction between "theoretical" and "applied" ethics is rendered meaningless. Moreover, because relationships such as friendship and parenthood are matters of applied compassion, on this view the traditional boundaries of "applied ethics" are radically expanded.

The final goal is a model of ethical reasoning that makes sense of the common intuition that compassion is morally praiseworthy. This model will challenge some highly regarded theories in ethics and political philosophy (Rawlsian justice, for example) and will bear significant similarities with other theories (such as care ethics). The ethic of compassion I describe in the following chapters addresses the Rawlsian and Kantian concern for fairness, the utilitarian concern for satisfactory consequences, and the concern in care ethics for proper treatment of marginalized groups. I suggest that its capacity to do so makes it more than a viable tool for ethical decision making; one might well consider it to be a primary tool in this regard.

CHAPTER ONE

What Is Compassion, and What Is It Not?

Compassion, in a man who lives in accordance with the
guidance of reason, is bad through itself and useless.
—Spinoza, *Ethics*

IN EVERYDAY CONVERSATION, compassion is generally thought of as a
recognition or awareness of the existence of suffering in some other being,
coupled with the desire to alleviate that suffering. This is not a philosophical definition, nor is it particularly instructive from an ethical point of view.
Utilitarianism starts with the belief that suffering ought to be avoided or
alleviated; if we assume one must be aware of suffering in order to avoid or
alleviate it, then any utilitarian ethic would be a compassionate ethic, even
if no utilitarian thinker was interested in the nature of compassion as such.

There are potentially important differences between the lay understanding of compassion and the utilitarian maxim to minimize suffering. For one,
the moment of awareness, explicitly a part of compassion, is only assumed in
utilitarianism. Second, as it is typically spoken of, compassion is confined to
the suffering perceived in others, while utilitarianism does not face this restriction. But surely there is something more ethically significant to compassion, some sense in which it has its own ethical merit. Surely it is more than
a utilitarian intuition, for even those who do not subscribe to utilitarianism
commonly think of compassion as a praiseworthy trait. We hear people say,
"I don't want your pity," but compassion is something we do tend to want
from others. Empathy is something we want out of, say, our psychoanalysts,
and we can go shopping for cards that express sympathy, but as we commonly speak of it, compassion seems to go beyond both of these. Sometimes
people use these words interchangeably, but for many people compassion
holds more weight than the others.

What is it about compassion that sets it apart? As I have characterized it so far, compassion has two parts: It entails a kind of awareness and a kind of wish or desire. This two-part structure already distinguishes compassion from some of the other words associated with it thus far. It is not incoherent, for example, to say to someone, "I sympathize with you, but I don't want to help you." However, it *is* incoherent to say, "I feel compassion for you, but I don't want to help you."[1] Compassion includes a motivation to act in a way that sympathy does not. Similarly, one can love a person without knowing what that person is experiencing, as the parent of an alcoholic child may still love the child without truly understanding what it is to battle a chemical dependency. Compassion seems to demand that one digs deeper than this, so that once again it is incoherent to say, "I have compassion for you, but I really have no idea what you're going through."

Compassion can be further distinguished from other associated terms as a fuller account of it develops, and one way to do this is to address the other terms as they appear in the history of philosophy. There are too many words associated with compassion—and too many philosophers have written on them—for all of them to be considered here. Schopenhauer famously writes of pity, just as Adam Smith famously expounds on sympathy, but I shall not address either of them directly here, nor many other potentially worthy philosophers, though their thoughts may share interesting parallels with the thinkers I do analyze in the pages to follow. I draw upon only a smattering of philosophers whose insights make useful contributions to the conception of compassion I seek to flesh out. Elements of Schopenhauer's account of pity will shine through in my discussion of Nietzsche, and Smith's sympathy might have been used to make some of the same observations I draw upon Hume to make; I set these (and other) philosophers aside in the interest of brevity, and because I take the thinkers I draw upon to be sufficient to do the philosophical work required.

The Survey

THE SCHELERIAN TAXONOMY

Of all the philosophers of the Continental tradition, Max Scheler stands out for his attention to the complex of ideas encompassing compassion. The great problem for Scheler is not compassion itself but rather sympathy, and it is a problem that has both philosophical and scientific import. Scheler's *Nature of Sympathy*[2] is interspersed with passages expressing the need for further scientific research on the phenomenon of sympathy, as well as evaluations of the progress scientists have made so far regarding it and reports of field data concerning sympathetic interactions (NS xlvii, 21, 131, 175, 232). Regarding the ethics of sympathy, he says, "There is a whole range of basic disciplines in philosophy and science for which an elucidation of the relevant phenomena is of the deepest interest" (NS xlvii), and it is this need for further research that contributes to his ultimate rejection of an ethic of sympathy.

Nevertheless, *The Nature of Sympathy* is an attempt to synthesize and advance our understanding of sympathy and its related phenomena and concepts. In the end, "sympathy" serves as an umbrella term that includes almost all of the other items in his taxonomy—which is considerable:

1. Benevolence (*Menschenliebe*)
2. Commiseration/pity (*Mitleid*)
3. Community of feeling (*Miteinanderfühlen*)
4. Compassion (*Erbarmen*)[3]
5. Emotional identification (*Einsgefühl, Einsfühlung*)
6. Emotional infection (*Gefühlsansteckung*)
7. Empathy (*Einfühlung*)
8. Fellow-feeling (*Mitgefühl*)
9. Love (*Liebe*)
10. Rejoicing (*Mitfreude*)

Each of these terms has distinctive philosophical significance for Scheler, and though he explains each one in detail, not all of them are significant in exploring the nature of compassion. The less relevant terms include community of feeling (in which two people experience the selfsame emotional experience), emotional identification (ultimately a form of dysfunction), emotional infection (our capacity to be swept up in the emotions of those around us), and empathy (which is either projective, serving as a data-gathering device akin to Humean sympathy,[4] or aesthetic, as employed by an actor to identify more fully with a character).

I shall gloss over these, noting only that something like empathy is indeed required in order to have compassion. In order to be compassionate one must have some means of detecting the suffering and satisfaction of others. If empathy serves this role, then empathy—or something functionally similar to it—is a necessary part of the cultivation and expression of compassion. Whether it is a part of compassion itself or a complementary trait will be left for now as an open question, but any account of compassion that seeks to make the experiences of suffering and satisfaction in others available to the one who feels compassion must have some feature that serves the function of empathy.

The remaining traits on the list—with the lone exception of love—can all be understood as "grades of sympathy," and indeed Scheler writes of the possibility of "a fully-developed theory of the grades of sympathy, from identification to non-cosmic personal love" (NS 232). He is quite particular here in specifying "non-cosmic personal love" as one of the grades of sympathy, rather than love in general. To love as a general concept he attributes a higher metaphysical status, as well as greater efficacy. At times he sets up what is almost a dichotomy between the domain of sympathy and that of love, especially with regard to ethics. Take as an example his ultimate rejection of the ethics of sympathy: "The ethics of sympathy is also found wanting in that it clashes from the outset with the self-evident law of preference, whereby all positively valuable 'spontaneous' acts are to be preferred to merely 're-active' ones. But all fellow-feeling is essentially a reaction—as love, for instance, is not" (NS 6).

Whether or not this "law of preference" is indeed "self-evident" (a claim that may well be questioned), it is clear that sympathy, including fellow-feeling, is considered to be reactive, while love is contrasted with it as an active force. He reaffirms this elsewhere, asserting that "the ethics of sympathy does not attribute moral value primarily to the *being* and attitudes of persons *as such* . . . but seeks to derive it from the *spectator*" (NS 5). This much is perfectly intuitive: If one feels sympathy in what is determined to be a morally good way, it is one's own feeling of sympathy that is evaluated as good, quite independently of the moral status of the one for whom sympathy is felt.

That said, these reactive traits are worthy of deeper examination. *Mitge-*

fühl, Mitleid, and *Mitfreude* are closely interrelated concepts, connected linguistically by the *Mit-,* or "with" element, in each of them and also connected conceptually in Scheler's exegesis. *Mitgefühl,* or "fellow-feeling," entails both *Mitleid* ("commiseration," translated interchangeably as "pity") and *Mitfreude* ("rejoicing," perhaps better translated as "rejoicing-with"). *Erbarmen,* which is translated into English as "compassion," is defined by Scheler as the strongest form of commiseration (NS 135), and it is therefore also conceptually linked to fellow-feeling. *Erbarmen,* commiseration, and rejoicing-with can be thought of as points along the continuum that is fellow-feeling.

It is particularly important for English speakers to notice the continuity between *Mitleid* and *Mitfreude* because *Mitfreude* is so difficult to render in English as a single word. "Rejoicing" is not bad if one is willing to consider the etymology of "re-joicing," which is to say "feeling joy again" or "duplicating joy"; from here one must only expand this reading to include "duplicating joy with others." In this sense, the relationship of joy to rejoicing is quite similar to the relationship between misery and commiseration. But this is not the everyday sense of rejoicing, and so readers and writers of English must content themselves with such awkward locutions as "rejoicing-with."

The significance of this is more than philological. Of course one should not infer that, because of this absence in English and because of the way the prefix *mit-* functions in German, speakers of German are somehow more capable of sharing joy with others than are speakers of English. However, it is worthy of note that English, which has a larger vocabulary than any other language and which is now hastening the extinction of other languages at a rate unmatched in history, is without a word to describe the sharing of joy. That a language—especially English—readily communicates the sharing of suffering with others but does not have a term for sharing their joy may be indicative of the difficulty of the latter as opposed to the former.

Everyday experience often tells us that rejoicing-with is indeed more difficult than commiseration. If two friends compete for the same job and neither of them is selected, it is easy for each of them to express their condolences to the other. However, if one should be hired, it is often anything but easy for the other to express congratulations for the other's success. That "compassion" in the everyday sense of the word includes suffering but not joy and that our vocabulary is lacking a correlate of "commiseration" to describe sharing happiness is indicative of this difficulty. It is therefore significant that Scheler includes *Mitleid* and *Mitfreude* as two species within a common genus, so to speak. It is not the two species but the genus—namely, fellow-feeling—that receives the bulk of his attention, and it is the genus, not the species, that deserves his readers' attention as well.[5]

Yet in the first sentence of *The Nature of Sympathy*, Scheler insists that "an *ethic* which finds the highest moral value in fellow-feeling, and attempts to derive all morally valuable conduct from this, can never do justice to the facts of moral life" (NS 5). He supports this claim with the conclusions of several arguments. First, because fellow-feeling is outwardly directed—that is, because it is always feeling-*with*, suffering-*with*, rejoicing-*with*—it cannot recognize self-directed imperatives. If there is such a thing as a self-directed ethical imperative (such as the Kantian duties to self, for example), then these must arise out of something other than fellow-feeling, and therefore it is not true that "all morally valuable conduct" is derived from fellow-feeling. Second, fellow-feeling itself is morally neutral until it is assessed otherwise. Scheler reminds us that sadism is heavily dependent upon a certain degree of fellow-feeling: Enjoyment of another's pain is predicated on sensitivity to pain in the other. Therefore fellow-feeling itself is intrinsically neither praiseworthy nor shameful: Some other influence is required to imbue fellow-feeling with moral value.

One of the problems with fellow-feeling—and with sympathy and empathy—is that it is merely responsive, not creative in its own right. To use Scheler's own terminology, these traits are not "spontaneous" but rather "reactive" (NS 6). Fellow-feeling has been shown already to be an important feature of our ethical lives. "But," as Scheler says, "all fellow-feeling is essentially a reaction—as love, for instance, is not" (NS 6).

Here we see a marked difference between love and all the other traits and feelings expressed so far. Later Scheler asserts again that "love is above all a *spontaneous* act" (NS 142). Moreover, Scheler claims that love is not morally neutral, as fellow-feeling was shown to be. Fellow-feeling is required for one to become a good torturer as well as a good lover: Both demand that one be sensitive to the feelings of the other. But according to Scheler, love is unquestionably morally positive in its value:

> A genuine love of humanity does not discriminate between fellow-countrymen and foreigners, the virtuous and the criminal, the racially superior and inferior, the cultured and the uncouth or between good and bad generally. Like fellow-feeling, it embraces *all* men, simply because they are men. . . . This, however, does not alter the fact that fellow-feeling . . . differs from love of humanity, since the latter, like all forms of love, is associated with a positive evaluation, such that it conceives of the human as possessing special value. . . . In fellow-feeling this specific evaluation of the human as such is not yet present. (NS 98–99)

Scheler maintains that "all fellow-feeling is *based* upon love of some sort and vanishes when love is altogether absent: but the converse does not hold" (NS 142). He claimed earlier that fellow-feeling must be dependent upon something else in order to have positive moral content; it now becomes clear that what it depends upon is love. If love is intrinsically morally positive, then any fellow-feeling that is based in it should also be morally positive. The fellow-feeling of the torturer is still morally negative because it does not arise out of love but rather out of some form of ill will.

But for Scheler, the significance of love extends beyond the moral sphere. He attaches a great deal of metaphysical importance to love, maintaining that "love is an emotional gesture and a *spiritual* act" (NS 99, passim). There is a distinction between love (*Liebe*) and benevolence (*Menschenliebe*) in his thought, and it is significant that for him benevolence recognizes a distinction between human beings, animals, and the divine (NS 98–99). It is easy to see the influence of Christian metaphysics here. Nevertheless, it would seem to be possible to reject these metaphysical associations and yet adhere to Scheler's philosophy, claiming that *Menschenliebe* is simply and literally "love of humanity," which is namely that subcategory of *Liebe* that applies to human beings only.

But for Scheler, the spirituality of love entails more than Christian metaphysical beliefs regarding the place of human beings in cosmological hierarchy. Throughout *The Nature of Sympathy*, there is the recurrent idea—due to the influence of Schopenhauer, no doubt—that love (among other traits of Scheler's taxonomy) is capable of communicating to us "the unity of mankind as a species" (NS 99), and not only that, but "bring[ing] us closer to the *very foundation of all things*," "*the unity and constitution of the ultimate world-principle*" (NS xlix). Just as Scheler developed this theme as a result of his studies of Schopenhauer, Schopenhauer developed it from his studies of Indian philosophy. The function served by Scheler's *Liebe* is fulfilled in Buddhism by *karunā*, or "compassion," which co-arises with *prajñā*, or "wisdom." These two are the means by which one realizes one's interconnection with all things, just as *Liebe* is the means for Scheler and *Mitleid* is the means for Schopenhauer. If this is an accurate sketch of all three philosophies, it may seem strange that Scheler should choose love rather than compassion to serve this role, since he accounts for both within his taxonomy. Why not choose compassion, in accordance with the source?

In fact, there is one passage in *The Nature of Sympathy* that attributes a higher metaphysical stature to compassion. On one occasion, "the phenomenon of compassion [*Erbarmen*]" is described as "a heightened commiseration bestowed from above, and from a standpoint of superior power and dignity" (NS 39). However, this is not in keeping with the description of compassion as "the strongest form of pity," for pity was one of the two varieties of fellow-feeling (the other being rejoicing-with). Because fellow-feeling derives its moral value from love, at least according to the Schelerian taxonomy, it therefore follows that the moral value of *Erbarmen* is also derivative. *Erbarmen* is morally good only insofar as it arises out of love. On this view, it would theoretically be possible to experience morally negative kinds of "compassion." If one's fellow-feeling arose not out of love but out of ill will, and if one's pity arose as a function of this fellow-feeling, then the strongest form of that pity would be an *Erbarmen* still grounded in ill will. It is not easy to think of concrete examples of this, as the English word "compassion" does not lend itself easily to morally negative connotations. To wish someone ill and yet feel compassion for them is not hard to imagine; to wish them ill, to feel compassion for them, and for this compassion itself to also be grounded in ill will is quite a different thing. Nevertheless,

Scheler seems to allow for the possibility of the existence of morally negative *Erbarmen*—that is, of a form of *Erbarmen* that one *ought not to feel.*

It is hard to reconcile this logical conclusion with the description of *Erbarmen*'s heavenly origins. I would bring them together as follows. Because love allows us to recognize our unity with everything in the universe, it can properly be described as spiritual—or even divine.[6] There are two varieties of fellow-feeling: those arising out of love and those originating in something else. Pity is a subspecies of fellow-feeling and can be seen in either of the two varieties of fellow-feeling. *Erbarmen,* however, is only properly described as the strongest kind of that pity that arises out of the fellow-feeling inspired by love. Whatever we might choose to name the most intense pity that arises out of the fellow-feeling inspired by ill will, it should not be called *Erbarmen,* nor should it be translated as "compassion." Love and *Erbarmen* are both inspired from above, and *Erbarmen* proper—that is, Schelerian compassion—is therefore morally positive in its content.

The Christian cosmology entailed in Scheler's accounts of love and *Erbarmen* is, in the end, dispensable. In other words, the belief that Scheler's taxonomy is an accurate description of some significant parts of human experience is independent of the belief that a metaphysical hierarchy exists in which human beings are superior to all other animal life and inferior to a real divine power. Other unstated metaphysical assumptions are also latent in Scheler's work, imported through his reading of Schopenhauer. Schopenhauer clearly derived his account of pity (*Mitleid*) from what he understood of Buddhism and Brahmanism. As will be discussed in more detail in the following chapter, *karuṇā* is inseparable from *prajñā*, both of these being defined in Buddhism in a soteriological sense. The idea is that when one gains the insights of true *prajñā* and *karuṇā,* one understands the interdependence of all existences in such a way that one's own existence cannot be separated from the existence of any other thing. This Indian concept is echoed in Scheler's account of love. Schelerian love evidently has divine origins. It is therefore associated with soteriological power, has the capacity to reveal the unity of all things, and is ultimately rooted in Schopenhauer's ruminations on pity.

Thus in a certain sense, Scheler is doing comparative philosophy. Focused on sympathy and its sister concepts as he was, he does not offer an argument for or defense of the metaphysical assumptions underpinning his account of love. If this is a deficit, it is a deficit in a position that is otherwise broadly appealing, having roots in both Indian thought and Judeo-Christian thought. But Scheler had other influences as well: namely, the Greeks, whose influence no European philosopher can claim to be entirely free of, and among whom Aristotle stands out as having the most to say about concepts related to compassion. It is to Aristotle that the survey turns next.

ARISTOTLE ON PITY AND FRIENDSHIP

According to Lee M. Brown, "Since Aristotle, compassion has been characterized as a feeling of empathy that is accompanied by a desire to enhance the fortune or reduce the misfortune of the person for whom empathy is felt."[7] This may be a more or less accurate encapsulation of how we think of compassion, but it does not accurately reflect Aristotle's thoughts. The passages Brown cites to support his claim are found in the *Politics* and the *Rhetoric*.[8] The passage from the *Rhetoric* begins as follows: "Let us now consider Pity, asking ourselves what things might excite pity, and for what persons, and in what states of our mind pity is felt" (R 1385b10).[9] "Pity" here—what Brown seems to be translating as "compassion"—is the Greek *eleos*. As Aristotle defines it, *eleos* is "a feeling of pain caused by the sight of some evil, destructive, or painful, which befalls someone who does not deserve it, and which we might expect to befall ourselves or some friend of ours, and moreover to befall us soon" (R 1385b10–15).

There are two salient features of this definition. First, it includes experiences of pain and excludes experiences of pleasure. Therefore, if I celebrate with my brother for his having won the lottery, my sharing in his feelings cannot be described as *eleos*. Second, *eleos* incorporates a certain function of imagination. When I see something ill befall another person, what elicits *eleos* is the possibility of that kind of event happening to me. If I cannot project myself or those close to me into the situation of the afflicted person, I do not feel *eleos*.

The first feature of *eleos*—its exclusivity of pleasurable experiences—

stands in clear contradiction to the account of "compassion" Brown ascribes to Aristotle. It also suggests that readers of English translate *eleos* as "pity" (or perhaps "commiseration") rather than as "compassion," since in English pity and commiseration are associated only with feelings of suffering, while compassion need not be construed so narrowly—or so, at least, runs the central argument of this book. It may be unconventional to speak of having compassion for my brother as he delights in having won the lottery, but it is not, strictly speaking, contradictory; "com-passion" is literally feeling-with, not suffering-with. Thus if I can share in my brother's joy with him, I am feeling-with. On the other hand, it is simply incorrect for me to describe my sharing in his jubilation as having pity for him; like *eleos,* pity has nothing to do with sharing experiences of joy.

The second feature of *eleos,* its imaginative component, has something in common with Scheler's projective empathy. In projective empathy, one imaginatively projects oneself into the situation of another and envisions what one's own reaction would be in the other's situation. The first half of Brown's description of compassion is "a feeling of empathy"; we might well read him as having something like Schelerian projective empathy in mind, for if he does, then he has correctly recounted at least this much of Aristotelian *eleos.*[10]

But we must keep in mind that, at least according to Aristotle, *eleos* is not an *aretē* (typically translated as "virtue," though I prefer "excellence"[11]). Evidence of this is found in Aristotle's exploration of what exactly an *aretē* is. In the second book of the *Nichomachean Ethics,* Aristotle says that since the *aretai* arise in the soul, they must fall under one of the three categories of conditions that arise in the soul: feelings, capacities, and states (NE 1105b15–30).[12] Ultimately he finds that the *aretai* are states, or "what we have when we are well or badly off in relation to feelings" (1105b26). Pity, however, does not fall under this category and in fact is used as an example of a feeling (along with anger, fear, confidence, envy, joy, love, hate, jealousy, and longing). One's ability to feel pity counts as a capacity, but neither pity nor the capacity to feel it can be an excellence.

What follows from the fact that *eleos* is not an excellence? First, Aristotle tells us that "we are neither praised nor blamed in so far as we have feelings," and our excellence should not be measured in terms of our feelings (NE 1105b29–31). To feel pity for a wounded animal, for instance, is wholly unworthy of moral praise; such a reaction to suffering is no more admirable than feeling happy on the day one's child is born and not entirely different from feeling thirsty after a long run. Pity would not be a matter of decision (as an *aretē* would) but rather a matter of reaction or of impulse.

Further, if it is a feeling, then like all feelings *eleos* must be properly governed, and the governance of feelings falls under the domain of certain excellences. Temperance is the excellence that controls instincts for physical satisfaction, such as hunger, thirst, and the libido. However, since pity is not pleasurable, nor is it necessarily bound to the physical (though experiences of pity may be accompanied by physical sensations), presumably pity would be governed by some other excellence. We might call it self-control, or composure, or serenity. Whatever its appellation, when cultivated this excellence would ensure that pity be expressed at proper times and in proper amounts, just as it might similarly regulate anger or jealousy.

There is some reason to believe that pity must be governed and that too much pity could be a bad thing. One has a problem if one so empathizes with the characters of a drama that one bursts into tears in the middle of the theater whenever tragedy strikes one of the players on the stage. Similarly, pity for a wounded animal on the side of a highway should not be felt to such an overwhelming degree that one can no longer safely drive, nor should a surgeon be so overcome by pity for a patient's condition that it becomes impossible to operate. But for Aristotle, this is true of both states and feelings. All *aretai* admit of excesses as well as deficiencies, and so if pity were construed as an *aretē* rather than as a feeling, all of the caveats above would still apply. Why then is pity construed not as an *aretē* but as a feeling?

Recall the definition of pity in the *Rhetoric:* It is a feeling we have for characters on the stage. Indeed, Aristotle holds that we *cannot* have pity for those who are near and dear to us: "The people we pity are: those whom we know, if only they are not very closely related to us—in that case we feel about them as if we were in danger ourselves" (R 1386a18–19). Aristotle offers the example of one Amasis, who did not weep when his son was taken away to be killed but did weep at the travails of a friend: "The latter sight was pitiful, the former terrible, and the terrible is different from the pitiful" (R 1386a21–23).

Here Aristotle seems to be recognizing something deeper than the feeling of *eleos*—some state or feeling through which we identify ourselves with those who are nearest and dearest to us. There are a number of Greek terms that describe feeling-with or sharing in a feeling, be it suffering with another or rejoicing with the other. Aristotle uses *sunēdesthai, sunkhairein, sullupeisthai,* and *sunalgein,* the prefix *sun-* connoting "with" (much as *com-* does in "compassion"). A friend, for instance, can be defined as one who shares one's suffering (*sunalgei*) and pleasure (*sunēdetai*).[13] Sharing in these experiences can be "terrible" but not "pitiful."

Eleos is not merely something one feels while watching a stage play, but neither is it a worthy source of moral guidance, for it does not apply to those who are closest to the subject. Moreover, as David Konstan argues, Aristotle would not recognize the possibility of self-pity, for on this account of *eleos* the pitier and the pitied must be distinct and to some extent even distant.[14] If *eleos* applies neither to ourselves nor to those who are closest to us—and if this inner circle, centered on the agent, is the very focus of Aristotelian ethics—then we should hardly be surprised if Aristotle finds it cannot serve as a source of moral guidance. Aristotle takes the excellences as moral guides, and as *eleos* cannot be one of their number, neither should it be of their kind.

Yet there is an excellence by which we may share the suffering and satisfaction of those who are close to us. What conveys to Amasis the "terrible" fact of his son's imminent demise is the excellence of friendship (*philia*). We rejoice and commiserate with our loved ones in a way that does not parallel the pity we feel for fictitious characters; for them, we feel not *eleos* but *philia*. Indeed, one standard by which a friend is defined is as "one who shares his friend's distress and enjoyment" (NE 1166a8–9)[15]—a definition very much in keeping with that of compassion as it is being treated here.

Philia is a necessary excellence because having friendships is a necessary condition for living well (*eudaimonia*). Aristotle justifiably contends that "no-one would choose to live without friends even if he had all the other goods" (NE 1155a5), and it is the excellence of friendship that makes individual friendships possible. Aristotle distinguishes many different types of friendships, the kinship shared between parents and children—such as that between Amasis and his doomed son—being just one species. Aristotle also ranks differing kinds of friendships in what is ultimately a moral hierarchy. Significant disparity in social power proves to be an obstacle for friendship, and so the *philia* between unequals is not the highest kind;[16] nor are friendships of utility, nor friendships that exist purely for enjoyment.[17] The best friendship, the kind of relationship that leads all participants in it to higher moral excellence, is the "complete friendship" of "good people similar in virtue."[18] Aristotle's virtue ethic is one that depends on the relationship between role models and emulators, and good friends can be role models to each other, mutually supporting each other's self-cultivation.

An interesting feature of Aristotle's *philia* is that it can be self-directed; in other words, one can befriend oneself. In fact, Aristotle maintains that "the defining features of friendship that are found in friendships to one's neighbours would seem to be derived from features of friendship towards oneself" (NE 1166a1–2). Aristotle lists five defining features of friendships and compares them to features of the self-love of a virtuous person (Table 1.1).

Of course, both self-love and friendship are only good if they are seated in a virtuous character. In a corrupt or base person, self-love amounts to nothing more than selfishness. But those who understand the human *ergon* of contemplation can love the contemplative and virtuous parts of themselves and of their friends, and this is the highest kind of love.[19] Herein lies the excellence of *philia*.

Philia, then, may be construed as a kind of compassion that extends both inwardly and outwardly, but its outward reach is quite limited for two reasons. First, only a very small number of people are capable of the most virtuous form of *philia*.[20] Second, by its very nature, *philia* of any variety only extends to those who are closest to the agent. *Philia*'s domain is close personal relationships, and beyond that sphere it is *eleos* that informs the agent of others' feelings.

Therefore neither *philia* nor *eleos* is truly suitable as a foundational principle of an ethic. *Eleos* failed because it is not an *aretē* but a feeling and therefore not subject to moral evaluation (though it is subject to the control of some *aretē* that can be morally evaluated). *Philia* fails because it is too

Table 1.1. Parallels between friendship and self-love

DEFINING FEATURES OF A FRIEND	DEFINING FEATURES OF SELF-LOVE
Someone who wishes and does goods or apparent goods to his friend for the friend's own sake.	[The excellent person] wishes goods and apparent goods to himself, and does them in his actions.
One who wishes the friend to be and to live for the friend's own sake.	He wishes himself to live and to be preserved. . . . For being is a good for the good person, and each person wishes goods for himself.
One who spends time with his friend.	[The excellent person] finds it pleasant to spend time with himself.
[One who] makes the same choices [as his friend].	The excellent person is of one mind with himself, and desires the same things in his whole soul.
One who shares his friend's distress and enjoyment.	He shares his own distresses and pleasures, more than other people share theirs.

Source: Aristotle, *Nichomachean Ethics* 1166a1–29, trans. Terence Irwin.

limited in scope. Were an ethical system to be founded on *philia,* its imperatives would only extend to family and close friends—the very people toward whom it is supposed to be least difficult to behave ethically. For most people, it is easy to be good to those who are nearest and dearest; indeed, according to Aristotle, "if people are friends, they have no need of justice" (NE 1155a27). Aristotle is correct to say that *philia* is "most necessary for our life," but he is equally correct in not declaring *philia* to be the chief excellence of his ethical system.

AGAPĒ

"Love thy neighbor as thyself" seems to be as succinct a mandate for compassion as one could ask for. If one truly loves one's neighbor just as one loves oneself, the boundary between altruism and egoism disappears—at least with regard to the neighbor in question. Unlike the Christian pity despised by Nietzsche, this maxim of Christian love is not obsessed with negativity;

one's neighbors are to be loved during their triumphs as well as their sorrows. If "neighbor" is construed broadly enough, it does not suffer the limitations of scope seen in the Aristotelian accounts of pity and horror. This love is not reserved for remote spectators, as is the sympathy of Hume, nor is it exclusively other-directed, as is the fellow-feeling of Scheler. In other words, the love of the "eleventh commandment" would appear, at least prima facie, to be the most similar so far to the Buddhist account of compassion.

But to be precise, we must question whether love and compassion are significantly different. As suggested earlier, I cannot sensibly say, "I have compassion for you, though I have no idea what you're going through," while I can say I love you in that context. Compassion entails attentiveness to the well-being of the other, whereas love is sometimes described as being unconditional (and therefore not dependent on attending to another's well-being). In a purely secular sense, unconditional love is dysfunctional: If I say I love you unconditionally, I love you no matter what you do to me, no matter how abusive you may be to me. But *agapē*—divine Christian love—can be appropriately unconditional. God's love is said to be unconditional—no matter how wretched I may become, I am still loved—and humans' love for the divine is supposed to be unconditional, for nothing about the divine is unlovable. Compassion does not function this way. First, it seems nonsensical to suggest that humans can have compassion for the divine. (What might an omnipotent god's well-being be like, and how could we possibly advance it?) Second, unconditional compassion is only compassion in the loosest, most abstract sense, for I cannot have any concrete sense of compassion for you if I have no idea whether you're suffering or satisfied.

The primary Christian virtue would seem to be not compassion but love. Paul writes of love's primacy in his oft-quoted passage, "So faith, hope, love abide, these three; but the greatest of these is love." His next sentence begins, "Make love your aim." And there is the passage from John, the most quoted of all: "For God so loved the world. . . ."[21] One might argue that I am splitting hairs, that what Paul and John had in mind is compassionate love, or that Christian love is inseparable from Christian compassion. I would grant that it is probably impossible to love and to deny compassion where compassion is possible; at any rate, I cannot imagine denying compassion to a person I love. But it does not follow from this that love and compassion are synonymous.

We may compare Christian thought with Buddhist thought on this point. Jesus of Nazareth and Siddhartha Gautama have a great deal in common philosophically, and much has been made of this in Buddhist-Christian dialogue, the details of which I will not go into here. (I am no theologian.) I will confine myself to the modest suggestion that, upon analyzing the thought of those two men as recorded in the earliest writings of their religions, one will find that compassion receives considerable philosophical development in the Buddhist tradition and that compassion in the Christian tradition follows from love, rather than being the object of philosophical explication.

There are two overarching Christian maxims regarding love: the eleventh commandment and the first, which is to love God with all one's heart. Anders Nygren refers to these as "the double commandment" (AE 61) and points out that they have long been thought of as representing the highest order of obligation in Christianity's ethics as well as its soteriology. The "love" of the double commandment is *agapē* (or *caritas* in Latin), which is to be compared to and contrasted with such other forms of love as *philia, storgē* (Latin *dilectio*), *erôs* (Latin *amor*), *koinonia* ("the fellowship of the faithful"), and *cupiditas*.[22]

In Nygren's classic study *Agape and Eros, agapē* is characterized as "Divine love," "indifferent to value," "a value-creating principle," "spontaneous and 'unmotivated,'" "utterly self-forgetful and self-sacrificial," "the initiator of fellowship with God," and "God's way to man" (AE 78, 77, 78, 75, xiv, 80, 81). All of these descriptions are to be contrasted with *erôs,* which is "acquisitive desire," "a human love for the Divine," "a longing and a striving after something man lacks and needs" (AE 210, viii, ix). To sum up, "Eros *recognizes value* in its object—and loves it," while "Agape loves—and *creates value* in its object" (AE 210).

Agapē is a creative force because it is divine in nature; it is the love of the divine for human beings. According to Nygren, human beings cannot express *agapē* toward the divine—such love may more accurately be called faith (AE ix)—but by imitating the divine, they can express *agapē* toward each other. There are therefore two senses of *agapē:* God's love ("Agape in the fullest sense of the term" [AE ix]) and the simulacrum of *agapē* that is the closest approximation of divine love of which human beings are capable. Human *agapē* must still be "unselfish love," a kind of "sacrificial giving" (AE 210) that loves regardless of whether its object is worthy of love or not.

C. S. Lewis concurs, drawing a distinction between "natural love" and "Divine love." Human beings naturally experience love, but, very much in keeping with Nygren's thought, Lewis says that natural love "is always directed to objects which the lover finds in some way intrinsically lovable."[23] On the other hand, divine love is what enables a human being "to love what is not naturally lovable: lepers, criminals, enemies, morons, the sulky, the superior and the sneering."[24]

Nygren also refers to "Divine love," repeatedly emphasizing that "the Divine love is unmotivated, the human motivated" (AE 96). The motivation for human love all too often boils down to selfishness. As Hannah Arendt puts it, "Self-love is the root of all desire."[25] We love what we love because it does us some good; we love what benefits us. Even the idea that our love should be requited is selfish in a certain sense: We want something back for our love. In Nygren's view, "Agape means the death, not of the self, but of selfishness; it is the antithesis, not of selfhood, but of self-centredness, which is the deadliest enemy of true selfhood. Man realises his true self just in so far as he lives by and in Agape" (AE xiv).

Very much in accordance with the fifteenth-century Dutch monk Thomas à Kempis, who described the love of Jesus as "free from all self-interest" and "retaining no trace of self-love,"[26] Nygren characterizes *agapē* as being "opposed to all forms of selfishness" (AE xiii). However, this characterization earns him a few detractors. As Stephen G. Post contends, "The western tendency to idealize selfless love devoid of even the slightest iota of self-concern is an aberration from the valid ideal of unselfishness in fellowship. Selfless, purely one-way love may be an understandable exaggeration of unselfishness, but its impact is essentially negative in that it undermines the circular flow of giving and receiving in which agape is sustained and supported."[27]

Post follows the Jewish theologian Abraham J. Heschel "in pointing out that the selfless image of the divine is erroneous."[28] Heschel maintains that Judaism is neither a religion of "self-satisfaction" nor of "self-annihilation,"[29] and this is as true of the divine as it is of humans. Yahweh does not will its own negation. Similarly, "the image of Jesus as beyond all self-concern is really quite superficial,"[30] says Post, who problematizes the "assumption that nonrequital [of divine love] was both desired, necessary, and good."[31]

The problem with this assumption, and consequently with Nygren's account of love as being "opposed to all forms of selfishness," is that it renders the relationship between humankind and the divine more shallow than it should be. If Jesus of Nazareth were absolutely selfless, the crucifixion would not have been much of a sacrifice. Moreover, if no requital is sought for the divine love for human beings, then suddenly the first commandment takes on an entirely different character. To be commanded to love is entirely different from loving in response to received love. Even Nygren agrees that "if we start with Agape ... as something *demanded,* we bar our own way to the understanding of the idea of Agape" (AE 61, emphasis mine). Post and Nygren concur that *agapē* must be freely chosen in order to count as *agapē,*[32] but Post maintains that even divine *agapē* must be accompanied by the *hope* for requital—even if it should still go unrequited. He says, "Mutual love is inextricably linked with freedom, risk, and patience, but never with selflessness. The absence of requital is never intended or sought after."[33] If the crucifixion is not to be trivialized, and if humanity is to maintain a meaningful relationship with the divine, then divine love cannot be as selfless as Nygren makes it out to be.

Of course, to expect requital is not to be selfish. Rather, to expect requital is to refuse self-annihilation; some vestige of the ego remains, though not necessarily in an egoistic or self-centered form. Post and Heschel maintain that the expectation of requital is necessary if love is to be a good, not a detriment. The possibility of love's being harmful to the lover was a concern from the very beginning. When Augustine mourns the death of his friend Nebridius, he too writes of the dangers of loving: "For wherever the soul of man may turn, unless it turns to [God], it clasps sorrow to itself."[34] Of all things of beauty, including human friends and loved ones, Augustine says, "The love of them, which we feel, through the senses of the body, must not be like glue to bind my soul to them. For ... if the soul loves them and wishes to be with them and finds its rest in them, then it is torn by desires that can destroy it."[35] When Augustine loved Nebridius, he "lived in a fever,"[36] failing to foresee that, in dying, all impermanent things must ultimately disappoint the ones who love them. As he so aptly sums it up, "What madness to love a man as something more than human!"[37]

Both Lewis and Arendt comment on Augustine's mourning for Nebridius.[38] According to Arendt, "for Augustine the happiness of having is not contrasted by sorrow but by the fear of losing."[39] Lewis encapsulates Augustine's love for his friend along similar lines: "If love is to be a blessing, not a misery, it must be for the only Beloved who will never pass away."[40] (This, of course, can only be the divine.)

But this kind of love is dangerously close to the faith of Pascal's Wager—as Lewis himself observes: "Who could conceivably begin to love God on such a prudential ground ... ? Who could even include it among the grounds for loving?"[41] We do not love in order to satisfy some "congenital preference for safe investments and limited liabilities."[42] Bet-hedging love is "closer to Stoic 'apathy' or neo-Platonic mysticism" than it is to true *agapē*.[43] *Agapē* must be selfless in at least this regard: It must be willing to risk loss, injury, hardship, and a broken heart. As Lewis puts it, "To love at all is to be vulnerable,"[44] and to deliberately leave oneself vulnerable implies a degree of selflessness.

Thus, *agapē* is opposed to selfishness and does entail selflessness—but not to the extent Nygren suggests nor to the extent Augustine experiences at the death of Nebridius. The question remains as to whether *agapē* can serve as the foundation of an ethic. The double commandment has been interpreted as such, but Nygren maintains that real love cannot be commanded.[45] If *agapē* were treated as a virtue, a virtue ethicist could contend that there can be an ethical command to cultivate the virtue of love, and that once cultivated it will be freely expressed (as Nygren insists it must be in order to count as *agapē*). Yet the question remains whether *agapē* is a *desirable* foundation for an ethical philosophy.

There is an incompleteness to the eleventh commandment that makes its mandate to love unsuitable for the foundation of an ethic. If a person is gripped by self-hatred and wants nothing more than his own destruction, to love his neighbors as himself is to wish for their destruction as well—or at least to be undisturbed by it. To rule out this possibility, the commandment might be rephrased, "Love thy neighbor as thyself, and love thyself."

But now it may tip too far in the other direction. Self-love is not demanded by the eleventh commandment, perhaps because self-infatuation comes all too easily to us. Egoism is arguably our more natural disposition; it is selflessness that must be cultivated or commanded. If real self-love (and not self-infatuation or self-aggrandizement) should be commanded, one must then wonder to what extent self-love is ethically permissible. Here Augustine's lament comes to mind: It is folly to love human beings as something more than what they are. Yet self-love, when taken too far, does exactly this. The eleventh commandment is intended to curb egocentrism, not to foster it.

It is entirely plausible that there exists a happy medium between self-destructiveness and egocentrism, but it is hard to see how the notion of *agapē* by itself indicates where this golden mean might be. If *agapē* were an inherently utilitarian idea, this would be a relatively easy question to answer: Love oneself to the extent that one does not adversely affect the utility of one's neighbors. That is, love oneself to the extent that one can maximally love one's neighbors, where loving is construed in terms of utility maximization for oneself and others.

This is an unorthodox understanding of love to be sure, for love is not ordinarily understood in terms of the hedonic calculus, nor is it taken to be so focused on balancing egoistic and altruistic drives. If *agapē* is defined in utilitarian terms, then the balance between selflessness and self-love may be found, but without this framework imposed upon it, it is difficult to see how *agapē* can recommend itself as the foundation of a secular moral philosophy.[46] To get closer, we must turn away from love—and also away from the Christian tradition—to David Hume and his account of sympathy in ethics.

HUMEAN SYMPATHY

To understand the role of sympathy in Hume's moral philosophy, one must first understand the philosophers to whom Hume was responding. Hume's description of sympathy as "the moral sentiment" is his reply to the philosophies of the "moral sense." The prominent ethicists who immediately preceded Hume (Butler, the Earl of Shaftesbury, et al.) had developed the idea that human beings had a moral sense analogous to the physical senses; that is, there was a perceiver and an object to be perceived. In the case of the moral sense, a spectator would perceive the action of an agent and the reaction of the "receiver"—namely, the person affected by the action. Sympathy comes into play here because it is the means by which the spectator perceives the experienced effects of the action on the part of the receiver.

Building upon and advancing beyond this idea of a moral sense, Hume developed his model of sympathy along similar lines. For Hume, sympathy is the means by which an observer makes moral evaluations. Hume rejected the idea that moral evaluations were a function of reason, because for him reason analyzes states of affairs, and from actual states of affairs one could not derive any statement regarding the way those affairs *ought* to be. Prescriptions of this sort could only be emotional evaluations, and for Hume sympathy was the passion that generated moral evaluations.

It is important to recognize that this sense of sympathy retains a significant degree of distance. Although Hume rejects "cold, calculating reason" as the seat of moral evaluation, this brand of sympathy also remains "cool" to a certain extent. Sympathy does not enter into the relationship of the agent and the acted-upon; it is an observer's passion, and by employing it the observer makes moral evaluations. It is also important to note that in Hume's view, sympathy itself does not generate moral evaluations. Rather, by giving one access to the pain or pleasure experienced by the receiver, sympathy allows one to judge whether the action in question was agreeable or useful to the receiver. The standard of moral judgment is therefore utilitarian. An act is labeled right or wrong by a spectator depending upon what the spectator's "moral sentiment" tells him or her about the receiver's response to an act; the receiver labels the same act right or wrong using utilitarian considerations.

But there is much more to be said about Hume's model of sympathy, particularly about his ideas on its origin. According to Hume, sympathy arises out of pride. This is quite a novel connection to draw, considering that we generally think of pride as being self-directed and sympathy as being outwardly directed. Even when pride is not self-directed, such as when a parent is proud of a child, there is no hint of what we usually call sympathy in that sense of pride. However, in Hume's philosophy, pride and sympathy should both be treated as technical terms, not to be confused with the everyday uses of these words.

In the *Treatise,* Hume says that "nature has given to the organs of the human mind, a certain disposition fitted to produce a peculiar impression or emotion, which we call *pride:* To this emotion she has assign'd a certain idea, *viz.* that of *self,* which it never fails to produce" (THN 287). In other words, it is our sense of pride that *generates* our sense of self. As Annette Baier describes it, "The idea of the self ... is produced by one 'peculiar' sort of member of the bundle of perceptions comprising its object, that peculiarly reflexive impression of reflection, pride" (APS 130). (This model of the self as a bundle of perceptions is not so far from the Buddhist model of self as a bundle of *skandhas.* This similarity will be revisited in the discussion of Śāntideva in the following chapter.)

Though pride is the origin of the idea of the self, this is not a solipsistic sort of pride—and therefore Hume should not be misinterpreted as following in the footsteps of Descartes but substituting pride for doubt as the acid test. According to Baier, the Humean self is "complex, changing, *dependent on others* for its coming to be, for its emotional life, for its self-consciousness, for its self-evaluations" (APS 130, emphasis mine).

What precisely is the nature of this dependence? The self is dependent on others because it is through comparing itself with others that it comes to understand itself. There is an intuitive plausibility to this idea. The fact that I am six feet, two inches tall from head to heel says nothing at all about whether I am tall or short; such evaluations only have meaning in a social context. I cannot know whether I am bright or stupid, kind or wicked, athletic or clumsy, unless I can compare myself with other people. It is not at all clear that I can even know whether or not I *like* myself, for liking and disliking are also descriptions formed in a comparative context. Maybe none of this matters. In a social vacuum, perhaps it makes no difference whether or not am vicious, or intelligent, or full of self-loathing. However, it seems implausible that someone existing in a social vacuum (assuming that is even possible) could have the same depth and breadth of self-knowledge as a person with social relationships. In this sense, it may be said that one's sense of self does indeed depend on others.

Hume says the same principle is generally true of all things, not just selves: We "judge of objects more from comparison than from their real and intrinsic merit" (THN 291). This does not devalue the intrinsic merit of an object or a self in any way; it is merely a statement about how we come to understand things. Pride certainly depends upon comparison with others: Whatever else a runner may gain from being able to run a four-minute mile, he is only *proud* of it insofar as he is aware of how many other people are capable (or, more importantly, *in*capable) of doing so. But for Hume, pride's dependency is greater than this. Annette Baier captures the essence of it well:

> Our idea of ourselves must have greater "vivacity," [Hume] claims, than that of our idea of any other person, because of our constant consciousness of "ourself." This superior vivacity, invigorated by pride, overflows in sympathy to vivify our ideas of the feelings of others, indeed to raise them into impressions, into shared feelings. . . .⁴⁷ So our wheeling passions, even loving and sympathetic ones, do tend to come to rest in self-concern. (APS 143–144)

At last sympathy enters the picture. Sympathy "comes to rest" in self-concern—that is, in pride—because although it is through sympathy that one understands the feelings of others, pride compares these feelings to one's own in order to get a more detailed understanding of the self. Sympathy is the human being's natural (or to use Hume's term, "direct") impulse when confronted with the feelings of others. This is true partly because human beings naturally wish to understand more about themselves and partly because human beings are naturally concerned with the well-being of their companions, and sympathy is what makes awareness of this well-being possible. In other words, sympathy satisfies a moral instinct and a kind of curiosity at the same time.

Schadenfreude is a particularly good example of how sympathy and Humean pride relate in the moral domain. To take pleasure in another person's sorrow, one must have a capacity to recognize that the other is unhappy and also a capacity to compare that person's miserable state to one's own relative comfort, with the result that one takes joy in the fact that the suffering is happening to someone else. Or, even more viciously, the suffering one recognizes in the other sometimes directly generates happiness in oneself. Hume says that rivals work this way: The success of one is predicated upon the failure of the other, and the failure of one is often met with by glee on the part of the other (THN 377).

On the other hand, when two people are not competitors but partners in an enterprise, "the advantage or loss of one becomes immediately the advantage or loss of his partner" (THN 383). These kinds of rivalries and partnerships can most easily be exemplified in economic terms, where a person's financial loss spells doom for the partner and joy for the rival. However, it is easy enough to think of emotional rivalries and loving partnerships in the same terms. One's awareness of the other's suffering or elation—in a word, one's sympathy—alters what one feels about oneself because of the comparisons drawn by pride. But more than this, the need for pride to compare the self to the states of others is what gives rise to sympathy. Sympathetic awareness of others is definitive of the self, and pride, always in search of self-definition, provides motivation to be sympathetic.

Nevertheless, there is a point at which pride can interfere with or "block" sympathy. For Hume, sympathy remains "the moral sentiment" and therefore of particular interest to the ethicist, but "the principle of comparison" by which we feel sympathy will not always lead us in a morally laudable direction (as the example of *Schadenfreude* has already shown). Baier points out that "'comparison' is seen to presuppose our capacity for sympathy," but there are times when "comparison blocks sympathy" (APS 150, 149). It is not the case that comparison and sympathy are rivals, one preempting the other on a mutually exclusive basis.[48] Rather, sympathy is a natural, "direct" reaction to the satisfaction and suffering of others.

Comparison is also a normal response, so that when sympathy, fueled by the imagination, provides a representation of the feelings of another being, it is a completely spontaneous response to compare those feelings to one's own. Sometimes this comparison overwhelms the original sympathetic impulse altogether: Where one might first have been able to feel happy at the success of one's competitor, consideration of one's own comparative misfortune results in bitter feelings of envy or even malice. All the same, Hume takes sympathy to be the natural state of affairs for us, despite whatever efforts of imagination it may demand and despite the fact that "the moral sentiment" is occasionally—perhaps even frequently—overruled by the comparison that follows after it, a comparison that was only possible because of the initial sympathetic response itself.

One must realize, of course, that none of this happens at a conscious level; pride and sympathy are both described as naturally occurring within the human mind (THN 287, 317, 320). It is equally important to remember that Hume's usage of "pride" and "sympathy" is philosophically precise and should not be confused with whatever associations we may have to our contemporary uses of those words. For Hume, pride is a laudable quality, described by Baier as an "agreeable passion in which he thinks our minds tend to rest and invigorate themselves whenever possible" (APS 143). "Pride conscious of itself is conscious both of its dependence on others and of its line of communication with [the] esteem [of others]" (APS 145). Sympathy is one means of comprehending this esteem, and as such, sympathy is in no way degraded by the fact that it "comes to rest" in pride. Humean sympathy satisfies curiosity of an ethical as well as an epistemological nature, and by its nature it is morally good, though it can be overwhelmed by stronger, less commendable passions.

In conclusion, while Hume's understanding of sympathy plays an important and necessary role in his ethics and his philosophy of self, it cannot be said that Hume has developed an account of ethics based on or grounded in sympathy. His is a utilitarian system in which sympathy enables spectators to participate in moral evaluation. Humean sympathy is not equivalent to compassion, but certain features of it—most particularly the fact that comparative thinking can obstruct it—will prove extremely valuable in the account of compassion I will develop later.

ROUSSEAU'S COMPASSION

Jean-Jacques Rousseau is unique among the modernist philosophers in his concern for developing compassion (*pitié*) as a matter of education. (Rousseau's English translators render *pitié* interchangeably as "compassion" and as "pity," a convention I shall not seek to overturn here, save to note that both of these terms have connotations in English that Rousseau does not seem to have in mind and to note that the reader should not confuse Rousseauan pity with Aristotelian or Nietzschean pity.) Compassion receives Rousseau's attention in two works: the *Discourse on the Origin of Inequality among Men* (originally published in 1755) and *Emile. Emile* postdates the *Discourse* by seven years and presents a much more robust account of compassion, including a program for cultivating compassion in children. Although the compassion of *Emile* is better developed, I begin with the *Discourse* because for Rousseau the earliest roots of compassion should not be overlooked.

In the *Discourse,* compassion "comes before any kind of reflection,"[49] and indeed Rousseau says it *must* precede rational reflection, for "the human race would long have ceased to be, had its preservation depended only on the reasonings of the individuals composing it."[50] In this context, Rousseau is speaking of human beings in the state of nature and, indeed, even before that point, when we were too primitive to properly be called human beings. (It is worth mentioning that evolutionary biology makes a similar observation about the origin of human beings, an observation summed up by Peter Singer: "We were social before we were human."[51]) Social animals depend on their communities for survival, and one of the survival benefits conferred by community membership is compassionate attention and care.

In *Emile,* Rousseau explains why compassion comes so naturally to us, holding that compassion is born out of self-love (*amour de soi*). This is not surprising given that it comes from a social contract theorist. He begins with the assumption shared by Hobbes and Locke—namely, that human beings are basically selfish. According to Joseph Reisert, Rousseau takes *amour de soi* to be "the most fundamental principle in the human soul."[52] But Rousseau moves beyond Hobbes and Locke to show how compassion can be derived from selfishness. Allan Bloom analyzes Rousseau's project in *Emile* as follows:

> *Emile* is divided into two large segments. Books I–III are devoted to the rearing of a civilized savage, a man who cares only about himself, who is independent and self-sufficient and on whom no duties that

run counter to his inclinations and so divide him are imposed. . . . Books IV–V attempt to bring this atomic individual into human society and into a condition of moral responsibility on the basis of his inclinations and his generosity. (E 7)

Bloom also compares this approach of Rousseau's to John Locke, who

> has no category for the miserable other than that of the idle and the quarrelsome. The recognition of our sameness and our common vulnerability dampens the harsh competitiveness and egotism of egalitarian political orders. Rousseau takes advantage of the tendency to compassion resulting from equality, and uses it, rather than self-interest, as the glue binding men together. Our equality, then, is based less on our fear of death than on our sufferings; suffering produces a shared sentiment with others, which fear of death does not. (E 18–19)

For Rousseau, there are two passions basic to the human heart: self-love and fear of death. Self-love takes two forms, *amour de soi* and *amour-propre*, both of which may be translated as "self-love," but *amour-propre* connotes pride and vanity. He comments on both forms of self-love in the *Discourse on the Origin of Inequality*:

> Amour-propre and amour de soi, two passions very different in their nature and their effects, must not be confused. Love of oneself is a natural sentiment which inclines every animal to watch over its self-preservation, and which directed in man by reason and modified by pity, produces humanity and virtue. Amour-propre is only a relative sentiment, artificial and born in society, which inclines each individual to have a greater esteem for himself than for anyone else.[53]

Thus for Rousseau, the opposite of self-love is not altruism; instead, two forms of self-love are each other's opposites, *amour de soi* being morally good and *amour-propre* being morally neutral but given to badness.[54]

Rousseau's strategy for teaching compassion to his imaginary pupil Emile is to never lose sight of basic human selfishness. As such, Emile will begin with a Humean sort of competitive pride: "Since my Emile has until now looked only at himself, the first glance he casts on his fellows leads him to compare himself with them. And the first sentiment aroused in him by this comparison is the desire to be in the first position. This is the point where love of self turns into amour-propre" (E 235). This follows his earlier observation: "If the first sight that strikes him is an object of sadness, the first return to himself is a sentiment of pleasure. In seeing how many ills he is exempt from, he feels himself to be happier than he thought he was. He shares the suffering of his fellows; but this sharing is voluntary and sweet" (E 229).[55]

"The desire to be in the first position" does not immediately strike one as a compassionate desire. By the same token, to see sadness and feel pleasure upon seeing it strikes one as being, if anything, anticompassionate. Emile's education does recommend itself insofar as it seeks to guarantee that he will never take his happiness for granted. Upon seeing the misery of others, he should always reflect on how lucky he is not to be in their stead. And it must be noted that Rousseau's compassion entails a three-step process of education, and thus far Emile has only reached stage one. Bloom describes the second stage as follows: "The second level of the education in compassion produces contempt for the great of this world, not a slave's contempt founded in envy, indignation, and resentment, but the contempt stemming from a conviction of superiority which admits of honest fellow feeling and is the precondition of compassion" (E 19).

Here again, "contempt" is not something we commonly link with compassion, and surely "a conviction of superiority" cannot be a precondition of compassion as we usually think of it. Perhaps Bloom has overstated the case, for Rousseau did say that, "although in general Emile does not esteem men, he will not show contempt for them, because he pities them and is touched by them" (E 336). Nevertheless, Rousseau does say that Emile reacts to sadness with pleasure, and he also reacts to the happiness of others with displeasure:

The sight of a happy man inspires in others less love than envy. They would gladly accuse him of usurping a right he does not have in giving himself an exclusive happiness; and amour-propre suffers, too, in making us feel that this man has no need of us. But who does not pity the

unhappy man whom he sees suffering? Who would not want to deliver
him from his ills if it only cost a wish for that? Imagination puts us in the
place of the miserable man rather than in that of the happy man. (E 221)

For the miserable to envy the happy is an understandable response, but
envy is typically described as being an inappropriate reaction—even an immoral one. But Rousseau is not without a defense for his account. First, innate human inclinations, if they are as selfish as he takes them to be, are not
the best imaginable foundation on which to build a model of compassion.
An account of compassion that arises out of selfishness is likely to yield results that conflict with our conventional understanding of compassion as
egoism's opposite. Second, Rousseau makes no claim that compassion as he
envisions it is a moral excellence. Indeed, on his account it is to be numbered
among the passions and not an excellence at all. As Bloom observes, "The
motive and intention of Rousseauan compassion give it little in common
with Christian compassion. Rousseau was perfectly aware that compassion
such as he taught is not a virtue and that it can lead to abuse and hypocrisy"
(E 18).

Nevertheless, it is still true of Emile that "he suffers when he sees suffering" and that this is "a natural sentiment" in him (E 251). Rousseau holds that
through his program of education, he has prevented as much as possible the
shift from *amour de soi* to *amour-propre* and has linked the *amour de soi* as
closely as possible to love for others:

> To become sensitive and pitying, the child must know that there are
> beings like him who feel the pains that he has felt, and that there are
> others whom he ought to conceive of as able to feel them too. In fact,
> how do we let ourselves be moved by pity if not by transporting our-
> selves outside of ourselves and identifying with the suffering animal,
> by leaving, as it were, our own being to take on its being? We suffer
> only so much as we judge that it suffers. It is not in ourselves, it is in
> him that we suffer. Thus, no one becomes sensitive until his imagina-
> tion is animated and begins to transport him out of himself.
>
>   To excite and nourish this nascent sensibility, to guide it or fol-
> low it in its natural inclination, what is there to do other than to offer

the young man objects on which the expansive force of his heart can act—objects which swell the heart, which extend it to other beings, which make it find itself everywhere outside itself—and carefully to keep away those which contract and concentrate the heart and tighten the spring of the human I? (E 222–223)

If Emile is at heart a selfish being, as the early social contractarians would have it, and if he learns the ability to find himself everywhere outside himself, then not only will he act with compassion but he will do so out of a sense of inclination, with no recourse to moral duty or obligation required. This was the aim of Rousseau's pedagogy: to elicit moral responsibility from the "civilized savage." And it seems he has successfully done so.

Despite his success, Rousseau's compassion cannot serve as a sufficiently stable foundation for building a system of ethics. First, compassion for him is not morally admirable in and of itself. It is prone to hypocrisy, and thus it cannot serve as the foundation of a moral theory. Second, central to this account of compassion is the fact that it works best in one direction: from the top down, so that one truly feels compassion only for those in a less fortunate position. This idea is so important to Rousseau that he made it one of his three maxims concerning *pitié:* "It is not in the human heart to put ourselves in the place of people who are happier than we, but only in that of people who are more pitiable" (E 223). An ethic of compassion must include the ability to rejoice with the joyful as well as the ability to commiserate with the miserable. Otherwise it will value the alleviation of suffering but will not value the advancement of happiness, and no moral philosophy that cannot value happiness is worth its salt.

Of course, these are not objections to Rousseau's moral philosophy, for Rousseau never proposed an ethic of compassion. In the end he says that *amour-propre* can be transformed into an other-regarding virtue (E 252) and that compassion (which arises from *amour-propre*) can therefore be virtuous and not a mere sentiment. But even in this case, he still prefers justice to *pitié:* "To prevent pity from degenerating into weakness, it must, therefore, be generalized and extended to the whole of mankind. Then one yields to it only insofar as it accords with justice, because of all the virtues, justice is the

one that contributes most to the common good of men" (E 253). Hence, even
after Emile becomes a compassionate, educated adult, Rousseau's counsel to
him will be to ground his ethics in justice, not compassion.[56] However, a full-
blooded ethic of compassion could certainly benefit from his understanding of how compassion can be cultivated even in the most selfish person. If
Rousseau's compassion cannot serve as the foundation of an ethical system,
it can assuredly serve as a valuable resource within the system.

NIETZSCHE ON PITY, LOVE OF THE
NEIGHBOR, AND COMPASSION

There can be no doubt that Nietzsche directed much of his philosophical
venom against pity (*Mitleid*). Pity is Zarathustra's "final sin" (TSZ 242, 327)
and also one of his "greatest dangers" (TSZ 185). It belongs to "grudge-joys
and drudge-boys"; it is "the deepest abyss" (TSZ 174, 157). Nietzsche saw pity
as deceptive, invasive, and ultimately harmful. But why should he single out
pity in particular?

"Christianity and modern morality exalt pity," at least according to Peter
Berkowitz, a point on which Nietzsche would undoubtedly agree.[57] It hardly
needs to be mentioned that in the arena of moral philosophy, Nietzsche took
Christian ethics and the conventional, "common sense" ethics of the average
citizen as his archenemies. Nietzsche does describe pity in ways that would
seem to support Berkowitz's claim, clearly associating it with "small men"
and with Christ and Christianity.[58] But if Nietzsche's sole grievance is this
sort of guilt by association, the philosophically minded reader must wonder
whether his rejection of pity is merely a pet peeve, a personal axe to grind,
rather than an issue of real philosophical import.

But the link between pity and Christian and conventional ethics is not
what makes *Mitleid* morally problematic for Nietzsche. This link is actually only a symptom indicating that both Christian and "common sense"
moral codes are infected with what is philosophically problematic about
pity. What is wrong with pity is that it is obtrusive, offensive, and deceptive.

"Verily, I do not like them," says Zarathustra, "the merciful who feel
blessed in their pity: they are lacking too much in shame. If I must pity, at

least I do not want it known; and if I do pity, it is preferably from a distance" (TSZ 88). As Zarathustra sees it, pity itself "offends the sense of shame" (TSZ 265). For one to feel pity, one must first look long and hard at the misfortunes of others, not unlike rubberneckers driving by a wrecked car on the highway. Only after having gaped at the unhappy event are condolences offered. Of course, it is impossible to offer one's condolences if one is unaware of situations in which consolation might be appropriate, but pity seems to require that one go looking through another's dirty laundry, so to speak: It demands that one pay attention to that in which the other places no pride. As such, pity essentially appeals to the prurient interest: "When the great man screams, the small man comes running with his tongue hanging from lasciviousness. But he calls it his 'pity'" (TSZ 218).

It is because pity fails to respect the privacy of others that Zarathustra says it is "obtrusive" (TSZ 265). The immodesty of pity is also a reason for Nietzsche to reject the Christian god: "He had to die: he saw with eyes who saw everything; he saw man's depths and ultimate grounds, all his concealed disgrace and ugliness. His pity knew no shame; he crawled into my dirtiest nooks. This most curious, overobtrusive, overpitying one had to die. . . . Man cannot bear it that such a witness should live" (TSZ 266–267).

But pity is more than simply obtrusive; it also entails a lack of respect for the one who is pitied. Zarathustra learns this from "the ugliest man," who is so inexpressibly hideous that he has fled from human society. But he fears neither their "hatred" nor their "catchpoles"; indeed, if these were their only means of persecution, the ugliest man says he would laugh at his fellow men and welcome their abuse. "But it is their *pity*—it is their pity that I flee. . . . [T]oday [pity] is called virtue itself among all the little people. . . . They have no respect for great misfortune, for great ugliness, for great failure" (TSZ 265).

Thus pity is not only invasive but also offensive, for it cheapens the life of the one who is pitied. The ugliest man has quite a unique status: No one on earth is uglier than he. The pity of "little people" overlooks his singular position entirely and transforms him into an object. Nietzsche was a man who could show pride in scars. He was proud to announce that "that which does not kill me makes me stronger," but pity, he says, pays attention only to that which failed to kill: the injuries, the sicknesses, and not the fact that one becomes stronger for them.

Not only is pity obtrusive and offensive in these ways; it also deceives the one who experiences it. This is a dreadful weakness for one who espouses self-overcoming and the will to power. Zarathustra's final sin is his pity, and pity is the final obstacle he overcomes (TSZ 242, 327). (Indeed, it is on the very last page of *Also sprach Zarathustra* that he finally overcomes it.) Berkowitz holds that "pity, or compassion for the downtrodden, is harmful because it saps the energy and strength of the healthy and well-constituted and preserves what is ripe for destruction, the multitude of weaklings and failures."[59] This may be true, but it is only a secondary threat. The chief danger lying within pity is its propensity to deceive the one who pities by instilling a misplaced sense of pride. As Zarathustra puts it, "The lie of my pity was this, that I *knew* I could see and smell in everyone what was spirit enough for him and what was too much spirit for him" (TSZ 186, emphasis mine). For Nietzsche, to pity is to assume that one understands that which elicits one's pity: Pity is predicated on the belief that one understands the other's pain. This belief is, more often than not, erroneous and all too hastily formed by those who "feel blessed in their pity." To feel pity is to look into an abyss of suffering (TSZ 157); this should elicit sorrow, not self-satisfaction. Insofar as it does instill feelings of blessedness, it deceives and thereby weakens the one who feels pity.[60]

Even gods are laid low by pity's deceptive power. Zarathustra is felled by pity as if by lumberjacks,[61] and ultimately it was pity, not Zarathustra, which slew both Christ and his divine father.[62] In the end, Zarathustra is able to overcome his final sin by molting off the concerns with happiness and suffering that mire him in pity:

> "To my final sin?" shouted Zarathustra, and he laughed angrily at his own words; "what was it that was saved up for me as my final sin?" ... Suddenly he jumped up. "Pity! Pity for the higher man!" he cried out, and his face changed to bronze. "Well then, that has had its time! My

suffering and my pity for suffering—what does it matter? Am I concerned with happiness? I am concerned with my work." (TSZ 327)

It is significant that this realization strikes him on the last page of the book, and equally significant that in his youth and even later in his personal development, Zarathustra himself succumbed to occasional moments of pity.[63] For Nietzsche, the pity that obtrudes, derides, and deceives is an outmoded moral phenomenon that must be outgrown.

So too is love of the neighbor, another value clearly borrowed from the New Testament. "'Do love your neighbor as yourself,'" exhorts Zarathustra, "'but first be such as *love themselves*—loving with great love, loving with a great contempt.' Thus speaks Zarathustra the godless" (TSZ 172). His advocating self-love is not advocating egotism or self-absorption. Nietzsche's concern is that love of the neighbor indicates a dissatisfaction with the self to the extent that one would rather be wrapped up in the affairs of others than be alone with one's own thoughts. It is with such concerns in mind that Zarathustra declares, "One must learn to love oneself—thus I teach—with a wholesome and healthy love, so that one can bear to be with oneself and need not roam. Such roaming baptizes itself 'love of the neighbor': with this phrase the best lies and hypocrisies have been perpetrated so far" (TSZ 193),[64] and "If this kind of self-love is a form of selfishness, it is a 'blessed' form, 'the wholesome, healthy selfishness that wells from a powerful soul'" (TSZ 190).

Walter Kaufmann points out that "Nietzsche repudiates only certain kinds of pity and love of the neighbor"—namely, those kinds that neglect or weaken the self.[65] In cases of those who do not love themselves, what good is their love to their neighbors? Theirs is a needy kind of love; their pity is prurient, lascivious, and prying. Pity and self-love that pour out too much leave the self empty and hollow. Still worse—as was shown before—they also do damage to their objects.

It is because of this that Zarathustra ultimately rejects this kind of pity and neighborly love in favor of an austere form of compassion: "But if you have a suffering friend, be a resting place for his suffering, but a hard bed as it were, a field cot: thus will you profit him best" (TSZ 89), and "Your com-

passion should be a guess—to know first whether your friend wants compassion. Perhaps what he loves in you is the unbroken eye and the glance of
eternity. Compassion for the friend should conceal itself under a hard shell,
and you should break a tooth on it. That way it will have delicacy and sweet-
ness" (TSZ 57). Nietzschean compassion makes no room for mollycoddling.
It does not highlight injuries and ugliness. It weakens neither the object of
compassion nor the compassionate subject. The one for whom compassion
is felt is not placed below the one who feels compassion; rather, the object
and the subject regard each other as equals. Zarathustra himself describes
the ugliest man as "inexpressible" and "scarcely like a human being" (TSZ
263), but at no point does he consider him to be crippled or deficient. If pity
offers a crutch, compassion offers a firm handshake—no assistance, just appropriate recognition.

"Verily, I may have done this and that for sufferers," Zarathustra admits
(therein confessing to past experiences of pity), "but always I seemed to have
done better when I learned to feel better joys. As long as there have been
men, man has felt too little joy: that alone, my brothers, is our original sin.
And learning to feel better joy, we learn best not to hurt others or to plan
hurts for them" (TSZ 88). In the end, one of the fundamental flaws with
pity—and, by association, one of Nietzsche's fundamental concerns with
both Christian and "common sense" moral codes—is that it is bound up in
negativity. Zarathustra's final solution to the problem of pity is to stop playing the game altogether, to stop trying to weigh pleasure against pain, happiness against unhappiness, and to absorb himself in his *"work."* His final
concern becomes only that which teaches him to feel better joys. Yet he does
not pursue these joys for utilitarian reasons; they are merely by-products of
his pursuit of his work.

It is difficult to get an ethic out of this position. Indeed, to even make
such an attempt might well be seen as contradictory to the philosophy of the
self-described "immoralist." Nietzschean compassion is not the same as our
conventional understanding of the term, but it certainly has its merits. One
of the pitfalls of compassion is its tendency toward overprotection, which in
the end can do more harm than good.[66] With Nietzsche there is no risk of
pampering. But to gain a fuller sense of what compassion is, we must look

beyond Nietzsche. My survey closes with an examination of what contemporary philosophers have added to the subject.

CONTEMPORARY PHILOSOPHERS ON COMPASSION

Outside of Buddhist studies, only a handful of philosophers have devoted their attention to compassion in recent years. Lawrence A. Blum published a short analysis of it in Kruschwitz and Roberts' *Virtues: Contemporary Essays in Moral Character.* Robert C. Solomon draws on Blum's account of compassion in his *A Passion for Justice,* where he argues that compassion is a necessary basis for our feelings of justice. Nancy E. Snow's article, "Compassion," uses Blum as a cornerstone and is arguably the best contemporary article on compassion. In "Compassion and Societal Well-Being," Lee M. Brown responds to what he sees as shortcomings in Snow's account, and Martha C. Nussbaum offers an alternative account of compassion in her book, *Upheavals of Thought,* and in a later article entitled "Compassion and Terror." If other analytic philosophers have given enough attention to compassion to devote articles or books to it, they are few and far between. This in itself is evidence of how seriously contemporary analytic philosophy takes compassion.

I begin my survey of them with Solomon and Snow, for they capture the essence of Blum and set the stage for later commentators such as Brown. Solomon's focus is on justice, not compassion, but he maintains that "without care and compassion, there can be no justice."[67] Solomon summarizes Blum's account of compassion as "a felt concern for another who is in some serious or grave conditions" (ibid. 232). Solomon also describes compassion as "fundamentally other-regarding rather than self-regarding" and says it requires "some 'imaginative reconstruction' of the other's condition" (232, 234). It is already apparent that what Solomon has in mind when thinking of compassion is limited in certain respects that have already been discussed: It excludes the feelings of the person who experiences it, and it excludes the positive or happy feelings of others. Nevertheless, Solomon's conception of compassion is useful in that he understands compassion not as an emotion. Rather, he describes it as "a mode of having emotion." He categorizes compassion, pity, sympathy, and others not "merely" as emotions but as "engagements

with the world. . . . Compassion and its kindred emotions focus our attention on the world, on the person or creature who is suffering. Compassion,
pity, and sympathy are feelings, but they are not 'mere' feelings" (232, 233).

Solomon opposes Spinoza, saying (contrary to the idea expressed in the
epigraph of this chapter) that compassion is a moral good because it gives
us access to the pain of the other. He gives the example of a military com-
mander who feels distress over having to send soldiers to their deaths. "At
such times," says Solomon, "it is good to feel bad, and to avoid the pain is,
in some sense, immoral" (233). Spinoza deemed compassion to be useless because it multiplies disutility; Solomon deems it a moral excellence for the
same reason.

Indeed, for Solomon, we would have no feelings of justice or injustice
were it not for painful experiences and the emotions that accompany them,
emotions that are typically deemed to be negative or even immoral. For him,
"wrathful anger is just as much a part of the emotional basis for our current
sense of justice as benign compassion" (277). "Our sense of justice . . . has its
origins in such emotions as resentment, jealousy, outrage, and revenge as well
as in care and compassion" (244). It is not only justice that is tied up with
these feelings. Compassion too is intimately linked with them: "To pretend
that one can be compassionate and fair-minded without at the same time
giving outrage and even hatred their due is to eviscerate the moral sentiments" (245).

For some people, this may be an accurate description of their feelings of
compassion and of justice. However, compassion as I think of it has little if
anything to do with resentment, revenge, or wrathful anger and still less to
do with hatred. Solomon is fully aware that connecting compassion to hatred and anger is unorthodox to say the least, and he treads carefully when
exploring such connections, but even with this in mind one cannot say that
his sense of compassion is akin to that of, say, the Buddhist tradition. Indeed, Solomon mentions the Buddha, finding him exceptional in that, in
many accounts of his life, he developed a sense of justice without ever having
experienced injustice. As a counterpoint, Solomon offers Jesus as one who
suffered the ultimate injustice. It is worth noting that, at least in many ac-

counts, the Buddha was also without anger, or at least without outbursts of anger, whereas the same cannot be said of Jesus (who overturned the tables of the money changers in the temple, for example). I do not wish to imply any necessary connection between anger and compassion or anger and justice in the Buddhist or Christian traditions; my only claim here is that Solomon's compassion, because it is linked to anger, is not the compassion I have in mind.

Nancy Snow takes a different view of Blum's compassion. Snow calls compassion "a morally significant emotion" and seeks to "defend the rationality of compassion as an emotional response."[68] Moreover, Snow seeks to demonstrate that, as a rational emotional response, compassion is a better foundation for society than Hobbesian rational self-interest. A civil society will do better, Snow suggests, if compassion motivates its members to assist one another than if they assist one another only insofar as it is in their best personal interests to do so.

Snow rejects the widely held view that compassion is contingent upon the ability of the one who feels compassion (whom she calls the "C-feeler") to imaginatively identify with the object of compassion (which she calls the "C-object"). As seen earlier, imaginative identification played a role in the thought of both Hume and Scheler, and Snow does not deny that it is possible for a C-feeler to employ the powers of imagination to identify with a C-object, despite the obvious epistemological difficulties this presents. If I say, "I feel your pain," clearly I cannot mean it in the literal, phenomenological sense, but Snow is satisfied (as are Hume and Scheler, among others) that the imagination allows us to recreate the experiences of others with sufficient accuracy to identify with them and "feel with them." (It is also worth noting, though none of the aforementioned philosophers remark on it, that sometimes observers have better knowledge of a subject's emotional states than the subject has. Think of a teenager, convinced of being in love, whose parents identify their child's youthful infatuation for what it is. As the parents' experience is broader than the teenager's, so too is their ability to accurately describe—albeit through their imaginations—what their teenager is experiencing.)

But Snow goes further than the others when she asserts that

the identification essential for compassion can also be effected through
beliefs, held by C-feelers, about their own similarities to C-objects, who
are frequently victims of misfortune, suffering or distress. I argue that
a particular set of beliefs about one's own vulnerability and consequent
liability to misfortune can make it rationally possible for a C-feeler to
identify with a C-object's plight, and thus is sufficient to warrant compassion as a rational response in many situations in which it is felt.[69]

Snow says her thought is in keeping with that of Aristotle, who describes
eleos in similar terms (cf. *Rhetoric* 1385b12–1386b8). For Snow, it is a belief
in mutual vulnerability that prompts us to feel compassion for others, and
this is a perfectly intuitive position to adopt. When we hear of people killed
by drunk drivers, our thoughts can easily drift to all the times we ourselves
have been on the road. It does not take much reflection to realize that what
separates us from the victims of drunk driving is little more than dumb luck.
By the same token, a common defensive mechanism is for people to refuse to
think about their similarities to those who experience misfortune. Soldiers
are taught to think of the enemy as inhuman objects, and indeed one can
hardly imagine someone learning to fire a weapon by considering the human
dignity inherent in the target. In the heat of battle, the last thing military
commanders want is for their infantry to consider how much is held in common with the infantry of the opposing side.[70]

"Central to compassion," Snow says, "is the belief, 'that could be me.'"[71]
Beliefs are indispensable to compassion in part because they distinguish
compassion from other emotions. "The feeling of pity, for example, is phenomenologically indistinguishable from that of compassion or grief, barring
reference to beliefs." But pity and compassion are importantly different for
Snow. Like Nietzsche, Snow holds that pity "includes a stance of superiority
toward the object of emotion that is often expressed in condescension." On
the other hand, she defines compassion as "a 'suffering-with' another that
includes an altruistic concern for the other's good." She goes on to say that
"There is an immediacy or urgency about compassion that pity lacks. . . . We
can pity someone while maintaining a safe emotional distance from what he

or she is undergoing. When we feel compassion this emotional distance is crossed. We desire to relieve the other's plight, and in so doing, relieve ourselves of the burden of sharing the trauma caused by his or her condition." This is very much in keeping with the common understanding of what compassion means. It is not only an awareness of another's suffering but also a desire for the alleviation of that suffering. Snow limits compassion to suffering only and to relatively significant forms of it: Indigestion does not count (196–198).

This account of compassion is sufficiently robust, according to Snow, to serve as the basis for a society. Here she follows Hobbes' project, but she holds that in the state of nature it is not rational self-interest but rational compassion that will lead to the best kind of society. Snow maintains that, "all things considered, rational persons would prefer living in a society in which compassion is fundamental to living in a society in which social allegiance is generated only to the extent to which persons' rational self-interest is served."[72] She says her compassion-based model "views weakness not as actual lack of ability, but as potential lack of ability. It recognizes the fact that each person is vulnerable. . . . Rational persons are aware of this limitation."[73] Hence, rational persons will choose a social model in which their vulnerability is minimized. This, Snow says, will be a society based on compassion—that is, "one in which persons are more likely to view their fellows as intrinsically valuable moral equals who are worthy of compassionate care and concern."[74]

Lee Brown argues that Snow's account of compassion is ultimately incapable of supporting what she would have it support—namely, a viable society—because compassion itself is unreliable. Brown forwards four points against Snow's position: first, that compassion is frequently either irrational or irresponsible; second, that compassionate relationships do not require certain traits necessary for maintaining a viable society; third, that compassion's unpredictability yields unpredictable results; and fourth, that compassion cannot be legislated and is therefore incapable of serving as the basis of obligation in a civil society. I shall consider each of his four points in turn.

Brown claims that, "although compassion can be viewed as a rational emotional response, it is not invariably a rational emotional response."[75] This may well be so, but it is not at all clear that Snow includes irrational compassion within her compassionate model of social philosophy. In fact, the point of her establishing compassion as a rational emotional response is arguably to remove from her discussion the kind of irrational compassion Brown has in mind.[76] (Solomon, following Blum's usage of the word "compassion" as Snow does, also links compassion with rationality, thereby ruling out Brown's irrational compassion: For Solomon, "the significance of compassion is that it ... provides rationality with a heart."[77])

This problem recurs in Brown's response to Snow: He criticizes her on positions she does not hold. Brown relies on a Hobbesian account of rationality that Snow explicitly challenges, then argues that Snow's rational compassion fails by Hobbesian standards. He deems "feelings of empathy"[78] as being unreliable bases for realizing social justice, but Snow has nothing to say about feelings of empathy. He says, "A recognition of misfortune is not always followed by feelings of ... compassion, or by compassionate behavior,"[79] yet Snow's account of compassion is not grounded in recognizing misfortune but rather the recognition of mutual vulnerability. Thus much of his criticism fails because it is not aimed at the right target.

Brown's second objection is that "a compassion-based theory of a civil and political society can fail to have features that are essential for grounding a viable civil and political society and that such a theory will have features that undermine the viability of a civil and political society."[80] This is a two-part objection, and the first part of it is arguably not a problem. That a theory *can* fail to have some feature or other is not problematic provided that it does not *in fact* fail to have it. The specific feature Brown speaks of with regard to Snow is the rationality of compassion[81]—that is, compassion's capacity to be irrational—but since Snow is speaking only of compassion as a rational response, the potential gap has been closed.

The latter part of Brown's second objection cuts deeper. Because compassion turns on the C-feeler identifying with the C-object, compassion is limited by the extent to which compassionate agents can identify with C-objects. But because, as history so often reveals, those in power often cannot or will not identify with the disempowered, those who are most in need of compassion are the least likely to receive it. What oppressed people need is justice, and Brown contends that compassion, because it hinges on identification, will not provide that.

I think he makes a strong point. However, it is important to keep in mind that social oppression is not a given; one might even suggest it occurs *because* the oppressors are uncompassionate. Hence much of the problem lies not with compassion itself but with the absence of it (and the presence of certain vices, no doubt). But there is a legitimate tension here between compassion and justice, for justice claims to be impartial while compassion does not. The question of partiality and impartiality will arise throughout the following pages and will be addressed in greater depth in chapter 4.

Brown's third objection, that compassion is unpredictable, appears to turn on his commitment to a Hobbesian rational self-interest. The objection is therefore question begging, for as Brown would have it, predictability arises out of that very conception of rationality. It is worth pointing out that, in addition to being question begging, the objection is double edged, for rationally self-interested agents also act unpredictably.

His fourth objection is arguably false. Brown claims that "one cannot be held accountable for the feelings that one has," for "feelings and emotions are involuntary responses."[82] This position seems particularly odd coming from Brown, a practicing Zen Buddhist, given that the Eightfold Path demands right feeling. Morally appropriate emotional responses are also important to Aristotle, who maintains—as will virtually every virtue ethicist—that moral evaluation must examine not action but action coupled with the dispositions, beliefs, and feelings that motivate the action. Take racism as an example: Many people—including Aristotle, the Buddha, and one would have thought Brown—would agree that if I harbor viciously racist feelings but am too scared to act on them, I am nevertheless immoral in my racism. Even if no one other than me ever perceives my racism, in principle I still ought not to feel the way I do. It is strange that Brown should overlook this, given the numerous examples of racism, homophobia, and other social biases he cites in support of his second objection. Perhaps a state cannot legislate feeling—that is, cannot literally write it into an enforceable law—but feelings can certainly be demanded of us by our moral systems.[83]

But just because Brown's objections fall short does not mean that Snow's position is without fault. As was stated earlier, Snow openly claims to be following Aristotle in her thinking on compassion. In her words, "Aristotle calls the emotion that he discusses 'pity' [*eleos*], but it resembles in essential respects what I call 'compassion.'"[84] But *eleos* was previously shown to be insufficiently sturdy to guide moral decision making by itself. Snow's only evident concern is with suffering, but ethics—as well as the social and political philosophy she writes about—must take satisfaction into its purview as well. Ethical life is about more than the escape from suffering.

Martha Nussbaum breaks down compassion rather differently. She too limits compassion to "another person's suffering or lack of well-being,"[85] but for Nussbaum compassion consists of four distinct kinds of judgment. The first is the judgment of seriousness; like Snow, Nussbaum holds that trivial forms of suffering (indigestion, etc.) do not warrant compassionate responses (though they may elicit some less significant kind of sympathetic response). Second is the judgment of nondesert, for according to Nussbaum we do not extend compassion to those who are undeserving. (If I suffer a huge financial loss in the form of IRS fines for many years of tax fraud I knowingly committed, I should not expect compassion from you.) Third is the judgment of similar possibilities, which assesses whether the C-feeler and the C-object (to use Snow's terminology) are similarly situated in such a way that the C-feeler sees the suffering of the C-object and thinks, "It could have been me." Here Nussbaum and Snow are largely in agreement, though Nussbaum suggests that this judgment need not always be possible. (Humans can indeed feel compassion for, say, dairy cows on factory farms, though the probability that human beings will undergo similar maltreatment is safely close to zero.) Finally comes the eudaimonistic judgment: "namely, a judgment that places the suffering person or persons among the more important parts of the life of the person who feels the emotion."[86] Nussbaum warns her readers not to confuse eudaimonism with egoism, but as she sees it, "the things that occasion a strong emotion in us are things that correspond to what we have invested with importance in our account of what is worth pursuing in life."[87]

There is little trace of emotionality in these four judgments, but this is not necessarily problematic; Nussbaum wants to stay away from the idea that compassion is "just a warm feeling in the gut."[88] I take it that it is possible for us to cultivate the kinds of judgment Nussbaum speaks of, the last of them being perhaps the most important one to develop. If I cannot see your values as valuable, I cannot feel compassion when they are stripped from you, and then my compassion is in fact a moral impediment. An overly narrow sense of compassion amounts to bigotry. If we can cultivate Nussbaum's four kinds of judgment, then compassion can be seen as morally constructive.

That said, it is not clear that compassion ought to be confined as Nussbaum confines it. I see no reason why the judgment of seriousness is necessary. Why should we think it incoherent for me to say I feel a very tiny amount of compassion for those who experience very tiny amounts of suffering? Perhaps I feel none, but then again, in some cases perhaps I ought to. In any case I think the judgment of seriousness is not a particularly serious feature of a coherent account of compassion.

More significant, as has been remarked already, is the recurrent tendency to restrict compassion to the negative. The Greek *paschein,* from which the word "passion" is derived, means "feeling," not "suffering," and "com-passion" is therefore better thought of not as "suffering-with" but "feeling-with" (or perhaps, as Solomon would have it, "feeling for"[89]). It is an odd locution in English to say that I feel compassion for my brother when I learn he wins the lottery (and indeed, Solomon suggests this is an inappropriate use of the word[90]), but ethically speaking it is arguably quite important for me to feel it—most especially when one considers the other emotions I might feel (envy being a likely candidate). But more shall be said on this later.

The second judgment, that of nondesert, may be a factual description of how we experience compassion, but it is not clear that this is morally acceptable. Suppose I knowingly commit tax evasion and am sentenced to prison. I am miserable there but suffer no unjust treatment at the hands of my warden, guards, or fellow inmates. That is, my mother can rightly say of all of my suffering, "He had it coming." Will she not still feel compassion for me? Will she not try to alleviate my suffering (for instance, by sending letters or paying me visits)? And in fact, is there not a sense in which she is doing the right thing when she does so? Letters and visits may well be supererogatory, but they are no less compassionate for being so.

Turned the other way, and assuming that compassion does indeed extend to feelings of happiness as well as feelings of woe, we might think of examples of deserved and undeserved pleasure. Suppose my sister wins the lottery, which she does not deserve any more than anyone else who bought a ticket. She then invests her newfound wealth in, say, a trip around the world, which she writes a book about, which then gets published. If she did not deserve the trip, she certainly deserves the pleasure of seeing her efforts at writing come to fruition. If I am happy for her when she accepts her enormous check, and I am happy for her at her book signing, it seems odd to suggest that one of these feelings is less compassionate than the other, and equally odd to suggest that one of them is inappropriate because of the causes underlying my sister's happiness.

Nussbaum's most important contribution, at least in my estimation, is the eudaimonistic judgment, for this is the principal means by which we see the world through the other's perspective. We truly feel compassion for the other when we value what the other takes to be valuable. Only then can we rejoice with the other when value is gained and commiserate with the other when value is lost.

To summarize, then, we have collected a number of contributions from contemporary philosophy. Snow argues that compassion is a rational emotional response, and Solomon can bolster this position with his observation that compassion is not merely an emotion but rather a mode of having emotion. To this we may add Nussbaum's eudaimonistic judgment and the accompanying idea that to be truly compassionate, we must be able to appreciate what people value as valuable, even when we see no value in it ourselves. Having finished the survey, what remains is to sort out what can be learned from it.

The Upshot

If it is possible to found an ethic on compassion, then it seems that compassion should not be subject to any of the problems highlighted by the foregoing thinkers. Each of these figures can be drawn upon to provide a set of parameters within which compassion must be defined—that is, a set of parameters beyond which an account of compassion must not extend if it is to be considered a viable foundation for an ethical framework.

Scheler points out that fellow-feeling cannot be the sole foundation of an ethical system because ethical imperatives are not always directed at our fellows; some imperatives are self-directed, and it would be impossible to generate self-directed imperatives without recourse to something other than fellow-feeling. Therefore, any account of compassion that is to found an ethic should also be capable of generating self-directed as well as other-directed imperatives.

Aristotle was correct to reject both *eleos* (pity) and *philia* (love) as primary virtues in his ethics. *Eleos,* he said, was not an *aretē* but a feeling, to be controlled by one of the *aretai* (such as temperance, for example). The moral significance of *eleos* is therefore indirect: If one's pity is expressed in such a way that is morally bad, one is held morally culpable not for the pity itself but for one's lack of self-discipline in tempering it. Excesses and deficiencies of pity are symptomatic of what is directly significant to the moral project: an underdeveloped excellence. If compassion is to found an ethic, its ethical significance must be direct, not indirect; it must be the primary trait, not a secondary one.

Aristotle also rejected *philia* as ethically primary, but for different reasons. Aristotle maintains that *philia* is limited in scope: We only truly love those who are nearest and dearest to us. I may wish all the best for the other people who happen to ride the bus with me, but it cannot be said that I feel *philia* for them—that is, that I *love* them. Yet they still have ethical entitlements that I must respect, entitlements that *philia* by itself cannot recognize. Any account of compassion that seeks to avoid this problem must construe compassion broadly enough that it recognizes as morally relevant all the people and all the things (possibly including animals, the environment, corpses, material possessions, etc.) that we wish to include in our moral consideration.

Nietzsche rejected Christian pity because he felt it undeservedly elevated the one who felt pity while debasing the objects of pity. Using pity to create the illusion of superiority above those for whom pity is felt is so obviously problematic that it needs no elaboration. Any serviceable account of compassion must avoid this pitfall and must therefore locate the agent who feels compassion and the object of the agent's compassion on a level playing field, neither made superior or inferior to the other by compassion itself.

Another criticism Nietzsche directed against pity was that it seems to celebrate suffering and cultivate a lascivious curiosity toward the sorrows of other people. Pity is therefore bound up in negativity. "Grudge-joys" is the name he gives those who pity, for they become so caught up pitying others that they actually come to begrudge those who have found contentment. Nietzsche reminds his readers that there is more to life than suffering, more to ethics than the problem of suffering, and this should be recognized by definitions of compassion as well. Just as utilitarianism would be incomplete if it sought only to minimize suffering and never to maximize satisfaction, so too an ethic of compassion should be as celebratory of happiness and contentment as it is concerned by pain and sorrow.[91]

Humean sympathy was seen not to be the ground of an ethical system, but nevertheless he did recognize its importance. The same was true of Rousseauan *pitié*. Sympathy and *pitié* facilitate our concern with others and thereby propel us into the ethical arena, so to speak. Solipsism is no ethical view, and on one level sympathy and *pitié* both call solipsism into question. On another level, sympathy and *pitié* enable spectators to take part in the ethical evaluation of others' actions, and in this sense they actually call relativism into question. But there is a certain pitfall regarding sympathy: Because it is a spectator's trait, and because it is basically comparative in nature, sympathy can lead us astray by wrapping us up in comparisons with others. Sympathy must not be allowed to pit one in a utilitarian competition of sorts, in which one measures one's satisfaction and suffering only in relation to those of one's rivals. The same is true of *pitié,* which is part of the reason Rousseau says it must yield to justice. A functional account of compassion must also avoid this kind of hedonic competitiveness; it must fight against comparative measurements of this sort.

Because "com-passion" is literally "feeling with," the very foundation of an ethic of compassion must take this "with" into account. A viable model of compassion should challenge the assumption that the self can be abstracted from all social relationships and identified independently. Existing as it must in socially situated individuals, compassion must strike a balance between self-love and love of the other. The Christian concept of *agapē* reveals a danger in loving unconditionally, at least outside of the context of the divine. Compassion too must not risk self-annihilating excess. And as Robert Solomon, Nancy Snow, and Martha Nussbaum point out, compassion is both emotional and rational; in an ethic of compassion, there should be interaction between affective and cognitive faculties.

In sum, the following eight conditions can be identified that a robust account of compassion must meet if it is to avoid the problems raised so far:

1. It must be an ethically primary trait.
2. It must recognize the role of affective as well as cognitive activity in moral decision making.
3. It must be capable of generating personally directed imperatives.
4. It must recognize from its very roots the irreducible relationality of human existence.
5. It must be as concerned with the promotion of satisfaction as it is concerned with the alleviation of suffering.
6. It must not degrade its object.
7. It must not be essentially comparative or competitive in nature.
8. It must not be so narrow in scope that it fails to encompass all those worthy of moral consideration.

An account of compassion that meets all of these conditions will not run afoul of the problems that have plagued earlier accounts of pity, sympathy, love, and so on, and it will therefore stand a much better chance of being able to provide useful ethical guidance. Perhaps most contentious among them, at least throughout most of the history of so-called Western philosophy, may be the fourth condition, which draws into focus the *com-* of compassion. The next chapter explores the nature of this *com-*, or being-with, in the process of seeking suitable foundations for a theory of compassion that meets all eight conditions.

CHAPTER TWO

What Is the *Com-* of Compassion?

Whoever longs to rescue quickly both himself and others should
practise the supreme mystery: exchange of self and other.
—Śāntideva, *Bodhicaryāvatāra*

IN SEARCHING FOR the *com-* or "with-ness" of compassion, a good place
to start is with analyses of those philosophical traditions that question the
discreteness of "self" and "other." Numerous thinkers and texts reject this bifurcation either implicitly or explicitly, and among them I select those whose
views may be synthesized into a model of compassion that meets the eight
conditions listed in the previous chapter.

Like the last chapter, this one will begin with a survey. I first take up
Śāntideva, whose *Bodhicaryāvatāra* serves as "one of the principal sources
of Mahāyāna philosophy,"[1] and whose meditations there on the nature of
the self—or better said, the insubstantiality of it—serve as an ideal starting
point. From there I move on to Dōgen Kigen, whose ideas, though removed
from Śāntideva by some five centuries and three thousand miles, expand
upon Śāntideva's thought and set forth a method by which one may realize
the insubstantiality of the self and thereby become compassionate. Much as
Buddhism links no-self with compassion, Confucianism can be seen to link
its version of compassion with its conception of the human self. I therefore
move on to an analysis of Confucius and Mencius to provide a different perspective on the self and on compassion. Lastly I take up the *Daodejing* and
the *Zhuangzi*, both of which provide a critique of the Confucian account
and therefore another perspective on the same issue.

The Survey

BUDDHIST COMPASSION, AND A CASE FOR IT FROM ŚĀNTIDEVA

"Buddhism may claim a unique position among all religions and ethical systems which teach benevolence as a virtue," writes S. Tachibana, "for it lays special stress upon it. It regards it as comprising all virtues, the root and basis of all virtuous conduct."[2] The "benevolence" Tachibana refers to here is a family of Buddhist philosophical terms, including *mettā, karunā, muditā, anukampā, anuddaya, ahimsā,* and *avera,* which can be translated respectively as loving-kindness, compassion, delightfulness, sympathy, nonviolence, and nonhatred. The first two of these will be the main focus here, though two other terms on Tachibana's list are worthy of note. Tachibana observes that *anukampā* is both etymologically similar to the word "sympathy" and serves a nearly analogous role in Pāli as sympathy does in English.[3] He defines *anukampā* as "the feeling which we experience at the moment when we see another in pain or distress and imagine ourselves in the same situation."[4] Understood in this way, *anukampā* bears similarities to Humean sympathy and to Schelerian commiseration (*Mitleid*).[5]

The second noteworthy point is Tachibana's association of *mettā* and *karunā* with *ahimsā,* a concept made famous by Gandhi. Tachibana maintains that Buddhism can claim the singular status of being more dedicated to nonviolence than any of the world's other dominant religious traditions (though he takes this claim too far when he says the history of Buddhism is "free from any bloodshed";[6] it seems he is overlooking the *sōhei,* or warrior-monks, of his own country's past). Given the bulk of Buddhism's history, as well as its central precepts, it is certainly appropriate to associate the practice of nonviolence with the cultivation and exercise of compassion.

Two classical Buddhist terms are commonly translated as "compassion": the Pāli *mettā* and the Sanskrit *karunā. Mettā* is also translated as "loving-kindness," and the distinction between it and *karunā* is important. *Mettā* is participation in positive experiences, while *karunā* is participation in negative experiences; the two could be translated as "rejoicing with" and "commiserating with."

The Japanese brought the two together, for in Japanese Buddhism the term for "compassion" is *jihi* (慈悲). According to Nakamura Hajime, *ji* (慈) corresponds to *mettā*, while *hi* (悲) corresponds to *karunā*. That the two of them are expressed together in the Japanese word for "compassion" is significant: If one only commiserates with the other and does not rejoice when the other is joyful, one has not yet cultivated true compassion. And since for many people *karunā* comes much more easily than *mettā*, the cultivation of *jihi* is a more difficult ethical accomplishment.[7]

The self-abnegation implied by *jihi* is a reflection of the basic Buddhist belief in the empty, dependent nature of the self. But this is the nature of all things, so to recognize self as empty (*śūnya*) is effectively to recognize the other as empty as well. Since both self and other are empty, and since both self and other depend on one another to arise, what self-abnegation really amounts to is the negation of any conceptual barrier separating self from other. Indeed, the very terms "self" and "other" are metaphysically loaded insofar as they point to the reality of this barrier. Speakers and readers of English have this barrier constantly reaffirmed in words like "himself," "herself," "myself," and "yourself." It would be better to follow Freud and replace "the self" with "the I" (*das Ich*), if only it were not so stylistically cumbersome to replace "herself" with "her I" and so on. In English the word "self" is all but inescapable, and so I reluctantly continue to use it in the pages to follow. But *karunā* and *mettā* can still be properly defined selflessly: *Karunā* is a matter of casting off the ego and becoming completely devoted to the alleviation of suffering; similarly, *mettā* is a matter of casting off the ego and celebrating joy.

I will return to the notion of a combined *mettā* and *karunā* later, but in the main the Buddhist tradition has been predominantly concerned with *karunā*, "the *feeling* of the pain and confusion of other beings and a desire to eliminate it."[8] Śāntideva presents an excellent philosophical articulation of the Buddhist argument for compassion in the eighth chapter of the *Bodhicaryāvatāra*. His argument is founded on two basic theses: that suffering is bad by definition, and that this is true regardless of where the suffering is located. "If one asks why suffering should be prevented, no one disputes that! If it must be prevented, then all of it must be. If not, then this goes for oneself as for everyone" (BCV 8/103). (Of course, Śāntideva is hardly the only

Buddhist to hold this position. I focus on him here as a paradigmatic figure in Buddhism and a representative of the Mahāyāna tradition.)

To clarify Śāntideva's first thesis, the reader must note that he is speaking about suffering, not pain. Pain is not by definition bad; by definition, it is only painful. "No pain, no gain," the old adage goes, and it is easy to think of examples in which a particular pain is actually preferable to its absence. Mountaineers endure physical and emotional turmoil in their summit bids, but they would not exchange this pain for an escalator to the top. In some endeavors, the pain is the point. It is a challenge to be overcome, a forge from which one emerges as a stronger person.

Suffering should not be thought of in these terms. We can think of our very neurology as being equipped to inform us of pain so that we can minimize our suffering. My hand flinches away from a hot pot so that I do not hold it for a long time and maim myself permanently. Having touched the pot, I suffer from the burns on my fingers, but if my nervous system functions correctly, I will not suffer for the rest of my life as a result of losing the use of my hand.[9] As Śāntideva conceives of it, suffering is something one would prefer to be without and something one will prefer to minimize when given a choice.

The second of Śāntideva's claims entails that, regardless of whether or not one accepts his understanding of suffering as bad by definition, it is still unacceptable to rank some occurrences of suffering over others. Specifically, one cannot justify ranking one's own suffering as being more significant than that of another. If suffering is indeed bad, as Śāntideva maintains, then it is bad no matter where it occurs, be it in one's own body or in that of a ground squirrel halfway around the globe.

I say "if" because it is inaccurate to claim that suffering is always bad from a Buddhist standpoint. For one thing, in a nondualistic system one ought to be wary of claiming that *anything* is always bad, suffering included. Second, suffering has a certain salvific power within the Buddhist tradition. If I suffer greatly and because of this suffering I attain enlightenment, ought you to have *karunā* for me? This is not making lemons into lemonade; this is legitimate suffering, which I would rather be without and which precipitates my enlightenment. The purgative power of suffering, and its capacity to teach, should not be discounted. But Śāntideva's point is that this is true across the board. If it is a mistake to think of all suffering as necessarily and inherently bad, then this is as mistaken with regard to one's own suffering as it is for any other experience of suffering.

It is this last feature that constitutes the real Buddhist teaching and that challenges the everyday behavior of most people. I naturally prioritize my own feelings over yours because I do not have direct access to yours, and—more importantly—because while my own suffering directly impinges upon my ability to lead a satisfactory life, I can frequently achieve what I take to be contentment while entirely ignoring the existence of your suffering. What is interesting about compassion in the conventional sense is that it makes it impossible for us to be fully content when those for whom we feel compassion are suffering. If my brother and sister are unhappy, I find myself distressed.

What happens in the case of my siblings—and typically happens far less often in the case of the ground squirrel halfway around the world—is that I do not erect a firm conceptual barrier between their suffering and my own. There is a sense in which my brother's suffering is my suffering. However, this perspective is still too limited, as evidenced by the fact that in this case neither my brother nor I must necessarily be concerned about the suffering of ground squirrels. Rather than saying, "His suffering is mine," it would be better to say, "For him to suffer is for me to suffer." On this latter view, no ownership is claimed over the suffering. It simply exists as something to be alleviated.

Śāntideva makes the same point: "Without exception, no sufferings belong to anyone. They must be warded off simply because they are suffering" (BCV 8/102). The reason we put limitations on the suffering we seek to ward off is because we have become accustomed to thinking of ourselves as distinct wholes, a view Śāntideva emphatically rejects. He likens the suffering person—indeed, any person—to an army or a queue, neither of which is truly possessed of independent existence (*svabhāva*) (BCV 8/101). Neither the queue nor the army can be distinguished from the individuals who form it; in the same way, consciousness cannot be distinguished from the individual experiences that make it up. What one perceives as the persisting self is in fact nothing other than a bundle of *skandhas,* fleeting ephemera that are replaced by subsequent and equally short-lived ephemera.[10]

As was remarked in the previous chapter, Hume's concept of the self is not far afield from this account. Whether the bundle of *skandhas* that finishes reading this sentence is identical with the bundle that started it is up for debate even among the various Buddhist schools, but it is safe to say that all Buddhists will agree that the bundle that is typing these words will no longer exist by the time this chapter reaches its close. Thus Śāntideva declares, "The notion 'it is the same me even then' is a false construction, since it is one person who dies, quite another who is reborn" (BCV 8/98). Therefore, "Just as the body, with its many parts from division into hands and other limbs, should be protected as a single entity, so too should this entire world which is divided, but undivided in its nature to suffer and be happy" (BCV 8/91).[11]

Conventionally we think of self-preservation as a healthy instinct, but exactly the opposite is true in Śāntideva's thought. The very concept of the persisting self is a delusion, even a sickness, and the drive toward self-preservation can only lead one headlong into suffering. "If one does not let go of self," he says, "one cannot let go of suffering, as one who does not let go of fire cannot let go of burning" (BCV 8/135). Śāntideva makes this analogy with all seriousness: Just as fire is the source of the experience of burning, the notion of the self is the origin of the experience of suffering. The idea of the self as a real, unchanging thing gives rise to fear and ultimately gives rise to Woody Allen's quip that the two most beautiful words in the English language are "it's benign." The same idea motivates a similar fear of gray hair and wrinkles.[12] If one recognizes—as Śāntideva does—that there is no such thing as a persisting self, it becomes much easier to cope with the inevitable extinction of the collection of experiences that we conventionally call the self.

If self-preservation is abandoned as delusional, something must be adopted to replace it. Śāntideva is no nihilist, and he would likely have granted that *anātman,* taken by itself, might well lead to a kind of nihilism in which wanton suffering could be caused with impunity. If there are no selves to be hurt, why not go about causing hurt to one's heart's content? A nihilist of this sort extends the nonreality of the enduring self to suffering, concluding that suffering is unreal (and therefore morally unobjectionable). However, here the underlying assumption remains that suffering is attached to the notion of the ego; get rid of the ego and you get rid of suffering. But Śāntideva does not call the existence of suffering into question. For him its existence is a given, revealed by Siddhartha Gautama's first Noble Truth. What does not exist, what is truly empty, is the idea of suffering as an independent entity, unconnected from any other existence. Suffering does not have *svabhāva;* rather, it arises dependently as an experience in the context of other experiences. Noticing one's first gray hair is not inherently an experience of suffering: Suffering is but a reaction—one wholly dependent on who experiences it and the context in which it is experienced.

To put it briefly, suffering is defined in terms of sufferers and sufferers are defined in terms of suffering. To put it even more briefly, *pratītyasamutpāda:* Suffering, like everything else, arises dependently.[13] But suffering is given as factually arising in the world. It is the result of delusions, one of these being the delusion of the *ātman*—the real, permanent, unchanging ego. Hence, Buddhists such as Śāntideva embrace the concept of *anātman,* or non-ego, rejecting self-preservation as a worthy instinct and replacing it with the idea that suffering is to be warded off simply because of its inherent nature.[14]

This is all well and good in theory, but how is it to be practiced? The first step is to realize that the very notion of the enduring ego elicits suffering in the one who clings to it. "What wise person would want such a self, protect it, worship it, and not see it as an enemy? Who would treat it with regard?" (BCV 8/124). The wise response is to meditate on the ego until one understands its fundamental nonreality. "In the same way that, with practice, the idea of a self arose towards this, one's own body, though it is without a self, with practice will not the same idea of a self develop towards others too?" (BCV 8/98). Erasing the conceptual distinction between self and other is only a matter of practice along these lines. When one embraces *anātman,* the dichotomy between self and other disintegrates, for if the first half of it is negated, the oppositional pair ceases to exist. Self and other are no longer considered to be opposites; rather, they are mutually entailing and they arise dependently (*pratītyasamutpāda*). Simple meditation will reveal that all sentient beings share the experience of suffering in common (BCV 8/90).[15] "Therefore," says Śāntideva, "in order to allay my own suffering and to allay the suffering of others, I devote myself to others and *accept them as myself*" (BCV 8/135, emphasis mine).

This is how Śāntideva unravels "the supreme mystery," which, as the epigraph to this chapter states, is namely "the exchange of self and other" (BCV 8/120). Egoism is abandoned in favor of altruism. One's own body becomes no more than a tool to employ in the service of alleviating the suffering of others (BCV 8/184). This is the way to practice compassion, and this emphasis on throwing the body away for the sake of practice is echoed some five hundred years after Śāntideva by Dōgen Kigen.

DŌGEN'S COMPASSION

Dōgen's Sōtō Zen can contribute two things to the account of Buddhist compassion developed thus far. First, by expanding the notion of sentience, it radically expands the scope of what compassion can encompass. Second, it provides the basis for a methodology for extending compassion in this way. Dōgen makes these contributions through his analyses of "all sentient beings" (*issai shujō*, 一切衆生), "dropping off body-mind" (*shinjin datsuraku,* 身心脱落), "just-sitting" (*shikantaza,* 祇管打座), and what he calls *genjōkōan* (現成公案).

Genjōkōan is the title of what is probably Dōgen's most often-quoted work. It was the second fascicle he wrote for his *Shōbōgenzō* and can therefore be seen as a sort of gateway for him into his *magnum opus,* a work that helped him give direction to his masterpiece.[16] Even according to some of the best translators of Dōgen's writings, it is "impossible to give adequate English translation" to the term *genjōkōan.*[17] If adequate translation is impossible, we may at least examine what translations we have and approximate from those.

Kōan is an abbreviation of *kōfu no antoku,* a public notice board upon which new laws were posted in medieval China; this legal tradition is reflected in translations of *genjōkōan* such as "realized law" (by Nishijima and Cross[18]) and "first principle" (by Suzuki Shunryu, who explicitly refers to principles handed down by a monarch[19]). In the Zen tradition, the word *kōan* came to describe a paradox on which practitioners are asked to meditate. (Hee-Jin Kim's translation of *genjōkōan* as "the *kōan* realized in life"[20] reflects this long-standing Buddhist tradition.) A third interpretation of *kōan* takes the publicity of *kō* to suggest "parity" and reads *an* as "keeping to one's sphere."[21] On this reading, *kōan* can be translated loosely as "particular entities achieving parity with each other," an allusion to *pratītyasamutpāda*.

Genjō is literally "becoming manifest," but if one asks *what* is becoming manifest, the answer, according to Suzuki Shunryu (among others), is "everything."[22] Indeed, Suzuki says straightforwardly, "*genjō* is everything."[23] Combined with the third interpretation of *kōan*, *genjōkōan* would then be a further allusion to *pratītyasamutpāda*, with a possible translation of it being "particular entities achieving parity with each other by manifesting together." Of all the many translations of *genjōkōan*, T. P. Kasulis' "presencing of things as they are" comes closest to this reading of the term, and though his is a philosophical translation rather than a literal one, I will employ it because of the insights it contains into Buddhist compassion.

In *Shōbōgenzō Genjōkōan*, Dōgen says,

> To learn about Buddhism is to learn about the ego.
> To learn about the ego is to forget the ego completely.
> To forget the ego completely is to be confirmed by the myriad things.
> To be confirmed by the myriad things is to drop off body-mind of oneself and others.
> If you get to this place, by doing so your every action will be presencing things as they are.
> If you get to this path, by doing so your every action will become presencing things as they are.[24]

For things to be present as they are (*genjōkōan*, or to use another phrase from Japanese Buddhism, *sono mama de*) is for them to be revealed as impermanence-Buddha-nature (*mujō-busshō*, 無常仏性). Dōgen says that any of my actions can make them appear this way to me, provided that I can drop off body-mind (*shinjin-datsuraku*, 身心脱落) and completely forget the notion of ego (*ko*, 己).[25] This awareness is certainly not restricted to meditative states; though Dōgen's Zen is founded on the doctrine of just-sitting (*shikantaza,* 祇管打座), the point of *zazen* meditation is to develop this awareness and then carry it beyond the meditation hall to daily life.

Dropping off body-mind is as important to Dōgen's thought as are *genjōkōan* and *shikantaza* (or, more broadly, *zazen*). Indeed, each one of these presupposes each of the others. Together, the three of them form a process: By just-sitting (or by doing *zazen* in general, while sitting or while doing something as ordinary as cutting vegetables), one is able to drop off body-mind so that things presence themselves as they are. To drop off body-mind is to drop off the notion of ego and realize non-ego (*muga,* 無己). Realizing non-ego must not be understood solipsistically (since the very idea of one distinct ego must be abandoned); just as there is no ego in one's own embodiment (*jiko,* 自己), neither does ego reside in that of others (*tako,* 他己). Dropping these off completely, there remains only a continuity in which all existences are equally included. All existences co-arise dependently and ephemerally; in Dōgen's language, they are all impermanence-Buddha-nature (*mujō-busshō,* 無常仏性).

When one completely forgets the notion of the ego, one throws away conceptual barriers and effectively expands one's sense of personal existence to include everything within one's experience. As Francis H. Cook describes it, "The process of self-forgetting is simultaneously a process of encompassing more and more of experience as 'self,' and . . . such a process in the individual promotes an enhanced humanness, not a diminished humanness."[26] Cook later says, "The authentic self as concrete experience is profoundly immersed in experience, which is to say, the world. In other words, the life of the authentic self is none other than the life of everything."[27]

When Dōgen speaks of "everything," he often uses the term *issai shujō* (一切衆生), which is "all sentient beings." But Dōgen's conception of "sentient beings" (衆生) is idiosyncratic, for he includes mountains, rivers, motes of dust, and even synthetic things such as fences and roof tiles.[28] In short, for him "all sentient beings" extends to all existences. This is a challenge to the Buddhist tradition he inherited, and it can also be seen as a challenge to Śāntideva, whose argument for compassion focused primarily on suffering and therefore on "sentient beings" in the more conventional sense.

Thus, when Cook tells us, "The life of the authentic self is none other than the life of everything," he means it quite literally. Dōgen himself affirms this in *Shōbōgenzō Yuibutsu-yobutsu* ("Buddhas Alone, Together with Buddhas"): "What the buddhas mean by the ego is nothing other than the whole universe. Thus, whether or not one is aware of it, there is no universe that is not this ego."[29] In *Shōbōgenzō Genjōkōan,* he conveys the same message in a different way: "To carry the ego to the myriad things and to confirm them through practice is delusion. The myriad things advancing to confirm the ego through practice is enlightenment."[30]

This last line includes the idea of the process described before: Through just-sitting or *zazen,* one can drop off body-mind, and by dropping off body-mind and realizing non-ego, the myriad things presence themselves as they are. I will call this Dōgen's method for becoming compassionate, though the connection between this process and Buddhist compassion is perhaps not yet clear. Compassion is largely concerned with suffering, and few of us need to be taught the first of the Buddha's Four Noble Truths to come to the conclusion that there is indeed suffering in the world.[31] At any rate, Dōgen does not doubt it, and when he exhorts us to do *zazen* and drop off body-mind, he is asking us to erase the fictitious conceptual barriers that wall off the suffering of the world. We are without ego; we are all impermanence-Buddha-nature; we suffer together.

Now, to recall Śāntideva, no one doubts that suffering is bad, and though some may doubt that things like mountains and rivers can suffer, Dōgen would say that even these are not to be conceptually pigeonholed as being fundamentally different from the conventional sense of "sentient beings."[32] They too are impermanence-Buddha-nature, and indeed it is the very impermanence of things that frequently elicits suffering.[33] When body-mind is dropped off and non-ego is realized, as Cook puts it, "the self is experienced as encompassing the 'other' as self,"[34] and so the suffering of every other is realized as personal suffering. And because one is naturally inclined to desire the alleviation of suffering, Cook can accurately say that "for Dōgen, authentic selfhood is an authentic selfhood *for others*—that is, its proper function is that of eliminating suffering and struggle in the world."[35]

To this I might add that just as there is suffering, there is also happiness. When body-mind drops off and all existences are encompassed within one's own, one will realize immediately that joy is joyful regardless of location, just as suffering is painful regardless of location. Thus Dōgen's philosophy can be seen to promote not just commiseration but full-blooded compassion—*jihi,* the communion of *karunā* and *mettā.*

On the face of it, Dōgen's compassion and Śāntideva's compassion are not all that different. Both ground compassion in the refusal to draw divisions between one's own existence and the existence of other sentient beings. Any number of Buddhist thinkers throughout the history of the religion will agree to this much.[36] But Dōgen makes two significant contributions to this account of compassion. First, he radically expands the notion of "sentient be-ings" to the point that one must take the physical world into account when behaving compassionately. (This might not be important but for the fact that the environment has too often been neglected in moral philosophy, a trend that persists across almost every era and culture.) Second, Dōgen spec-ifies a method for becoming compassionate. He dedicated a great deal of his written work—and also the bulk of his daily activities throughout his adult life—to guiding practitioners in the proper way of meditation, so that they could drop off body-mind, realize non-ego, and cultivate wise compassion.

But no analysis of Dōgen would be complete if it did not take note of the fact that Buddhism came to Dōgen through China. Dōgen wants to return to the practice of Siddhartha Gautama, who also just-sat under a tree, but the influence of Chinese culture on his Sōtō Zen is inescapable—nor should one attempt to escape it, if one seeks to fully understand compas-sion. Though neither the Confucians nor the classical Daoists emphasize the vocabulary of compassion as the Buddhists do, as a concept compassion is vitally important to both of these traditions. And what the *Analects,* the *Laozi,* and the *Zhuangzi* have to contribute is significant and of great benefit to a fully fleshed model of compassion. Let us begin with Confucianism.

COMPASSIONATE CONFUCIAN PERSONHOOD
AND THE DYNAMICS OF *SHU* (恕)

A natural place to start looking for compassion within the Confucian tradi-tion is in the work attributed to Mencius, for within the *Mencius* one finds the most commonly quoted passage on compassion from the Confucian tradition:

My reason for saying that no man is devoid of a heart sensitive to the suffering of others is this. Suppose a man were, all of a sudden, to see a young child on the verge of falling into a well. He would certainly be moved by compassion, not because he wanted to get in the good graces of the parents, nor because he wished to win the praise of his fellow villagers or friends, nor yet because he disliked the cry of the child. (II.A.6)

The word translated as "compassion" here is *ceyin* (惻隱). Mencius takes *ceyin* to be one of the four incipient tendencies from which the four "sprouts" (*tuan,* 端) develop, and it is the four sprouts that make us human.[37] "The heart of compassion is the germ of benevolence," says Mencius; it is a natural propensity in human beings and one that must not be denied for fear of crippling oneself (ibid.). According to Mencius, it is in our nature to be compassionate and benevolent; indeed, "whoever is devoid of the heart of compassion is not human" (ibid.).

D. C. Lau tells us that "In [Mencius'] view man is basically a moral creature," and that "Mencius' name is, above all, associated with his theory of the goodness of human nature."[38] The heart of compassion provides evidence of this basic goodness. At the moment the child slips on the edge of the well, one feels one's heart leap. The natural human response is to cry out, to reach out, even if this reaching is purely emotional and never materializes into some physical action to rescue the endangered child. It is but a germ of compassion, and as Lau tells us, "In order to develop this into full-fledged benevolence, a great deal of nurturing is required."[39] Nevertheless, it is there, and it fuels Mencius' rejection of what was then the prevailing view that humanity was basically corrupt.[40] (Contrast "tender-minded" Mencius with "tough-minded" Xunzi, who held that "man's nature is evil; goodness is the result of conscious activity."[41])

But Mencius does little to describe the nature of *ceyin,* saying only that compassion gives rise to *ren* (仁)—frequently translated as "benevolence" —and that "A benevolent man extends his love from those he loves to those he does not love" (IV.A.27). *Ren* is one of Confucius' cardinal excellences (*de,* 德) and a cornerstone of the *Analects.* Thus to understand *ceyin,* one must turn to Confucius.

Now Confucius does not employ Mencius' *ceyin,* for the character of human nature was not a point of philosophical contention in his day as it was in Mencius' lifetime.[42] Nor does another term from the *Analects* leap to mind to take the place of *ceyin* as "compassion." However, one need not use a term explicitly in order to talk about what it represents, and though Confucius does not speak of compassion directly, there is evidence that he is in fact concerned with it, as seen in his discussion of another term in the *Analects:* namely, *shu* (恕).

David Hall and Roger Ames translate *shu* as "deference" and also as "placing oneself in another's place" (TTC 50; cf. *Analects* 4/15).[43] The latter translation points directly to compassion. Compassion entails the ability to understand the position of others, which one achieves according to Confucius by standing in the other's place and perceiving the world as much as possible from the other's perspective. This is why *shu* is understood to be the foundation for the proverbial Golden Rule: "Do not impose upon others what you yourself do not want" (*Analects* 12/2, 15/24). D. C. Lau's translation of *shu* as "using oneself as a measure in gauging the wishes of others" (LY 135n) supports this reading of *shu,* but according to Lau, *shu* by itself is not enough to bring about the morally praiseworthy acts and feelings that might be described as compassion. "Having found out what the other person wants or does not want, whether we go on to do to him what we believe he wants and refrain from doing to him what we believe he does not want must depend on something other than *shu*" (LY 16).[44]

In Schelerian terms, Lau's reading of *shu* corresponds roughly to fellow-feeling, a trait required to excel as a lover or as a sadist. Fellow-feeling and *shu* both allow one to predict what will cause pain in another and what will cause pleasure: It is then up to the agent to choose between eliciting pain or pleasure, and neither *shu* nor fellow-feeling by itself is sufficient to make this choice. According to Lau, *shu* must be accompanied by *zhong* (忠), or "doing one's best," in order to arrive at benevolence (*ren,* 仁) (LY 16).

Hall and Ames interpret the relationship between *shu* and *zhong* differently, holding that "*shu* is always personal in that it entails *chung* [*zhong*]: 'doing one's best as one's authentic self'" (TTC 287). On Lau's reading, *shu* is amoral in its content, serving more or less as a data-gathering device. On

Hall and Ames's reading, *shu* would seem to have positive moral content, with *zhong* serving as a personalizing force as well as another positive moral influence. According to Hall and Ames, "The methodology of shu requires the projection or recognition of excellence as a means of eliciting or of expressing deference. Shu as a methodology requires that in any given situation one either display excellence oneself (and thus anticipate deference from others) or defer to excellence in another" (TTC 287). Here *shu* itself is essential to harmonious relationships with others; it is not simply a means by which one gets to what is necessary for such relationships.[45]

Because *shu* is needed for maintaining harmonious relationships, it is immediately invested with moral value, for according to Confucius human relationships *are* the locus of ethics. Lau says that "Confucius certainly has far more to say about moral character than moral acts" (LY 10–11), and one's character is formed through the course of developing and maintaining relationships with others. As Confucius himself puts it, "In strolling in the company of just two other persons, I am bound to find a teacher. Identifying their strengths, I follow them, and identifying their weaknesses, I reform myself accordingly" (7/22). For the Confucian, it does not make sense to speak of a human being in isolation from social relationships. Human beings, properly speaking, are irreducibly social creatures, and should some member of the genetic group of *Homo sapiens* somehow become dislodged from *all* social relationships, that being would no longer lead a fully human existence.

It therefore becomes difficult to use the word "self" in a Confucian context, for that term is laden with a great deal of baggage (ranging from the notion of a permanent soul or psyche to the idea of the absolute separation of individuals, which is the genesis of the *problem of other minds*).[46] Moreover, neither "ego" nor "the I" will do as replacements. For the Confucian, it makes more sense to think of families than abstracted selves of this kind. Indeed, the bare fact that there is no linguistic distinction made between singular and plural nouns in Sinitic languages is already indicative of the problem: Even if the word "self" could and should be imported into Confucianism with all of its philosophical baggage in tow, in classical Chinese it would still simultaneously represent both "self" and "selves." If the word

"self" may be used at all in a Confucian context, it may only safely be employed while keeping such caveats in mind.

Roger T. Ames does exactly this when he goes about "articulating the
Confucian self as a 'field of selves.'"[47] Ames' "focus-field" model of selfhood
stands as a rejection of the most prevalent models of Confucian selfhood,
ranging from Hegel's caricature of China's "hollow men" to Chad Hansen's
part-of-whole (as opposed to one-of-many) model.[48] Employing the language
of William James, Ames develops an account of Confucian selfhood that
begins with the family: "The family . . . is articulated in terms of *lun* 倫, a
ritual 'wheel' (*lun* 輪) of social relations that 'ripple out' (*lun* 淪) in a field
of discourse (*lun* 論) *to define the person as a network of roles.*"[49] Both the
family and the individual may be thought of as foci within broader fields.
In the case of the family, the field is perhaps the village where the family
resides, and then the neighboring towns, and more broadly the province.
In the case of the individual, the field is the family itself, along with friends,
in-laws, coworkers, and anyone else with whom the individual maintains a
meaningful relationship.

In both cases, the field grows increasingly diffuse and indistinct as the
distance increases from the particular focus in question. The central government has a relationship to the family, for instance, but this relationship
generally recedes into the background of the field unless something out of
the ordinary brings it into focus. Individuals have fleeting relationships
with everyone they pass on the street, but these relations are only brought
into sharper focus by unusual events (a chance collision on the sidewalk, for
example, or a shared delay at the airport). Also common to both families
and their individual members is that there are multiple foci in any given
field, and that no one of them automatically gains precedence over any of
the others. Ames compares this to Rudolph Arnheim's observations on the
visual arts, in which "every visual field comprises a number of centers, each
of which attempts to draw the others into subservience."[50]

According to Ames (as well as David Hall), this focus-field relationship
is not only descriptive of Confucian familial and individual identities but
is also pervasive throughout Chinese thought in general. Ames and Hall's
translation of the *Zhongyong,* for instance, is entitled *Focusing the Familiar;*

in their view, the relation between *dao* (道) and *de* (德) is akin to that of focus and field.[51] And when Mencius says, "All of the myriad things are complete here in me" (VII.A.4), this too is interpreted as an expression of the field's being fully understood within the focus.[52]

How is the focus-field model of personhood related to *shu*? If a person is one particular focus in a field, it is not separable from the field and does not necessarily take precedence over any other focus. Just as museum-goers can devote their attention to various different points within the field of a particular artwork, so too does the attention shift from one focus to another in the social arena. The players in this arena need not be competing to "draw the others into subservience," as Arnheim has it with the visual experience, but nevertheless one must have the ability to discern when to defer to others and when others ought to defer to oneself. For Confucius this is done by putting oneself in the place of the other, attempting to see the world from the standpoint of the other.

Social rituals (*li,* 禮) provide invaluable assistance in adopting the perspective of others and deciding what sort of conduct *shu* demands. In many cases, it is easy for a first-grade teacher and her students to understand the direction in which deference should flow between them, for many of their interactions are already circumscribed by social rituals. On questions of mathematics, reading, or playground safety, the children should defer to her experience, and there are social rituals in place to facilitate this (the practice of hand raising and calling on those whose hands are raised, for instance). On questions of the students' own artwork (the subject matter of which is sometimes hard to determine), or on matters of their feelings, she should be the one to defer and offer a listening ear. Again, there are social rituals in place to make this easier and times and places in which the teacher is expected to be the listener. (Show-and-tell is a classic example.) Naturally, these social exchanges will not always be one sided. Students are to defer to their teacher by raising their hands, but the teacher is to defer to the needs of the students as well, perhaps by calling on someone who hasn't spoken recently, or even by ignoring those students whose hands are raised and calling on the one who will benefit most by being challenged by the question at hand.

There are some classes in which the lines of deference are not so immediately clear, such as a martial arts class full of adults, where no individual is visibly marked out as the teacher by something so obvious as physical size (as in the first-grade classroom); hence the introduction of ranking systems by belt colors. The rituals of donning a sash or *obi,* tying it properly, always wearing the color corresponding to the highest rank achieved, and so forth: All of these facilitate social relations between experienced practitioners and novices, between instructors and students, and even among the ranks of first-day neophytes. The rituals associated with belts and uniforms need not entail militaristic chains of command in which students must obey every demand of the master (though such dojos do exist). Rather, when students have questions about techniques, belts allow them to find the appropriate person to ask for guidance, and when a practitioner sees someone performing a movement in an unorthodox manner, belt color again indicates whether the individual should intervene to correct the other's movement or stand back and try to learn something from it. In short, the ritual of a ranked belt system facilitates *shu* between students and teachers.

Shu precludes authoritarianism because authoritarians do not earn the deference of others by demonstrating personal excellence; they demand obeisance unconditionally. Rather, *shu* facilitates the recognition of deserved authority. To use the words of Hall and Ames, "The social condition necessary for the realization of legitimate authority involves the existence of myriad and fluctuating deference patternings grounded in intersubjective experience" (TTC 180). "Legitimate authority" is earned by those who author themselves, forging themselves into excellent exemplars for the other members of their communities. When one achieves excellence (*de,* 德), one earns the deference of others, who then ought to become emulators if they are to attain the same level of excellence. (Cf. *Analects* 12/19: "The excellence of the exemplary person is the wind, while that of the petty person is the grass. As the wind blows, the grass is sure to bend.") Hence, deference is not self-sacrificial but rather self-transformative. As Hall and Ames put it, "Deference is a response to recognized excellence. It cannot be forced. Deference . . . leads one to experience in and through another. The object of one's deference . . . experiences him or herself as a locus of value" (TTC 181). Hence one must always "recognize that both the claims to excellence and the exercise of deference have their basis in the notion of self-creativity" (TTC 181).

Compassion as we characteristically think of it is not a "response to recognized excellence," but it does require that one "experience in and through another." Hence, while as a methodology *shu* has the potential to cultivate compassion, *shu* by itself is not identical to compassion. To find a more exact correlate to compassion within Confucian philosophy, we must push deeper.

What kind of person employs this methodology of *shu?* For Confucius, it is the person who acts authoritatively (*ren,* 仁). One could make the argument that the goal of the *Analects* is to instruct, assist, and encourage its readers in becoming *ren.* Certainly Confucius would have been pleased if any of his audience achieved this goal, for at times he seems to doubt whether any such people exist at all. "Are there people," he asks, "who, for the space of a single day, have given their full strength to authoritative conduct? I have yet to meet them" (*Analects* 4/6).[53] Indeed, the Master sometimes wonders whether he himself is an authoritative person (7/34, 14/28). Yet the goal is not so very far away: "How could authoritative conduct be at all remote? No sooner do I seek it than it has arrived" (7/30). But to make this commitment, to will oneself to stay on this path, is the obstacle most people cannot overcome (7/34).

The etymology behind the Chinese character for *ren* (仁) is relevant here. *Ren* is composed of two elements, the left radical signifying "person" or "persons" (人) and the right radical denoting "two" (二). Thus, upon seeing *ren,* readers of Chinese characters are immediately confronted with the visual image of two people: that is, relationality. The communal inclusiveness latent in the very character for *ren* is present in Confucius' own discussions of *ren:* "Authoritative persons establish others in seeking to establish themselves and promote others in seeking to get there themselves" (6/30).[54] For one who is authoritative, individual personhood is already inclusive of others; the authoritative person always conceives of him or herself as embedded in a community. As Hall and Ames put it, "The authoritative person is one who not only extends his sphere of concern to embrace and serve the interests of his community, but who literally extends himself to take in his com-

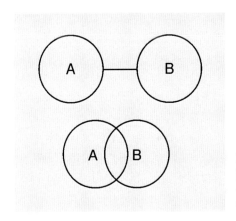

Figure 2.1: The relationship
between substantive persons
versus the relationship between
"eventful" persons

munity (TTC 122)." Herbert Fingarette sums it up saying, "For Confucius, unless there are at least two human beings, there are no human beings."[55]

Roger Ames and Henry Rosemont Jr. illustrate this diagrammatically in their explanation of the inherent metaphysics latent in Sinitic languages as opposed to Indo-European languages. In Indo-European languages, the definite article is intrinsically indicative of a substance ontology: When one says "*the* mountain," one already suggests a permanent thing, and by referring to "it" one suggests that the mountain is the selfsame mountain it was the last time "it" was referred to—and here I use the word "self" deliberately; the mountain is thought to possess enduring selfhood. But in classical Chinese, one says not "the mountain" but simply "mountain," and the word can serve both as a noun and a verb, so that mountains can be mountaining. Ames and Rosemont characterize this as a difference between "essential" languages (such as English) and "eventful" languages (such as classical Chinese), with the corresponding inherent metaphysical presuppositions being a form of substance ontology of essences versus a process ontology of events.[56]

If this kind of thinking is extended to human beings, one arrives upon two rivaling conceptions of personhood: the essentialistic, substantive person versus the episodic, ever-changing, "eventful" person. Relationships between these two species of self may be diagrammed as shown in Figure 2.1 (Note that Thomas P. Kasulis employs diagrams like these to great effect, elaborating upon them where necessary and applying them to a wide range of philosophical issues.[57]

In the top diagram, two substantive or essential persons, A and B, share a relationship, represented by the bar connecting them. Should the relationship dissolve, the two individuals remain unchanged; no essential part of the ego itself is lost. In the lower diagram, A and B share a relationship, but on this model—the Confucian model—the relationship is an ongoing event that is partially constitutive of those who are involved in it. A and B are not atomic individuals but foci in a field. If the relationship should be broken off, both A and B are diminished, for they are both constituted by each other.[58]

The lower model describes some of the most important relationships in our lives. A widow, having lost her husband of fifty years, may very well liken his death to the loss of a limb (or even a lung). Sickeningly sweet Valentine's Day cards with clichés like "You make me whole" suggest the "eventful" model of personhood as well. Indeed, even Aristophanes' mythological account of the separated lovers in the *Symposium* is suggestive of "eventful" personhood: When two lovers destined to be together find each other at long last, their relationship makes them whole.[59] Everyday conversation supports this model of personhood as well, for we regularly define ourselves and other people by virtue of their relationships: "I'm Don's grandson"; "this is my friend, Alex"; "that's Denise; she works with Michele." We speak of our relationships as self-transformative: We "*make* friends" and "*change* each other's minds."

For the Confucian, these relationships are ultimately more real than anything else we use to define ourselves as individuals. This fundamental reality of our relationships is not diminished in any way by the fact that our relationships frequently change according to context: A may avoid introducing B as his boyfriend in settings where others don't know A and B are gay, and he will certainly avoid it in contexts where the two of them are actively hiding this fact. Depending on the social circumstances, B may be described as "my coworker," "my friend," "my lover," "my partner," or even "that jerk I used to go out with." On the "eventful" model of personhood, as the relationship between A and B changes over time, A and B both undergo transformations, and as A and B move from one social context to another, their various relationships with any number of others come into or slip out of focus. Their perceptions of each other, the way they are perceived by third parties, and even their very self-perceptions may change. A gay man who is closeted to his family is arguably a different person with his lover than with his parents; this is accurately depicted by the Confucian "eventful" model of the person.

How does one choose how to introduce another in a given social circumstance? Putting the question another way, how does one go about defining oneself and others? For Confucius, one must do so with appropriateness (*yi*, 義) and ritual propriety (*li*, 禮). Though each of these deserves pages of explication in its own right, the point may be put briefly by saying one takes part in the creation and definition of oneself and others on a contextual basis by keeping the interests of all parties involved in mind. If social interactions are what persons are made of, then one goes about creating oneself—and takes part in defining how others create themselves—every time one interacts with other people. As Hall and Ames put it, "Person making requires a taking in of others into one's field of concern," and from this "it follows that there is a close relationship between the advancement of the interests of others and the cultivation of oneself" (TTC 123). This is why the authoritative person "literally extends himself to take in his community" (TTC 122). It is also why "the concern that Confucius has for the relational self and the communication that effects it is a major theme throughout the *Analects*. The identification and articulation of interests and importances is the basis for person building and the inclusion of others in one's field of selves" (TTC 123).

All of this points to a Confucian understanding of compassion. Authoritative personhood (*ren* 仁), seen etymologically and visually to symbolize the smallest possible community, describes relationally constructed persons as diagrammed and elaborated upon by Ames and Rosemont. In it, the border between altruism and egoism is blurred: It is no longer possible to refer to self-interest as being distinct from others' interests, for the others in question are partially constitutive of the ongoing process that is selfhood. One does better when one's associates do better. Add to this the Confucian excellence of *shu*, through which one puts oneself in the other's place, attempting to see the world from the perspective of the other. To attempt to perceive the world from another person's perspective and to refuse to separate the advancement of that person's interests from the advancement of one's own is not a bad definition of compassion.

From the outset, the conventional understanding of compassion was defined as having two parts: One must perceive that another is suffering and one must wish for that suffering to cease. What we have here in the combination of *ren* and *shu* is a clearer articulation of those very conditions. If one can place oneself in the other's place, one should be able to perceive the other's suffering. And, because one dislikes suffering (by definition), and because one does not erect a conceptual barrier between one's own interests and that of another, one will automatically desire that the suffering of the other should cease.

But the combination of *ren* and *shu* expands beyond this. *Ren* and *shu* demand not only that one wish for the other's suffering to cease but also that the joys of the other continue and multiply. As Confucius said, "Authoritative persons establish others in seeking to establish themselves and promote others in seeking to get there themselves" (6/30). It is not enough that one is merely aware of the suffering of the other; Confucius values genuine feeling over understanding: "To truly love it is better than to understand it, and to enjoy it is better than simply to love it" (6/20). *Shu* and *ren* demand that one adopt the other's perspective and make the other's suffering one's own. This brand of compassion comes up time and time again in the *Analects,* permeating other excellences beyond the ones already discussed. For example, in 12/22, "Fan Chi inquired about authoritative conduct (*ren* 仁), and the Master said, 'Love others.' He inquired about realizing (*zhi* 知), and the Master said, 'Realize others.'"[60]

Naturally, *ren* and *shu* are not without their limits. The closer A is to B, the more readily A can identify with B's perspective through *shu* and the easier it will be to refrain from constructing a conceptual barrier dividing B's interests from A's. If A and B have little in common, it becomes more difficult for A to express *ren* or *shu* to B. Suppose they are simply riding the same bus together, and B's eyes remain fixed in a book; A's capacity to interact authoritatively or deferentially with B is sharply curtailed. But until now there has been no suggestion that compassion is without limits, and, indeed, the limits of *ren* and *shu* may be instructive in discovering what the limits of compassion may be. Though neither *ren* nor *shu* should be translated as compassion, the two of them together do much of the work compassion does, and practically speaking they constitute Confucian compassion.

But this account is not without criticism. When the early Daoists rejected Confucianism, one reason for this rejection was the idea that Confucian values appear to restrict themselves within human societies, which make up only a small part of the world. The full story is more complex than this, but as far as compassion is concerned, this one objection is sufficient reason to look to early Daoism for further insight into the nature of compassion.

COMPASSION IN LAO-ZHUANG DAOISM

Among the philosophical traditions mentioned so far, classical Daoism is perhaps the most difficult school to which to ascribe an invested importance in compassion. Even vocabulary is an obstacle. There is no one term that can be accurately rendered into English as "compassion" and that also appears frequently in either the *Daodejing* or the *Zhuangzi*. The closest option may be the character *ci* (慈), which Lau, Henricks, and Ames and Hall all translate as "compassion." *Ci* does not feature prominently in the text, but it does arise several times in *Daodejing* 67, which begins,

I really have three prized possessions that I cling to and treasure:
The first of these is compassion,
The second, frugality,
And the third is my reluctance to try to become preeminent in the world.[61]

Daodejing 67 goes on to say that "It is because of my compassion that I can be courageous,"[62] and that "to forsake compassion for courage . . . is sure to end in death."[63] It also says, "When nature sets anything up / It is as if it fortifies it with a wall of compassion."[64] Roger Ames and David Hall shed light on this confusing passage: "In nature's own story, each thing emerges within a cocoon of familial feelings as a first line of defense that buffers it against a sometime hostile world."[65] In the context of classical Daoism, *ci* can be thought of as akin to motherly love, a love that is warm but also potentially self-abnegating. Ames and Hall's example of ci in nature as "a first line of defense" is a good one: Think of mother animals defending their nests or dens even against hopeless odds.

A dissenting opinion with regard to translation (among other things) can be found in the work of Russell Kirkland, who translates ci as "solicitude *or* due consideration."[66] Regarding *Daodejing* 67, he says, "This passage is significant because it is one of the few passages in the Daoist classics that clearly commends concern for others. A key element is the term ci, which is usually translated as 'compassion.' But our modern term 'compassion' has lots of ideological 'baggage,' and no one, to my knowledge, has meaningfully explained what this passage really says."[67]

Ames and Hall offer just such an explanation:

> Finally, and most fundamentally, I must be compassionate. In the Daoist epistemology of unmediated feeling, what makes frugality and noncontentiousness appropriate for dispositional interactions is that both entail *taking other things on their own terms*. Compassion funds the concrete network of affective relationships that constitutes one in a particular nexus. *Feeling each other is how we really know each other.* All effective transactions are affective transactions, and require recourse to these invested relations.[68]

The epistemological approach here is suggestive of the interpretation of Humean sympathy as a solution to the problem of other minds. But there is more going on here. To take other things on their own terms is the best way to really know them, but it is often the way to avoid contention with them as well, and this noncontentiousness is best described as an ethical stance. Moreover, Ames and Hall's explanation of compassion is of interest to the metaphysician as well, for compassion (i.e., taking other things on their own terms, knowing them, not contending with them) makes possible the relational network that is constitutive of both oneself and the other.

Bearing all of this in mind, consider the following passages from the *Zhuangzi*:

> Without an Other there is no Self, without Self no choosing one thing rather than another.

"Other" comes out of "it," "it" likewise goes by "other."
What is It is also Other, what is Other is also It. . . . Where neither It
nor Other finds its opposite is called the axis of the Way.[69]

These lines speak to the metaphysical, ethical, and epistemological concerns
raised above. In brief, they constitute a rejection of every kind of essential-
ism. They highlight a fundamental philosophical error inherent in drawing
hard and fast distinctions between oneself and the rest of the world. To fall
prey to this error is to fail to recognize that one is embedded in the world,
and that one cannot be oneself without being a feature of the world. To
divorce "it" from "other" or "self" from "other" in absolute terms is, for the
authors of the *Daodejing* and the *Zhuangzi,* to fail to understand the nature
of one's existence. This is why "the axis of the Way" is "where neither It nor
Other finds its opposite." As a midpoint between "self" and "other," the axis
of the Way suggests that it is realistic to take both "self" and "other" into
account at once.

Thus to do well in making one's Way is to recognize the error in divorcing
oneself from others. This recognition is the foundation of compassion. We
are most compassionate when we do not divide ourselves fully from those
for whom we feel compassion. Thus it is easier to feel compassion for a lover
than for a total stranger: The closer the other's interests are to one's own, the
harder it becomes to distinguish between egoism and altruism. It is in this
spirit that the *Zhuangzi* affirms, "The utmost man is selfless."[70]

It is hardly necessary to point out the strong similarities between this line
of reasoning and the Buddhist argument for compassion based on non-ego
and the dependent co-arising of all existences.[71] However, another parallel
between the Buddhist position and the Daoist position should be noted.
The *Zhuangzi* passages quoted above are all too prone to be understood as
highlighting an epistemic problem, not an ethical one. In this context, however, no line should be drawn between the two. In Buddhism, the realization
of *anātman* and *pratītyasamutpāda* is on one level a matter of *prajñā,* or
wisdom; acting on this realization is then conceived as a matter of *karuṇā,* or
compassion. Nevertheless, *prajñā* and *karuṇā* are two sides of the same coin;
the epistemology and the ethics cannot be separated from each other. Similarly in the *Zhuangzi,* the fact that the passage makes an epistemological

observation in no way precludes ethical commentary from being included within it, and indeed the division between ethics and epistemology must be recognized as one that has little relevance in the classical Chinese tradition. (More will be said about this in chapter 3.)

Though some may say that "ethics" is a modern term that has no place in Daoism, others contend that Daoist ethics have no place in modernity. Many scholars, including some prominent philosophers and Sinologists, call into question the viability of whatever ethic Daoism may be putting forth. According to A. C. Graham, the *Zhuangzi* presents an "uncompromising moral relativism,"[72] and Herrlee Creel seems to agree, for he claims that for the Daoist, "'right' and 'wrong' are just words we apply to the same thing depending on which partial point of view we see it from."[73] And if uncompromising relativism were not bad enough, consider the following characterization of Daoist thinking by Russell Kirkland:

> Because there actually *is* a benign natural force at work in the world, any extraneous action on the part of humans can logically only cause further disturbance. So, from the Daoist perspective, the "conscientious moral agent" is not, as James Rachels has argued, someone who deliberates carefully and then "is willing to act on the results of this deliberation." Rather, the responsible person is someone who is willing *not* to act on the results of moral deliberation.[74]

Kirkland's position is supported by Holmes Welch, who ultimately concludes that "Lao Tzu is not the kind of thinker to whom twentieth-century Americans would turn for advice."[75]

The charge leveled against classical Daoism is essentially one of ethical quietism. The difficulty this poses with respect to the question of compassion is this: Compassion would seem to demand some form of ethical intervention, and quietism is antithetical to interventionism. Thus, if it is true that the Daoist embraces ethical quietism, then rather than having room for compassion, Daoism would actually seem to be opposed to the cultivation of compassion.

The charge of quietism, however, is arguably grounded in a mistaken understanding of a very important Daoist term: *wu wei* (無爲). When rendered into English as "do-nothing" or "dumb inaction" as some translators have done,[76] *wu wei* could easily be seen to entail a kind of isolationism or quietism. But one would do well to challenge such a translation of this important term.

Wing-tsit Chan issues just such a challenge with his translation of *wu wei* as "taking no unnatural action."[77] On this reading, *wu* suggests not the absence of action but rather the absence of any attempt to force natural processes to alter course. This interpretation is also supported by David L. Hall and Roger T. Ames' rendering of *wu wei* as "noncoercive action in accordance with the *de* ('particular focus') of things."[78] According to these translations, action is not only allowable but necessary, for it is arguably quite unnatural for human beings to abstain from action.[79]

This reappropriation of *wu* is justified by two important appearances of it in the *Daodejing,* in which it appears not simply as *wu wei* but *wei wu wei* (爲無爲). *Daodejing* 3 says, "It is simply in *doing things* non-coercively (*wei wu wei*) that everything is governed properly."[80] And in *Daodejing* 63, the reader is advised to "*Do things* noncoercively (*wei wu wei*)."[81] In both cases we are urged to go about our business—that is, to take some action.[82] *Wei wu wei* is neither inactivity nor a form a quietism; rather, it is an admonition not to interrupt the natural flow of events with inappropriate personal agendas.

The next question, then, is whether or not the exercise of compassion is an inappropriate interruption of natural processes. We have already seen one passage from the *Daodejing* that suggests it is not: According to chapter 67, "When nature sets anything up / It is as if it fortifies it with a wall of compassion [*ci,* 慈]."[83] But this passage is the exception, not the rule, for it is difficult to find other lines in either the *Zhuangzi* or the *Daodejing* that clearly describe concern for the joy and suffering of others. Characteristically, compassion is this very concern, and the classical Daoist texts offer little direct evidence of it. Some (such as Kirkland and Welch, perhaps) might take this as sufficient evidence to convict Daoism of quietism. But this is premature. There remains another question to be addressed: Namely, *why* do the *Daodejing* and the *Zhuangzi* lack an extended, explicit commentary on suffering and happiness, and what might such an absence imply?

Two comments from J. J. Clarke point toward an answer to this question. According to him, "Daoism is engaged in combating a particular form of ethical theory which gives priority to rules and names," and he describes the Daoist sage as "[one] who, through mirroring and cultivating in himself the way of nature, the *dao,* exemplifies but does not specify in law-like terms the way for others."[84] The reason the classical Daoist texts say little about suffering in an explicit manner is that their authors have seen so many thinkers before them attempt to deal with the subject and have deemed every such attempt to be a failure. The problem for the Daoist is not that there is suffering. That much seems to be given. The problem lies in how we *approach* suffering: how we mistakenly try to alleviate it by classifying it in ways it cannot be classified.

Support for this claim is found throughout the *Zhuangzi,* particularly in those passages concerned with cripples and mutilated criminals. Amputees receive neither pity nor disgust; instead, they are honored for their insights into the Dao. Dismemberment and disfigurement are ordinarily thought of as reasons for despair, but in the *Zhuangzi* the dismembered and disfigured have been given a new perspective and should be respected for the wisdom this can bring them. Their suffering is largely needless, brought on not by the injury itself but by inappropriate responses to the injury. (Here one recalls Zarathustra's encounter with the ugliest man, who also undergoes needless suffering as the object of others' pity.)

The *Zhuangzi* identifies similar inappropriate responses in the face of death, as seen in the classic story of Master Sanghu's funeral. Zigong, a Confucian, is mortified to see Sanghu's Daoist friends singing joyfully with the corpse right at their feet. Horrified, Zigong asks whether their conduct is in accordance with the rites (*li*). They respond, "What does he know about the meaning of the rites?"[85] Zigong comes to mourn at the funeral because that is what social rituals demand of him. The Daoists, on the other hand, mourn only when they are mournful, not when it is expected of them.[86]

According to A. C. Graham, for Zhuangzi "to lament is to make the mistake of distinguishing the disliked from the liked."[87] For this reason Zhuangzi tells of Master Ziji, who says of himself, "Alas! I lamented the man who had lost himself, then I lamented the lamenter of the man, then

I lamented the lamenter of the lamenter of the man, and afterwards I withdrew further every day."[88] There is a clear concern with suffering here, both in one's own experience and in that of others. The Daoist does not claim that injuries and the passing of loved ones are not to be lamented, but he does maintain that many forms of suffering are simply lamenting the fact that one is lamenting and that this is foolish and selfish.

The Daoist texts are not explicitly clear on how one should avoid this unnecessary suffering, but this absence of a concrete prescription is in keeping with one of the most basic of Daoist precepts: Once you start dealing with such things in a fixed manner, you've already lost track of them. Clarke sums it up well: "Like an artist, [the sage's] self-creative activity should inspire rather than be imitated."[89] For the Daoist, the problem of suffering is no different from any other problem: Attaching fixed names and solutions to it will never avail you, so its resolution will always be a matter of adopting the appropriate perspective—or, as Ames and Hall put it, a matter of "taking other things on their own terms" in order to really know them.

The same advice holds on the matter of happiness. The presumption that the Daoist has no interest in happiness and welfare, despite the fact that all of the rest of us are concerned with them, stands in clear contradiction to the Daoist texts. Both the *Daodejing* and the *Zhuangzi* contain passages written with a sense of humor, and the point of humor is not to entertain its writer. No, the wittier passages of the texts are intended to amuse the reader, and this itself is evidence of a concern for the reader's happiness.

Another instance showing a concern for happiness—and a humorous one, as it happens—is found in the famous parable of the fish in the river Hao. Zhuangzi, looking down on the fish in the river, comments on how happy they are, and his companion Huishi asks how, since Zhuangzi is not a fish himself, he could possibly know that they are happy. Zhuangzi says, "You aren't me; how do you know I don't know that they're happy?" This is not the last of the witticisms in the story, but something else is important here: The parable begins and ends with the *happiness* of the fish. Zhuangzi could just as easily have remarked that the fish are bored, but that was not the story the author wished to tell.

Finally, it is not clear that a person with no concern for the welfare of others would bother to write a book at all. The Daoist texts are prescriptive; they are political treatises, written in order to help others resolve problems. True quietists don't write instructional manuals about being quietistic; to do so is to violate the precepts of quietism.

At this point we may return to the question of whether or not compassion plays an important role in Daoist philosophy. Russell Kirkland phrases the question this way: "How, one wonders, can one be expected to be 'compassionate' when one is elsewhere urged to treat all humanity as 'straw or dogs'?"[90] This is not exactly right—the text speaks of the *sage* treating people this way, for heaven and earth do likewise—but since the presumptive goal is to strive for sagacity, let us take Kirkland's point as he has phrased it. He has actually come far closer to hitting the mark than he thinks he has, though in all probability he is unaware of it, for it seems he does not understand exactly what the mark is. One consequence of the Daoist's nondifferentiation of "It" and "Other" is that, as Kirkland points out, humans are not to be divided categorically from entities such as straw and dogs. But whereas Kirkland sees this as a demotion of human beings to the level of "lesser" things, the authors of the *Zhuangzi* and the *Daodejing* will see this as a promotion of all things to the level of human beings. In the eyes of the classical Daoist, the common mistake is not so much that we overvalue human beings and human endeavors but that we fail to accord just as much value to the nonhuman. We accept lessons from human teachers more readily than from water, wind, or the fish in the river Hao. If we are urged to "treat all humanity as straw or dogs," the real command is to reject what Ames and Hall call "human exceptionalism" and instead to "treat all things and all people with parity, even the seemingly least among them."[91] As Ames and Hall observe, from the Daoist perspective, "even a clutch of straw is entitled to reverence at the proper time and place."[92]

Now the criticisms leveled against a Daoist ethic can be revisited. Kirkland's various objections have already been dispelled. Arthur Danto described the Daoist as "necessarily a loner,"[93] but now this must be called into question. The focus-field model of personhood proposed by Ames and Rosemont would seem to be relevant in a Daoist context, for when Zhuangzi says, "Without an Other there is no Self, without Self no choosing one thing rather than another,"[94] he is embracing a mutual, relational defining process of Self and Other. On this conception of the person, there is no such thing as a loner.

Graham held that the *Zhuangzi* presents an "uncompromising moral relativism,"[95] while Creel said that for Daoists, "'right' and 'wrong' are just words we apply to the same thing depending on which partial point of view we see it from."[96] It is important to recognize that the second of these claims can be true while the first is false. There is a difference between relativism and perspectivalism or pluralism, and while Graham is speaking of the former, Creel may not be, and however one reads Creel, one should not read Daoism as resolutely morally relativistic.[97] Daoism takes a firm stance against unnatural, coercive action, and insofar as it does this, it rejects relativism.[98] However, it will certainly reject moral absolutism as well, and it will not readily compromise on this point.

If there is such a thing as a Daoist ethic, it is a perspectivalist ethic— and this is quite in keeping with a Daoist account of compassion. To adopt the perspective of another and attempt to know what the other is experiencing is the first step of Daoist compassion (the second step being a concern with the other's well-being, a concern I have argued to be an important part of classical Daoist philosophy). Daoist compassion consists in a refusal to divorce self from other, an embracing of perspectivalism, a rejection of anthropocentrism, and a concern to bring about overall well-being (this being inclusive of both oneself and others), all of which must be accomplished spontaneously and noncoercively.

This is markedly different from the Confucian account of compassion discussed earlier. In the *Daodejing,* compassion arises naturally, and indeed we can take many aspects of nature as our instructors in becoming compassionate. But for Mencius, compassion is a fragile germ that must be carefully cultivated if it is to flourish. On both readings, compassion is a natural occurrence, but it seems that for the Daoist, compassion will bloom if left to its own devices (that is, if we do not interfere with it), whereas for the Confucian, compassion must not be left alone lest it wither away.

Buddhist compassion differs from both of these, but whatever the difference in philosophical nuance, compassion is a necessary ingredient in early

Confucianism, Lao-Zhuang Daoism, and the Mahāyāna tradition from seventh-century India through thirteenth-century Japan. These models of compassion will be helpful in chapter 3, where the rubber meets the road, so to speak, for there I seek to explain and apply the ethics of compassion. But before moving on to that, let us consider one more important question regarding compassion's role in the history of moral philosophy.

The Upshot

I have shown that compassion holds a significance in the predominant philosophical traditions of Asia that is unparalleled in the thought of any Greek or European philosopher examined thus far. This is not to suggest there have been no detractors within the so-called Western traditions. There have been many, and their criticisms have been sharp. John Dewey and George Herbert Mead both suggest that human beings are fundamentally relational. Carol Gilligan and the care ethicists that follow her challenge the primacy of reason, contending that caring relationships should be the central paradigm for ethical thought. But these challengers arise in traditions that have never given compassion or compassionate relationships pride of place. The question now arises: Why not?

I will not claim to offer a definitive explanation, but I can suggest a potential answer. Ever since Plato made the reasoning part of his tripartite soul the charioteer and the spirited and appetitive parts the horses to be controlled, a certain rationalistic bias has been favored by any number of his successors. Since Plato, reason has stood largely unchallenged as the arbiter of moral judgment, and from Aristotle to Kant to contemporary thinkers such as John Rawls, many (and perhaps even most) philosophers in the traditions that followed Plato have rejected emotions or passions—compassion being included among these—as capable of governing moral deliberation.

But it is premature to ascribe this tendency to a rationalistic bias, for presumably any bias toward rationalism would have risen from the absence of a satisfactory contender to rival reason in this role, rather than the other way around. Indeed, we saw that Aristotle, Nietzsche, Scheler, and the others all had good reason to reject the various traits they rejected; all were fraught with problems that did not plague the Buddhist ideal of *jihi* or the Confucian excellences of *shu* and *ren*.

What, then, is the explanation? I contend that it lies not in such concepts as compassion, pity, sympathy, or love, but rather in the concept of the self or person in which these feelings take place. The common strand running through Buddhist, Confucian, and Daoist thought is that no bifurcation is made between "self" and "other." The refusal to make this division happens in different ways and is supported by different philosophical foundations, but in every case "self" and "other" are seen to be mutually entailing. If persons are posited as atomic, isolated, or independent entities, then compassion is a step that must be made; in other words, it requires work, for a bridge must be built between oneself and the other. If persons are understood to entail each other, then compassion registers automatically; no philosophical work is required.

It would be incorrect to claim that all of the thinkers examined in chapter 1 subscribe to the atomic model of personhood. Aristotle stands out as a counterexample: He defined the human being as a *politikon zōon,* and the political nature of the human animal is fundamental to his thought. (His ethics, to cite an easy example, hinge upon the interplay between role model and emulator; it follows that for him, the good life must necessarily be a social life.) Because Aristotle links the *telos* of a human being to human *eudaimonia* as a social and political being, a person outside of all social relationships is not, precisely speaking, a human being in the way the rest of us are: That person is without the *telos* and the corresponding *eudaimonia* that the rest of us have as our goals. However, even Aristotle does not claim (as Dōgen does, for instance) that in truth there is *no difference* between you and me or, more broadly, between "other" and "self." Even according to Aristotle's conception of the political animal, compassion effectively remains a kind of bridge to be built between selves.

It is not a gross oversimplification to claim that, in the predominant ethical schools of European and Anglo-American cultures, the central figure of moral reasoning is the "I." The concept of sin is instructive here. In the

Abrahamic religions, sin mars the soul of a particular person, and no amount of sin *I* can commit will doom *you* to damnation. There are denominations within Islam and Christianity alike that emphasize the importance of missionizing and thus of expanding the community of the faithful, but in the end we are all said to be judged individually.

Kantian pure reason also belongs to individuals and is applied by them in individual cases. Indeed, Kant would have it applied in such a way that our unique social relationships are ignored; we are to treat each other as rational beings and to bracket out whatever private inclinations our relationships might inspire. Utilitarian analyses may be applied to laws or the decisions of groups, but there it is the *decision* that is weighed as maximizing or failing to maximize utility, and such decisions ultimately fall to individuals. The very notion of locating moral reasoning not in the "I" but in the "we" is a relatively recent phenomenon in the moral theories of the analytic philosophical tradition.[99]

Again, a prime example of one who has challenged the assumption that the "I" is the natural locus for moral responsibility is Aristotle. For him the ultimate goal of morally good conduct is the ultimate goal of all human beings: *eudaimonia,* or living well. Aristotle says that whether or not one can be said to have lived well depends in part on the conduct and fortunes of one's family and friends after one has passed away. If after my death my children fall into wickedness and my estate falls into ruin, it might be said that my life fell short of the mark of *eudaimonia* (NE 1100a5–1101b1). But Aristotle does not say the same of the moral excellences. If I was held to be brave in life, or generous, or kind, Aristotle would be hesitant to strip me of such descriptions even if my children should turn to viciousness after my death.

Consider this account of moral excellence in contrast to the Confucian account. Confucius holds that if the child fails to behave responsibly, the parent's authoritativeness might well be called into question.[100] He lauds the moral excellence of villages as well as individuals.[101] Twenty-five centuries later, the Japanese philosopher Watsuji Tetsurō, drawing heavily upon the Confucian and neo-Confucian traditions, explicitly locates his ethics not in the individual person but in the betweenness (*aida, aidagara,* 間)

connecting person and person.[102] This accurately and succinctly captures the classical Chinese conception of the person as a socially and collectively constructed entity and is also fully in keeping with the Buddhist rejection of a firm self-other dichotomization. In other words, for Confucius, Watsuji, Śāntideva, and Dōgen, it is only natural to locate ethics in the "we." The "I," strictly speaking, is a foreign concept to them.

It should now be apparent why compassion has enjoyed a certain pride of place in the Confucian, Daoist, and Buddhist traditions: The *com-* of compassion suggests the "we" that is already the locus and the focus of their ethical reasoning. Philosophers who begin with the "I" seem to drift naturally toward rationalism, Kant's pure reason being the epitome of this trend. For thinkers who begin with the "we," it seems equally natural to drift toward compassion or to something close to it (such as the care of contemporary feminist care ethicists, for instance).

This is not to suggest that every person in Confucius' village was a compassionate person. Compassion requires more than simply growing up under a certain set of ontological assumptions about humanity. The point, rather, is that if one thinks about oneself as being constituted by one's relationships with others, then compassion is already implicit in the way one thinks about relationships. It is no more than implicit—a sprout in need of cultivation—but it is already there. If, on the other hand, one thinks of oneself as being wholly independent of others, then compassion is not implied at all. Rather, it is a kind of bridge to be built, a connection to be created between atomic individuals (assuming, of course, that other individuals exist; solipsism is at the very least a live option—and potentially a logical necessity). In thinking about myself and other people, if I begin where Descartes begins, I can still be compassionate, but I must overcome daunting epistemological obstacles to do it. If I begin where Confucius begins, I can still be uncompassionate, but to do it I must ignore what will seem to me to be obvious facts about human existence. Belief in the relational nature of human beings is neither necessary nor sufficient for becoming a compassionate person, but having the belief helps and not having the belief is a hindrance.

The previous chapter concluded with a summary of eight conditions that an account of compassion should meet if it is to be deemed capable of meaningful ethical guidance. Many of these have been addressed implicitly in my analyses of the Confucian, Daoist, and Buddhist models of compassion. The project of the next chapter is to explicitly address the eight conditions in developing a workable model of compassion and then to flesh out how a compassionate ethic might work.

CHAPTER THREE

Defining Compassion

We should all agree that each of us is bound to show kindness to his parents and spouse and children, and to other kinsmen in a less degree; and to those who have rendered services to him, and any others whom he may have admitted to his intimacy and called friends; and to neighbors and to fellow-countrymen more than others; and perhaps we may say to those of our own race more than to black or yellow men, and generally to human beings in proportion to their affinity to ourselves.
—Henry Sidgwick, *The Methods of Ethics*

THE EPIGRAPH POINTS to several ideas that are fundamental to an understanding of compassion. First, it says we are *bound*. All of the models of compassion laid out in the previous chapter also suggest a bonding, one that is part and parcel of human existence. Second, it says that the nature of these bonds is dependent upon the social context in which they are situated. That our obligations to others rise commensurately with their relational proximity to us is an intuition common to Confucianism and to Sidgwick. Third, by revealing a conceit largely endemic to Sidgwick's day—namely, the "our," which suggests that the practitioners of philosophy (i.e., Sidgwick's readers) are exclusively white—the passage reveals a failure to take seriously the perspectives of groups outside of the author's own.[1] The final phrase, laden with anthropocentrism, indicates the same failure. But the adoption of foreign perspectives is vitally important to the cultivation and exercise of compassion, as was indicated by the classical Daoist interpretation. It is a means by which sympathy or fellow-feeling is infused with wisdom to become *jihi*—wise compassion.

Sidgwick, of course, is talking about kindness, not compassion, but we can see in his words a concern with much of what was discussed in chapter 2.

It is now time to draw upon those ideas to lay down a philosophical account of what compassion is and how it works. Let compassion be defined as *an attentiveness to suffering and satisfaction, coupled with the will to bring about the alleviation or cessation of suffering and the continuation and multiplication of satisfaction.*

Four things must be noted about this definition. First, it is of two parts, or what I shall call the two "moments" of compassion: the moment of attentiveness and the moment of will. This is in keeping with the notion of wise compassion (or alternatively, "compassionate wisdom"; if *karuṇā* and *prajñā* are two sides of the same coin, it does not matter which comes first). It is important to recognize that compassion begins with attentiveness, for this is compassion's epistemic component.

Second, this definition is not an attempt at essentializing compassion. It does not say that compassion is the same thing in all cultures. It only says that compassion has two moments, and that compassion is concerned with alleviating misery and multiplying happiness. Its bipartite nature separates compassion from traits like pity or sympathy, while its concern for satisfaction as well as suffering is necessary for providing moral guidance in all the ways it must (even if this necessary connotation has fallen out of the conversational usage of the word). The previous chapter demonstrated that Confucian compassion, Daoist compassion, and Buddhist compassion are not identical. There is no reason to believe that any of these would be identical to properly construed accounts of Muslim compassion or Jewish compassion. This definition says only that compassion, properly understood, is bipartite and is concerned with overall well-being.

Third, although it speaks of suffering and satisfaction—the characteristic concerns of utilitarian ethics—this definition of compassion is not necessarily utilitarian in nature. One of the basic tenets of utilitarianism is that suffering is bad and satisfaction is good, and to maximize the latter while minimizing the former is defined as being morally right. Compassion as it has been defined in this context is also concerned with maximizing satisfaction and minimizing suffering, but it is not implicit in this definition that compassion is good *because* it maximizes utility or *insofar as* it does so. On this definition, compassion may be interpreted in purely utilitarian terms—according to which the maximization of utility is both compassionate and right—but it may also be interpreted otherwise. In other words, it may be that compassion is good for reasons other than its potential as a utility-maximizing influence. This is an important feature of this definition, for it allows adherents of any number of ethical systems, not just utilitarians, to employ this account of compassion in ethical decision making.

Fourth, compassion as defined here is concerned with satisfaction as well as suffering; rather than *karuṇā*, think of *jihi*, the confluence of *karuṇā* with *mettā*. As Nietzsche emphasized, it is important for ethics to incorporate our happiness as well as our sorrow, and an ethic of compassion must not fail on this point. It is an odd use of the word—though not a misuse of it—to say that I can show *compassion* for those who are joyful, but this is exactly what an ethic of compassion will demand. If anything, this demand is a greater ethical challenge than the demand to show compassion to those who suffer, for many people find it quite difficult to find contentment in the contentment of others. As both Hume and Rousseau observed, to the extent that we are competitive, we tend to hear echoes of our own discontent when we hear of another's success.

Perhaps the fact that it is often more difficult to feel compassion for the fortunate is the reason why it sounds odd to use the word "compassion" in those circumstances. Rejoicing with those who are close to us is one thing, but it is more difficult to come up with concrete examples in which one has compassion for a stranger who realizes success, as compared to examples in which one has compassion for a stranger who suffers. This is true in my case at the very least; despite my efforts to strike a balance, I find that the examples I write of tend to describe compassion for the suffering more often than compassion for the satisfied. Perhaps this is because I want to use strong examples, and compassion for the suffering is often quite dramatic. Perhaps it is because suffering itself is often more dramatic than satisfaction, thereby lending itself to better examples. This hypothesis is not without evidence. The best works of fiction are usually about people in trouble; contented people just don't hold an audience's interest. In actual fact we tend to have— in popular American culture, at least—many more conversations about our turbulent relationships than about our satisfactory ones, and indeed in a

satisfactory relationship there is often nothing to report. At any rate, compassion as defined here is as concerned with satisfaction as it is with suffering, even if my examples in the pages to follow tend to describe the latter
more often than the former.

Attentiveness

Attentiveness is the epistemic component of compassion. It is what alerts
one to instances in which one's compassion is called upon. Indeed, compassion can be thought of as a kind of attending-to. Attending physicians are
entrusted with the well-being of all the patients in a hospital ward. A flight
attendant attends to and attempts to meet the needs of passengers. We also
speak of attention to detail, such as that of a glassblower, who must attend to
the temperature of the fire, the movement of the glass, and its distance from
the flame in order to produce works of beauty. It is this kind of attentiveness
that I have in mind: a creative attending-to of needs. Specifically, it is a creative attending to the needs of avoiding suffering and achieving satisfaction,
both of these being considered in light of the relationally dependent nature
of who and what we are.[2]

Buddhism has long linked compassion to highly focused attentiveness.
Zazen can be understood to be this kind of practice. By attending to the impermanence of all sentient beings and also to their craving for permanence,
one comes to have compassion for them. This attentiveness must become a
habit, an ordinary feature of everyday life, if it is to fulfill its purpose. This
is true in the Buddhist tradition—seen, for instance, in Dōgen's *shikantaza* (祇管打座, "just-sitting" or *zazen*-only)—as well as in the thought of
any number of moral philosophers, a virtue ethicist such as Aristotle being
a good example. Aristotle's emphasis on the role of habituation (*hexis*) in
moral development is directly relevant here, as habituating proper attentiveness is a necessary stage in habituating proper compassion.

What, then, is proper attentiveness? It might best be understood by first
examining improper attentiveness, which is also the product of habituation. Selfishness leads me to attend to the needs of those who can benefit

me. Therefore, as a child I quickly learn to evaluate my parents' moods, even if only to get the things I want, and as a young adult I learn to compliment those who can do me favors, to laugh at the jokes of those I want to like me, and so on. On the other hand, altruism leads me to attend to the needs of others simply because the needs exist. Therefore as a child I have trouble understanding, even after the DARE officer comes to my school to talk about drugs, why people sell street drugs at all if they are so harmful to other people. To habituate proper attentiveness—that is, compassionate attentiveness—is to habituate oneself to become aware of needs regardless of location and also to look beyond any personal advantage potentially attached to those needs.

When it works well, attentiveness leads one to wisdom. Wisdom is an excellence extolled by Buddhism, Confucianism, and Daoism, and if there is compassion in any of these, it will be a wise compassion.[3] On the model of compassion being developed here, attentiveness is the means by which such wisdom is acquired.

At its highest level, or when it is performing best, attentiveness bears strong similarity to what people call identification.[4] When I identify with another, I understand the other's experiences as intimately as possible. When the other rejoices, I react in kind. The same is true when the other suffers, and opportunities to bring about the other's joy or avert the other's suffering do not escape my attention any more than they do in my own case. That is, when I have the opportunity to help, I do so as often as I would have helped myself. At this level of attentiveness, I do not divide the other's interests from my own. And once proper attentiveness becomes a habit, compassion can also become habitual.

Because attentiveness serves a crucial epistemic function, compassion is not—as Spinoza charged—devoid of rationality, nor must an ethic of compassion jettison reason entirely. Indeed it must not. However, an ethic of compassion will challenge the notion that cognition is the only operator in the ethical decision-making process. Contra Kant, who holds that in ethics "the ground of obligation . . . must be sought a priori solely in the concepts of pure reason"[5] and that "the teachings of morality . . . command for everyone, without taking account of his inclinations"[6] (compassion being included among these[7]), an ethic of compassion contends that ethics is a matter of emotion as well as cognition.

Hume made a similar suggestion when he said it is not, strictly speaking, contrary to reason for him to prefer the destruction of the whole world to the scratching of his little finger. Reason by itself is not enough to compel us to act morally. It can perform the hedonic calculus, it can apply the categorical imperative, but he says it cannot, having arrived upon what is right, motivate us by itself to actually *do* it.

Hume's suggestion is supported by contemporary cognitive psychology. Psychologist Daniel Goleman describes the case of Elliot, a man whose personality underwent a radical change after the removal of a brain tumor.[8] Elliot's rational abilities remained fully intact, but his *emotional intelligence* (the title of Goleman's book) was drastically impaired. After the operation, "Elliot was virtually oblivious to his feelings about what had happened to him . . . unable to assign *values* to differing possibilities. Every option was neutral."[9] Elliot could rationally understand that people prefer satisfaction to suffering, but he could not prefer their preference himself. Unsupported by the ability to make emotional commitments, Elliot's reasoning mind could not draw such preferences at all.[10]

> Ecofeminist philosopher Karen Warren observes that on many versions of classical liberal moral theory (e.g. Kantian), Elliot-after-surgery seems to instantiate the (Kantian) ideal of the rational, impartial, detached observer! But Elliot's emotional intelligence was seriously debilitated: *Without the ability to feel or to care about any of the options available to him, Elliot was incapable of moral reasoning.*[11]

In compassion, the moment of attentiveness includes this ability to feel or care. Attentiveness is more than belief formation and more than the reasoned weighing of options—for even Elliot remained "able to make every step in the calculus of a decision."[12] Attentiveness is an emotional investment (in this sense linked to the *passion* of compassion), and, if Warren and Goleman are right about the role of emotional intelligence, it is what ultimately makes moral decision making possible.

The present account of compassion, beginning with attentiveness, reflects what we know about human decision making and reflects our habitual emotional investment in our ethical lives. But belief formation is still a part of it. When I attend to those around me, I perceive happiness and I perceive pain. In so doing, I instinctively form beliefs: "She is pleased;" "he is hurting;" "I am troubled." Compassion entails a concern for these states—I want her satisfaction to continue, his suffering to cease, and my mind to be at ease—which then prompts the will to motivate action.[13] Reasoning has not been cropped out of the picture, for I must still evaluate which of my options to pursue. Which of these calls on my compassion, which shall I answer first, and how? This sort of question is one our rationality excels at answering, but this can only happen with a prior emotional investment—namely, an investment of compassionate attention.

Therefore, an ethic of compassion does not seek to supplant cognition, but it does ask reason to "share the throne" with emotion. Attentiveness includes both cognition and emotion: A successful attending physician is capable of making dispassionate decisions and is simultaneously capable of showing warmth at a patient's bedside.

But if compassion does not supplant cognition, then perhaps one might think that cognition is supporting compassion and that in fact compassion is ultimately something extraneous laid on top of reason—philosophical "dead weight," so to speak. Perhaps the insights of Goleman and Warren offer a more accurate picture of the mechanics of the decision-making apparatus, but this is more of a contribution to cognitive psychology than to ethics. (Small wonder, one might suggest, considering that Goleman is not an ethicist but a psychologist.) But compassion must not be understood so narrowly. The traditions most heavily drawn upon in developing this account of compassion all emphasize wisdom, but none of them advocates a form of reason akin to that espoused by thinkers such as Kant or Rawls. Wisdom is grounded in particularity, while Kant and Rawls strive to "cleanse" the ethical decision-making process of the particular, the empirical, and the contingent. In their later works, both Kant and Rawls relax on this point, but their initial "cleansing" instinct is entirely alien to the Buddhist, Confucian, and Daoist accounts of wisdom.

Two examples may serve to clarify the difference and to highlight the importance of compassion in the process of ethical evaluation. Kant famously took a firm stance against all forms of lying, even in the case of a so-called white lie to save another person's life. "To be truthful (honest) in all declarations," he said, "is . . . a sacred and unconditionally commanding law of reason that admits of no expediency whatsoever."[14] As an opposing example, consider *Analects* 13.18, in which Confucius hears of a man nicknamed "True Person," who, with headstrong honesty reminiscent of Euthyphro, has turned in his father for a crime. Confucius responds saying, "Those who are true in my village conduct themselves differently. A father covers for his son, and a son covers for his father. Being true lies in this." One must grant that, given Kant's original premises, his conclusion concerning dishonesty is valid. However, it also recommends a course of action so aberrant from the norm as to seem almost deranged. Normal, healthy people do not avoid telling white lies to would-be murderers when an innocent human being's life hangs in the balance.

Now it is not necessarily problematic that an ethic should prescribe behavior that flies in the face of social norms. The Holocaust and the institution of American slavery arguably could never have happened without the complicity of normal, healthy people.[15] But white lies have no place on a list of such atrocities. Kant's conclusion is fanatical, but it follows from his premises because of the notion of abstract reason on which his moral system is founded. Compassion, grounded in wisdom and an attention to particularity, avoids such fanaticism. What it will say about sons and their errant fathers is still up for question, and the answer for True Person may well differ from Euthyphro's, for while True Person's father stole a sheep, Euthyphro's father was involved in a person's death. But because its attentiveness is an attention to particularity, an ethic of compassion can respond to the novel and ever-changing circumstances in our ethical lives.

The last question regarding attentiveness concerns its subjectivity. Wisdom and reason differ in that, while philosophers such as Kant and Rawls hold reason to be objective, wisdom is commonly understood to be subjective. An ethic based on reason is held to be impartial, while an ethic based on wise compassion is open to being described as subject to partiality. Consider

Kant and Confucius once more: Kant is concerned with objective truth, while Confucius is concerned with being true to one's family. Indeed, impartiality is not generally associated with compassion at all. An ethic of compassion will admit of partiality to a much greater degree than will an ethic of justice. This issue of partiality will doubtless be one of the most contentious points of an ethic of compassion, and I shall take it up again in greater detail in chapter 4. For the present, let it only be noted that the ethics of compassion will call into question not only the possibility of impartiality in ethics but also the desirability of impartiality.

With the moment of attentiveness more fully fleshed out, we may direct our attention to the second component of compassion, the moment of will.

Will

Rainer Maria Rilke wrote, "Work of the eyes is done, now / Go and do heart-work."[16] One could say that the moment of attentiveness is akin to the "work of the eyes"; the moment of will, then, is the "heart-work."

The first point to understand about the moment of will is that, like attending, willing must become a habit if one is to cultivate the excellence of compassion. A second important point concerns the difference between willing and acting. Will frequently motivates action, but a compassionate will does not always translate into compassionate action. It is possible to be compassionate without *doing* anything. In this sense, compassion is similar to Kant's idea of a good will: Even if I am bound and gagged in a prison cell, unable to take any action, I may still be considered to have a good will and also to be compassionate. It is too strong to claim, as Kant does of a good will, that neither compassion's usefulness nor fruitlessness can enhance or decrease its value, for compassion always seeks to be put into practice. However, it may still be deemed to be an excellence even if for some reason the agent should be incapable of acting on a compassionate will.[17]

The moment of will is one of the critical differences between compassion and other associated traits such as pity, sympathy, or empathy. As was mentioned in chapter 1, it makes sense to say, "I have sympathy for you but I do not wish to do anything to help you," and there are many other traits (including empathy and pity) that may replace the word "sympathy" in this statement. However, it is contradictory to say, "I have compassion for you but I do not wish to do anything to help you." Compassion includes a motivation to alleviate suffering and prolong satisfaction; that is, it includes the will to help.

The moment of will must be included in an effective model of compassion in order to make compassion stronger than sympathizing, empathizing, pitying, or feeling sorry for. None of these is sufficiently solid to serve as the foundation of an ethic. However, the moment of will may also appear to be in conflict with one of the principal sources on which this account of compassion is based. Buddhist compassion is said to be desireless, for the pursuit of enlightenment is concomitant with the pursuit of extinguishing the desires. The present account of compassion is not committed to any particular philosophical or religious tradition—deliberately so—but it should be committed to avoid excluding any of them explicitly, especially one it draws upon so heavily. Is the moment of will at odds with desireless *karunā*?

I think not. I have deliberately avoided describing the moment of will as a kind of desire, couching it instead in terms of a motivation to act. Even bodhisattvas must be motivated by something. The question of enlightenment and desire is a long-standing problem in Buddhist philosophy. Enlightenment would not appear to be different from any other difficult goal: Only the most motivated can reach it. Those who pursue it wholeheartedly certainly appear to have a desire to attain it. To solve the paradox, one might suggest that in the pursuit of enlightenment there is a desire but none who desires it. The desire for enlightenment is wholly selfless. There is reason to believe that compassion might also be a selfless pursuit—especially when it is couched in a tradition in which wise compassion is associated directly with enlightenment.

This, of course, is only of interest to those who embrace Buddhism, and though the present model of compassion draws on Buddhism, it is not confined to Buddhist compassion. Any account of compassion, I think, must include both attentiveness and will (or something closely corresponding to them), and I think that compassion is best accounted for when compassionate agents are described as fundamentally social beings rather than fundamentally isolated ones. I contend that however strange it may sound, one *can* feel compassion for oneself, but in the end compassion both arises in relationships and is most often extended toward those with whom one shares in relationships. The next step is to model how compassion functions in such social relations.

The Concentric Ring Model of the Compassionate Self-in-Community

Compassion can be thought of as having a "flow." It flows between persons and through them, connecting them. It is a social and psychological mechanism by which we are alerted to joy and suffering in our communities. But just as there is flow, one can also think of barriers to that flow. Sheer physical distance was already proposed as a potential barrier. Racism, misogyny, homophobia, and cultural elitism all act as more complex barriers to compassion. Intimacy and familiarity have the capacity to break such barriers down: We know from everyday experience that it is easier for us to attend to and will to help those who are closest to us, those with whom we share the most of ourselves. (I shall call this closeness "relational proximity.") When we feel compassion most acutely, we identify so intimately with those to whom our compassion extends that the boundary between egoism and altruism all but fades away.

Figure 3.1 maps compassion's flow, the barriers to compassion, and varying degrees of relational proximity. The term "self" is employed here with hesitation and with the recognition that the word is laden with ontological presuppositions.[18] What lies at the center of this diagram will change with the various interpretations of the model that are to follow, and indeed any usage of the word "self" is risky when discussing something that blurs the distinction between self-interest and others' interests. Initially, let the center of the diagram be populated by the most pedestrian understanding of the self—those numerically distinct things to which we assign social security numbers, birthdates, speeding tickets, and so on (but note that even this sense of self is still self-in-community.) I begin with this concept of the self

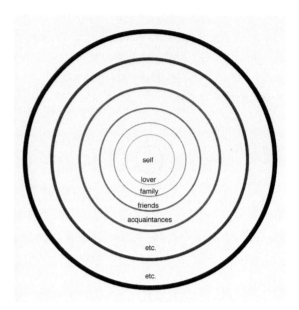

Figure 3.1: A concentric
ring model of the
compassionate self-
in-community

because it describes a very common way of thinking about human existence,
and as such it may prove useful in describing at least a preliminary sense of
how compassion works.

In the absence of cognitive or physiological abnormality, there are no barriers to compassion within this self. It sounds strange to speakers of English
to say one can have compassion for oneself, but speakers of Spanish readily recognize *autocompasión* as exactly that. Indeed, English has a locution
that comes close: I can feel sorry for myself, so why not compassion? Certainly I can attend to my own suffering and satisfaction, and certainly I can
will to eliminate one and prolong the other. Compassion requires no more
than this.[19]

Only the thinnest and most porous of barriers separates my interests from
those who are closest to me. In Figure 3.1, the closest orbit to the center, typically populated by lovers, spouses, or children, is walled off by the thinnest
and lightest ring. For those who occupy this ring, it is sometimes impossible
to discern many of one's own interests from those of the other. Identification is so strong at this level that attending to the well-being of the other is

automatic. The first time I saw my partner Michele take a bad fall while rock climbing, I winced instinctively. My heart leaped; the impulse to help was wholly unmediated. In fact, she recovered from the fall before I did; she was ready to climb before I was ready to resume belaying. Phenomenologically speaking, I did not experience the fright she experienced, but in the very moment she experienced hers, I experienced mine.

The population of any given ring, including the one closest to the center, is subject to change. The birth of a child may affect the intimacy between the mother and father. People grow apart; friends come and go; intense experiences draw people closer together. However the rings may be populated, one's immediate family and closest friends typically find their way to an orbit very close to the center. These are people whom one has known so long and so well that it is extremely easy to identify with them, attend to them, and wish for their well-being. One gives of oneself very freely when it comes to the people in this ring; there are few obstructions to compassion's flow.

Outer orbits are occupied by casual friends, extended family, acquaintances, coworkers, and so on. The walls separating these rings are increasingly thicker and darker in the diagram: This is to represent increasingly greater obstacles to the flow of compassionate attention and compassionate will. Again, the population of any given ring will vary from person to person. A police officer might take all other police officers into a closer ring, for some professions recognize a particularly strong internal fraternity. Pregnancy can have a similar effect, eliciting immediate rapport from strangers. The same is true of Harley-Davidson ownership, sorority membership, and countless other factors.

Moments of high emotion create temporary bonds of compassion: When the Cubs win, their fans are wont to celebrate with anyone they see wearing a Cubs jersey. Zealously patriotic people may extend their compassion more readily to citizens of their own country than to foreigners (much as Sidgwick suggests). For the most part, this latter example is not a weakening of the barrier that ordinarily stands between oneself and random strangers (as was the case with police officers and Cubs fans) but rather the conscious or unconscious bolstering of a barrier walling off those considered to be alien. Racism functions in much the same way with regard to compassion, as do misogyny, homophobia, and religious fundamentalism. Xenophobia of all kinds seeks to alienate and to protect (regardless of whether or not there is any real threat to defend against), and this kind of thinking erects formidable barriers against compassion's flow.

Xenophobic prejudices aside, there are beings whose physiological and psychological structure *is* alien to our own—namely, nonhuman animals—and this has historically been a significant barrier against compassion. Ethicists have rarely considered animals to be on par with human beings, and many philosophers have stated or implied that we do not have obligations to them except indirectly. Canonical ethical texts give me any number of reasons not to kick puppies, whether because such behavior will inculcate viciousness within me, because the puppies belong to someone and property damage is wrong, or because they are the creation of some divine being whose wrath I will incur by harming them. But none of these appeal to anything of moral significance in the puppies themselves; thinkers like Bentham (who appeals to their sentience) or Dōgen (who appeals to their Buddha-nature) are, comparatively speaking, rare.[20]

This is hardly a mystery. We are ethical beings because we are social beings, and very few people interact socially with animals in any way similar to the ways in which they interact with human beings. As far as compassion is concerned, it is much more difficult to attend to and understand beings whose bodies and minds differ from our own. Many of our compassionate impulses are based on inference: I see you bang your shin; I know that hurts when I do it; I wince. But I have no idea what it feels like for puppies to bang their shins, and with jellyfish I cannot even complete the analogy. That said, people do typically recognize an order within the animal kingdom, species with which they sympathize more than others. Puppies tend to outrank jellyfish, and indeed mammals generally seem to outrank everything else. This is unsurprising: They most closely share our own physiology. "Cute" animals also get high rank, mammalian or otherwise, and "smart" ones as well, possibly because these are the ones people tend most often to anthropomorphize. (The animals designated "smart" tend to be only those that mirror human intelligence most closely; very cunning animals whose intelligence bears little resemblance to our own—sharks, for example—are rarely included.)

We can draw a concentric ring diagram of sorts within the animal king-dom, and we can also find a place for nonhuman animals in the diagram mapping ourselves and other human beings. For most adults, this place tends to be beyond those rings that encircle all human beings, as was evi-dent in Sidgwick's passage concerning kindness, where nonhuman animals are not even mentioned. I say "most adults" because children are frequently unencumbered by the conceptual barriers that discern human beings from everything else; their capacity to feel compassion is similarly unencumbered. Of course, among adults there are also those whose compassion flows more freely toward nonhuman beings. People who are vegetarian to avoid inhu-mane treatment of animals have weakened the conceptual barrier walling off animals and have moved them closer toward the center of the diagram.

It is also worthy of note that some people prefer the company of certain animals to the company of any other humans in the neighborhood, and they are not necessarily antisocial for having this preference. The blind develop profoundly deep relationships with their seeing-eye dogs, just as K-9 officers do with their dogs and Jane Goodall did with her chimpanzees. Pet owners the world over can sympathize: A lot of human beings just aren't as nice as our Labrador retrievers.

The outermost ring, farthest from the center, will typically be where the nonsentient entities of the natural world are located. For most adults, plant life can be the object of compassion only in the loosest possible sense. (Again, children are not always limited in this way.) Science tells us what is good for trees and what is bad for them. Based on such insights, we can at-tend to the needs of trees, but most will say it goes too far to claim that we attend to their *suffering* or that if we tend to their satisfaction, that satisfac-tion is akin to our own (for our satisfaction includes career goals, love, family relationships, and so forth). Our compassionate will can have as its object the well-being of trees, but again that well-being is generally accepted to be on a different order than our own. For many people, this radical difference is an all but insurmountable obstacle to compassion, and so nonsentient things are viewed simply as resources to be consumed. Schools of thought that rec-ognize something of inherent moral value within nonsentient natural beings themselves (e.g., deep ecology) are, once again, relatively rare.

However, it is only rarely the case that a given barrier to compassion is wholly insurmountable. Moral education and shifting cultural values can erode certain barriers over time—witness the change in the social acceptability of racism over the past fifty years of American history—and traumatic events have the capacity to knock holes in the barriers, so to speak. The victim of a hit-and-run across the street immediately becomes the object of compassionate attention, even if the victim is a random pedestrian unknown to any of the passersby. I might even neglect the needs of those closest to me (say, by failing to be on time to my mother's birthday dinner) in order to attend to the needs of random strangers (say, by assisting the victim of a car accident), provided only that the stranger's need is sufficiently dire and sufficiently close.

For most of us, compassion is as Mencius described it: a natural tendency. However, there are other tendencies, arguably equally natural (and certainly easy to come by) that inhibit compassion: selfishness, mistrust, and even the simple desire to get through the day without crying. The Buddha's father tried to shield him from the suffering of the world, but the rest of us have no such protection: We are surrounded by misery and by happiness, and we cannot react to all of it equally. Indeed, Mencius might have argued that we *should not* react to all of it equally. Mencius rejected the Mohist concept of all-inclusive caring. For him, benevolence is modeled on familial relationships, and it makes no sense to try to care for all people as one's siblings or parents; to do so is to short-change one's family. Confucianism does maintain that exemplary persons (*junzi,* 君子) "take 'all under *tian* 天' as their provenance,"[21] but in the end, relational proximity matters—and, at least according to Confucian reasoning, it *should* matter.

It should be noted that the Confucians would not have interpreted Figure 3.1 as I have done so far. At this point, my discussion has been confined to what I have dubbed the "basic" interpretation of the concentric ring diagram. It maps compassion's flow from the standpoint of conventional morality, and I take it that it does not extend compassion too far. Perhaps it does not extend compassion sufficiently far enough, as some of the interpretations to follow will suggest. This "basic" representation of the compassionate self-in-community and the way in which compassion circulates is based upon what

I take to be fairly ordinary, "person on the street" sorts of presuppositions about human beings and the natural world. Human beings, for instance, are represented in the model as discrete, independently existing beings, but ones whose existence is couched in a network of relationships. The traditions discussed in chapter 2 challenged this assumption, and when the diagram is reinterpreted from the perspectives of those traditions, it may still be a useful heuristic, but what it represents will undergo radical change.

A CONFUCIAN READING

From a Confucian perspective, there is no single person at the center of the model. Rather, the entire model represents the person. In other words, I *am* that person whose relationships are mapped out in the diagram. For the Confucian, I am composed of my relationships, and this concentric ring model represents or maps them. The Confucian sense of compassion is grounded in analogies to the family and ultimately in familial love, obligation, and respect; all of these are closely duplicated by the concept of relational proximity in the concentric ring model.

To facilitate the Confucian reinterpretation of the model, I will employ a distinction between Steve and "Steve." "Steve" in my case occupies the center of the model and represents the most reductionistic understanding of who I am. "Steve" is six-foot-two, a hundred and seventy pounds, and was born in August of 1973. "Steve" is different from Steve, the "real me," as it were, the person represented by the whole diagram. Steve is Michele's partner, the son of Bill and Kathi, brother to Dave and Kris, like a brother to Alex. He is known best in terms of these relationships: who his acquaintances are, who his teachers are, and also his students, his coworkers, his neighbors. Confucian thinking emphasizes particularity in its ritualized roles and relationships, and so the population of the model's rings must always be very specific. I said before that the people named in the model were only intended to represent a typical sample. The Confucian would place particular emphasis on this caveat and would prefer to see as much specificity as possible in the diagram: not "family" but "Michele, Kathi, Bill, Kris, Dave, Alex"; not "friends" but another catalog of people. Indeed, on a Confucian model, a host of new rings might be introduced. All of us have a sense of those with whom we identify more closely; Confucian reasoning would prefer that every subtle difference in the flow of compassion be mapped out.

Of course, a map of relational proximities may change from day to day. Someone is shifted further out as the result of a quarrel; a shared experience brings someone else closer in. The model, in the end, will never be more than a heuristic tool. More important is the reinterpretation of what the model represents: not the relationships between persons but a person constituted by those relationships.

A DAOIST AMENDMENT TO THE CONFUCIAN READING

The classical Daoist would be much more willing to accept the Confucian understanding of the concentric ring model than the "basic" interpretation of it. Though the Daoists rejected what they took to be the petrification or stultification of social and moral behavior that seemed to accompany Confucian thinking, they did not reject the Confucian understanding of what human selves are and how they function.

However, according to the Daoist, the Confucian reading is still anthropocentric. The authors of the *Laozi* and the *Zhuangzi* would warn us not to forget about the close relationship humanity has to nature. As heavily as we depend upon our parents when we come into the world, surely we are at least as dependent on the world itself. Indeed, human relational existence itself would never have come to be without plants, stones, water, and so on.

An exceptional account of this dependence is to be found in the *Rinrigaku* (*Ethics*) and *Fūdo* (*Climates*) of Watsuji Tetsurō. The betweenness that is so important to Watsuji's analysis of *ningen* (人間) is not only a relational betweenness among human beings; it also exists between humanity and the world. In the *Rinrigaku,* he makes use of two prevalent terms for "world"—*seken* (世間) and *yo no naka* (世の中)—and both originally meant "the public,"[22] signifying that the Japanese have long thought of the world as the locus of human interactions, not as a quantifiable subject of the physical sciences. The earth is not simply a stone in space; it is the theater of human experience. For Watsuji, human beings are shaped by the world they live in—as is evident by diet, culture, language, and physiology—and they also take part in reconfiguring the theater of their experience—as evidenced by technological innovations in travel, communications, and energy production, to name but a few.

The classical Daoists would have applauded Watsuji's vision of the interplay between the world and the humans who dwell in it. They would also have urged us not to forget the other animals, of which Watsuji makes little mention. Now it is not easy for the average adult to empathize with, say, a bat (to use Thomas Nagel's famous example), and it is still harder to empathize with a mountain or a stream, but from the Daoist perspective, these things must also receive our compassion.

But to what degree is this possible? How does one even attempt to feel compassion for snow? Vertebrate animals are sufficiently similar to us that we can imagine what it might be like for them to feel pain, but even to extend one's compassion toward insects is already a stretch. Though it may be fallacious anthropomorphizing to believe that pulling a leg off a cockroach makes it suffer, it does seem reasonable to infer as much just to be on the safe side. Cockroach physiology is so alien to our own that we cannot know with certainty that maiming them causes pain, but when in doubt, it seems reasonable to abstain from actions that may well cause pain.[23]

Such inferences are generally reasonable when made regarding animals, and thanks to the agricultural and botanical sciences we even have a fairly good sense of what is good and bad for plants. A mountain or a stream can be seen as an ecosystem, and ecological theories provide different accounts of what is good and bad for an ecosystem—but what about the stones on a mountain or in a streambed? What about snow atop the mountain or alongside the stream? It is hard to imagine that snow *has* a good so that we might do or fail to do something good *for* it. The same is generally thought to be true of individual stones. Most of us would look askance at someone who wandered along a stream wantonly smashing stones with a sledgehammer, and we might even find such an individual morally blameworthy for this behavior. (A basic utilitarian argument might be that the stream was more pleasing for the rest of us before this strange person started smashing its rocks.) But at least according to the ethical theories that tend to dominate contemporary discourse—namely, some version or other of utilitarianism, contractarianism, or Kantian deontology—it seems odd to say that *harm* was done against any particular stone that fell under the hammer. "Harm," on these views, will constitute either loss of utility or some sort of violation of rights or dignity, and since stones can neither experience utility nor make claims to their rights or their dignity, it would seem to be true by definition that one cannot possibly harm a stone.

This view is not universal, of course. The Hawaiian word *pōhaku,* meaning "stone," includes the idea that the *pōhaku* has *mana,* or power. *Pōhaku* have *mana* in the same way that people have it, or trees, or rivers. One does right by *pōhaku* when one takes care in choosing, for example, which ones are to be used in constructing buildings. *Pōhaku* rich in *mana* are not to be disturbed, and so when investment groups propose to build things like golf courses on the Hawaiian Islands, they frequently meet with resistance from the Native Hawaiian community. It is not very hard to imagine a member of the investment group laughing this off as "local superstition" or something along those lines. But it is also not very hard to imagine the authors of the *Laozi* or the *Zhuangzi* sympathizing with the Native Hawaiians. (Incidentally, it is also not very hard to imagine children being more sympathetic to the Hawaiians than to the investors; as mentioned before, children are often less encumbered than adults by the limits to imagination that prevent many of us from understanding what compassion for a rock might be like.) Wanton rock smashing violates *zhiren* (自然) even if it does not violate any rights. Moving powerful *pōhaku* constitutes a similar violation.

The investment group is no more likely to be persuaded by the *Laozi* or the *Zhuangzi* than it was likely to be persuaded by the *mana* of the rocks where its golf course is supposed to go, but perhaps it might understand an argument from a philosophical tradition closer to home. Onora O'Neill distinguishes between two types of moral rejections. The excellence of justice rejects the principle of injury: That is, it rejects personal harm, property damage, rights violations more generally, and any other unwarranted injury. On the other hand, excellences like compassion, benevolence, or charity reject apathy and neglect.[24] Even if rocks have no rights—indeed, even if rocks are incapable of suffering any harm at all—one would hardly describe the wanton rock smasher as behaving in a caring way toward the rocks, and one could therefore reject the rock smasher's behavior as being apathetic or neglectful.

O'Neill's rejections of injury and apathy or neglect direct our moral attention to the nonhuman as well as the human. Daoism rejects human exceptionalism and bids us to pay attention the nonhuman in the same way that we attend to the human. Note that it does not say we should divide our attention *equally* between the human and the nonhuman. Bean counting is not the goal; rather, the aim is to pay attention where attention is merited. The first step of compassion is the moment of attentiveness, and Daoism would have such attention devoted appropriately, without preconceived conclusions of what deserves it and what does not.

As such, it is not clear that Daoist compassion will encompass snow, though if a snow-covered mountain were understood to have a good as an ecosystem, then the entire system might well become the object of compassion—snow, rocks, and all. Snow by itself might earn aesthetic attention but not compassionate attention. Compassionate attention, attention to suffering and satisfaction, will not be confined to the human sphere, but will be devoted wherever it is appropriate.

In the case of the person wantonly pulverizing rocks, from the Daoist perspective a case could be made that the appropriate object of compassion would be not the rocks but the one smashing them. If ever there was a case of someone acting coercively, this must be it. Wanton rock smashing and authentic way making are very likely at odds, and, moreover, it may well be the suffering on the part of the rock smasher (i.e., frustration, bottled-up anger, boredom, etc.) that has brought about such coercive activity. The compassionate thing to do, then, is to try to understand why the rock smasher carries on so strangely and to attempt to offer guidance toward a more natural and noncoercive kind of way making.

A BUDDHIST READING

The concentric ring model is reconfigured once again from the perspective of Buddhist enlightenment. From the standpoint of what Nāgārjuna would have called "conventional truth," the "basic" reading of the model is quite understandable. But as one draws closer to the "ultimate truth," one comes to realize that the independently existing ego at the center of the model is a conceptual fiction. This is not Nāgārjuna's viewpoint alone; every school of

Buddhism rejects a reified *ātman*. What is actually at the center is a collection of perceptions and memories whose continuity generates the illusion of an independent ego.

If the ego is only illusion, then the rings that barricade the ego from other existences are equally illusory. Indeed, belief in *ātman* can be thought of as two co-arising illusions: a belief in permanence and a belief in the rings, which represent the notion of independent existence (*svabhāva*). Naturally, the two of these are interrelated (because, for example, part of believing in a thing's permanence is believing that it endures independently of changes in the things surrounding it), but it is possible to temporarily isolate the latter from the former and consider it on its own terms.

The belief in one's own independent existence and in the independent existence of other entities arises quite naturally, even if only from the use of language. I speak, write, and think using nouns and pronouns, and these words cut up the world into distinct parts. It is certainly convenient to do so, and given an understanding of what nouns and pronouns represent, I can even evaluate sentences containing them as being true or false. This must be truth and falsehood in a linguistic or conventional sense, not in the ultimate sense, but so long as I am interacting with someone else who uses nouns and pronouns as I do, conventional truth will suffice.

But while erecting these conceptual barriers is convenient, it is an obstacle to understanding the ultimate truth. For the Buddhist, to realize the ultimate truth is to be enlightened, and from that standpoint there can be no belief in *svabhāva* nor in the *ātman*. Rather, there is dependent co-arising and no-self, or to put it even more succinctly (borrowing Dōgen's terminology), there is only impermanence-Buddha-nature. From this perspective, the concentric ring model of compassionate selfhood must be reenvisioned, as depicted in Figure 3.2.

At the center of the diagram is not self but no-self. All entities are without ego, but in this case, if the diagram is to represent me and how my compassion flows, then no-self refers to that bundle of perceptions, faculties, and memories (i.e., *skandhas*) that I conventionally call "me." The concentric rings of the diagram have been wiped away, along with the conceptual bifurcations they represented.[25] Instead, there is only compassion flowing out

no-self

Figure 3.2: The concentric
model reinterpreted from
the perspective of Buddhist
enlightenment

to all other existences. It is difficult to represent others on the diagram itself,
for to map them out as distinct from the no-self at the center is to reintro-
duce a self-other distinction that has already been eradicated. Instead, there
are lighter and darker regions of the diagram, with compassion flowing most
easily to the lightest areas, those closest to the center.

For no matter how completely no-self is realized, even the Buddhist can
admit to certain obstacles to compassion, not the least of which being sheer
physical distance.[26] (I say so assuming it is safe to set aside claims within the
tradition that one gains clairvoyance and other superhuman powers upon
approaching or attaining enlightenment.) Dōgen says that the enlightenment of one being is the enlightenment of all beings—and he does mean *all*
of them[27]—but I would argue that even he does not mean to say that in the
moment of enlightenment, a monk or nun in Eiheiji Temple can directly
perceive the enlightenment of a cockroach in Madagascar.[28] Rather, consider
the central message of *genjōkōan:* For the ego to advance and authenticate
the myriad things is illusion; for the myriad things to advance to authenticate the ego is enlightenment. Hence, all things take part in the enlightenment of one being, for it is their advancing to that being in their suchness
that constitutes its enlightenment.

Because of obstacles like physical distance, some entities will be closer to
the center of the diagram than others; that is, compassion will flow more
easily to some than to others, even for the enlightened. The Bodhisattva
Vow only states that "no matter how innumerable the sentient beings, I vow
to save them all"; it does not say that all will be saved simultaneously. One's
compassion should embrace all sentient beings sooner or later, but instant,
equal, concurrent salvation by compassion is not required.

Note, however, that after the diagram is reinterpreted from the standpoint of Buddhist enlightenment, no preference is given to family members
or loved ones, to say nothing of human beings as a species. Whereas Confucian thinking rejected the possibility of all-inclusive care, Buddhist faith
includes a belief in the possibility of universal compassion. And, whereas
things like snow or rocks will not necessarily become objects of compassion
in Daoist thought, according to Dōgen all things are sentient beings and
must therefore be encompassed by compassion.[29]

This last point raises the same question posed earlier: How does one feel
compassion for snow? Is one to rejoice when it falls and be sorrowful when
it melts? What is its good, so that it can be satisfied or dissatisfied? Is nuclear
waste to be included among sentient beings? If so, how does one feel compassion for one of the deadliest substances ever created by humankind, and
why should one do so at all?[30] To be sure, the answers to such questions may
rely to some degree on faith, for Dōgen and the patriarchs before him were
religious leaders, not Buddhologists but Buddhists. However, to properly address and answer these questions will digress too far from what this chapter
is intended to accomplish; it will be taken up again in chapter 4.

Cultivating Compassion: The Metaethical Foundation

In order to develop an ethic of compassion, certain metaethical presuppositions must first be accepted. The first is that compassion is a good thing.
There are many who will already assume this, but on the other hand we
have already encountered philosophers who reject compassion utterly. Recall
Spinoza's claim, cited as the epigraph in chapter 1, that "Compassion, in a
man who lives in accordance with the guidance of reason, is bad through

itself and useless." Consider Kant's position as well; agreeing as he does with Spinoza that to share in suffering is to multiply it, he holds that "there cannot possibly be a duty to increase the ills in the world and so to do good *from compassion* [*Mitleidenschaft*]."[31] Part of the problem is a matter of translation: What Kant and Spinoza are rejecting is better translated as "commiseration" than as "compassion" as it has been described here. But since wise compassion includes commiseration, this simple change in vocabulary is not enough to dismiss the objections.

It is easiest to build a case for the moral worthiness of compassion by beginning with the recognition that human beings are irreducibly social creatures. Because we are social beings, our well-being is affected by the well-being of those with whom we share relationships. As such, compassion is not entirely voluntary; it is, as Mencius described it, an incipient tendency. This, of course, says nothing of its inherent moral worth; there is no reason to believe that all of our incipient tendencies are morally good. But it remains true that many of the most fulfilling relationships in human life are compassionate ones—and they are arguably better relationships for being compassionate.

For example, if I am seeking a romantic partner, I have the option of seeking someone who offers me physical pleasure and as little else as possible. I can, as Kant describes it, "acquire" a spouse in a strictly legal sense: "that is, as the rightful consequence of the obligation not to engage in sexual union except through *possession* of each other's person";[32] I need not make any significant emotional investment in the relationship. Yet instead I seek someone with whom I can share emotions. I seek to build a relationship deep enough that should there be a death in my partner's family, I grieve for it and for the pain my partner experiences. I do not seek these things masochistically but rather as part and parcel of a fulfilling, healthy relationship in which we also rejoice with each other when we experience success and happiness.

Compassion holds with Shakespeare's old adage, contra Kant and Spinoza, that "a sorrow shared is a sorrow halved; a joy shared is a joy doubled." This sharing is only metaphorical—I cannot actually give my experiences away—but it remains true that we are changed by our relationships, most especially those in which we instinctively respond in kind to the happiness or suffering of the other. There is a real sharing taking place, not of the phenomena of pain and pleasure themselves but rather in the transformative process in which all parties of a relationship participate because of compassion.

But from a utilitarian point of view, there is still something strange going on here. Why would any utility-maximizing agent agree to enter into a relationship in which that agent stands to undergo greater suffering? I take it that this is the sort of thinking that fuels Spinoza's objection to compassion (and ultimately Kant's as well, though Kant, of course, is no utilitarian). The notion of the discrete individual motivated by reason is latent in the objection: We are not rational utility maximizers first and foremost, and we do not enter our relationships with anything like Kantian autonomy. Rather, we are born into some relationships and we seem to fall into others. Some we pursue actively, but it is only when we are welcomed by others that relationships begin to form. In every case, it is not one agent choosing to have a relationship with another but a plurality of people being transformed by one another, and this reciprocal authoring of personhood is what we call a relationship.

Yet compassion is still a strange phenomenon from a utilitarian perspective, for it is the only thing I can think of that motivates me to hope that my loved ones suffer. If someone in my family should die, I would prefer that my partner share in my sorrow, though in every other aspect of our relationship all I want for her is happiness. For me to *want* her to feel pain is a very strange thing.

A utilitarian might argue that in fact I do not want her to feel pain *on balance*. Instead, what I want is her happiness and mine, and we both tend to be happier in a relationship that requires significant emotional investment, even to the degree that each of us suffers when the other suffers. A utilitarian argument for the inherent moral worthiness of compassion could be constructed along these lines, concluding that (contra Kant and Spinoza once again) we tend to bring about greater utility on balance by cultivating compassion than by not doing so. For some, such an argument may not be necessary: Compassion's moral worthiness may be so apparent as to require no argument. In any case, the curious will want an explanation as to why human beings do in fact tend to seek compassionate relationships in some of the most fulfilling aspects of their lives, even when this brings about the risk of pain for loved ones, and this rough sketch of a utilitarian argument may serve in that capacity.

Assuming it is accepted that human beings are irreducibly relational beings and that for relational beings the cultivation of compassion is morally worthy of pursuit, the next question is, how does one cultivate compassion? Dōgen offers one method, which begins with the notion of the ego. In his Sōtō Zen, as in Buddhism in general, the independently existing ego is only a conceptual fiction. Once one realizes that the ego is without inherent existence but arises dependently instead, one is ready to work to extinguish egotism and selfishness.

Not everyone will accept Dōgen's basic metaphysical presuppositions, but the cultivation of compassion is not contingent upon their acceptance. A basic recognition of one's own social embeddedness is enough to realize the folly of unfettered selfishness. Aristotle gave us enough to recognize this much. Without even employing his idea of the *politikon zōon,* we are materially and formally caused in a social matrix; without our parents' genetic material, the products of farmers around the globe, or the oxygen-carbon dioxide exchange we engage in with plant life, we would not be what we are. All that is really required—from a secular, Sōtō Zen, or other religious point of view—is an awareness of the fact that there is never a point at which one exists in a social vacuum, followed by an awareness of the fact that one's well-being is tied up with that of other beings.

Buddhism holds that once no-self is embraced, compassion follows naturally. Suffering, after all, is to be avoided even after the notion of a discrete, egocentric self is abandoned. Satisfaction is still preferred (though what counts as satisfaction may change). One simply realizes that these things are true regardless of where the suffering and satisfaction arise. From this perspective, it is easy to wish to bring about the satisfaction and absence of suffering in all beings. Indeed, that is all that it makes sense to wish for.

Naturally, there are other methods for the cultivation of compassion, their bases ranging from other religious doctrines to simple prudence. I detail only the Buddhist method here because it already received attention in chapter

2 and because, once the relational nature of human existence is accepted, I take this approach to be a persuasive and effective one. Of course, it has not yet addressed the process of making ethical evaluations. That is the subject of the following section.

Putting Compassion into Practice: The Ethics of Compassion

Given the foregoing metaethical assumptions regarding compassion, one may adopt a concrete strategy regarding ethical evaluation. This will follow the lines of what philosophers call virtue ethics, though I will use the term "aretaic ethics" to avoid some of the connotations of the word "virtue." The preference in vocabulary is a considered one. "Virtue" shares its origins with "virility," the root *vir* meaning "man." Originally, "virtue" described one's ability to impregnate, and from there it was taken to describe only stereotypically masculine excellences. "Excellence" is not specific to gender nor even to species; Aristotle's *aretē* and Confucius' *de* (德), both more accurately translated as "excellence" than as "virtue," can be applied to animals and even inanimate objects. To avoid sexist connotations and to deliver what Aristotle and Confucius have in mind when speaking of *aretē* and *de,* I will use "excellence" instead of "virtue" and "excellent" or "aretaic" instead of "virtuous." (One set of exceptions will be references to contemporary philosophers or philosophical movements; in respect to their own philosophical preferences, I will use the language they use, referring to "virtue ethics," "virtue epistemology," and so forth where they do.)

COMPASSIONATE ARETAIC ETHICS

At this point it should not be surprising that, ethically speaking, compassion should be cast in terms of a moral excellence. An aretaic ethic grounded in compassion must take as its first and most basic assumption that compassion is in itself morally good and worthy of cultivation. Moreover, it must also assume that compassion ranks highly among the moral excellences, perhaps the very highest of them. The latter of these assumptions is the more difficult of the two to grant, and to provide a knockdown argument in support of it would be a remarkable achievement worthy of its own book. Here I will only show how, if compassion were to occupy such a lofty position, it might provide moral guidance. It is worthy of note, however, that Buddhism has long named its highest moral excellence to be compassion—or, more specifically, *wise compassion*—the twin excellences of *prajñā* and *karuṇā* (and also *mettā* in the Japanese tradition). As this parallels the model of compassion I have been arguing for all along, the history of Buddhism supports the idea that compassion could plausibly be placed at the head of an aretaic ethic.

If compassion is defined as the chief excellence, all other excellences and vices could be defined in terms of it. On this system, the excellences would be defined as those traits of character that facilitate or bolster the cultivation and exercise of compassion. Similarly, vices would be defined as those traits of character that inhibit, deter from, or damage the cultivation and exercise of compassion. According to these definitions, courage would be counted among the excellences, for there are times when it is daunting to assist those who are suffering. Avarice, on the other hand, would be defined as a vice because it encourages solely self-interested pursuits and thereby builds up barriers to the flow of compassion.

Any number of character traits can be analyzed in this way and counted as virtuous or vicious. Moreover, compassion provides a standard in cases where it is ambiguous whether the exercise of the trait in question is virtuous or vicious. Honesty, for example, is generally regarded as a moral excellence, but there are cases in which it seems cruel to tell the whole truth. Kant's famous prohibition against lying even to save a life[33] is not compassionate honesty, and so in a compassionate aretaic ethic, philanthropic lies would not be so stringently proscribed.

Holding wise compassion to be the standard by which all other excellences are defined, the catalog of excellences it defines is very similar to the list of excellences we recognize generally. Wise compassion dictates that we display honesty, bravery, generosity, temperance, kindness, intellectual curiosity, fidelity, persistence, thoughtfulness—and the list goes on. It demands that we abstain from indulging impulses to be greedy, derisive, deceitful, closed-minded, cowardly, and so on. Furthermore, of all the aforementioned excellences, none of them can supplant wise compassion and play its role. That is, none of these excellences can serve as a standard by which all other

excellences are defined—or at least they cannot do so in such a way that
the list of excellences they generate is one we commonly recognize as being
wholly and comprehensively good.

Suppose courage were taken to be the highest excellence, and all other
excellences were to be defined in terms of it. (Winston Churchill suggested
something like this when he said, "Courage is the first of human qualities
. . . because it guarantees all the others." Taken literally at her word, Mother
Teresa made a similar suggestion: "To have courage for whatever comes in
life—everything lies in that."[34]) Sometimes we refrain from doing ghastly
things not because we find them unkind or otherwise vicious but because we
find ourselves afraid to go through with them. How many crimes are left un-
done solely because the would-be perpetrators are afraid? If courage were the
prime excellence, such forbearance would be deemed vicious. Would kindness be an excellence within an ethic of courage? Think of stories of children cornering a wounded animal and torturing it. If a child is torn between
wanting to protect the animal on one hand and on the other the twin fears
of bloodshed and of appearing cowardly before a group of peers, an aretaic
ethic based on courage would very likely dictate not kindness but brutality.

I will not seek to present a conclusive argument proving compassion's superiority over all other excellences. Instead, I offer two less ambitious sug-
gestions. First, there seems to be a common instinct when thinking about
the excellences to propose one as governing the others, as Churchill did with
courage and Aristotle did with *theōria*—and, incidentally, as Rousseau did
with compassion.[35] Contemporary literature on virtue ethics indicates at
least one reason supporting that instinct: There is debate about whether
there is any clear-cut way to decide which of two excellences should govern
one's action should the two ever come into conflict.[36] A governing excellence
could help in resolving such conflicts.

Second, if one elects wise compassion as the highest of the excellences
and the standard by which other excellences are defined, it fills the role well.
On the one hand, the catalog of excellences defined by wise compassion will
make up a satisfactory list. By comparison, if Churchill's courage were placed
in the same role as the defining standard of the excellences, the catalog thus
produced is likely to include many dispositions we commonly consider to be

vices and is not likely to include many dispositions we commonly consider to be excellences. To put it succinctly, it is easy to imagine a legitimately courageous tyrant but not so easy to think of a legitimately compassionate one. An ethic of courage is more likely to encourage those dispositions that make one an excellent tyrant, whereas an ethic of compassion is more likely to count those dispositions among the vices.

On the other hand, wise compassion will serve as a standard by which at least some conflicts between excellences can be resolved. Supposing I have the option of cultivating *theōria* (perhaps by wandering alone in the mountains pondering questions of philosophy) or cultivating charity (perhaps by working with the needy): If compassion is my guide, I will typically choose to cultivate charity.

But this raises the question of whether *theōria* should even be counted among the excellences. Is contemplative wisdom compassionate? Because *karunā* entails *prajñā* and vice versa, one might reflexively include *theōria* among the excellences defined by compassion without further consideration. This is too hasty, for *prajñā* is not *theōria,* nor is it *phronēsis.* Nor is it *zhi* (和) for that matter, the kind of wisdom that Daoist sages sought in their solitary pondering in the mountains. Is there a place for solitary pondering in an ethic of compassion?

It should be pointed out that even Aristotle, who placed *theōria* at the apex of his hierarchy of excellences, granted that while the life of *theōria* could theoretically be a life of solitary contemplation, in order to live well the *politikon zōon* needs friends and associates, and some of the Aristotelian excellences are aimed at cultivating friendships.[37] The same is true in Daoism, albeit in a different way: The point of being alone in the mountains is to realize that one is not alone in the mountains. Thus even the most intellectual kind of wisdom, the wisdom most removed from daily struggles, still thrives in being-with.

Moreover, compassion is concerned with the well-being of the agent as well as that of other entities. Therefore, if theoretical contemplation leads to one's own satisfaction, then so long as it does not detract from the satisfaction of others or lead to their suffering, there is no reason why an ethic of compassion would not embrace it as excellent. It must be pursued in moderation, of course, since to devote oneself wholly to contemplation would result in neglecting one's neighbors. But for any endeavor that neither positively nor negatively affects the well-being of others, if it satisfies the agent, there is generally no reason not to engage in it. Thus there is not necessarily anything uncompassionate about purely intellectual pursuits, though anyone who recognizes the irreducibly social nature of human beings will also recognize that oftentimes such pursuits are best taken up dialogically.

Thus far an aretaic ethic of wise compassion has been described mostly in ethical terms. Now the groundwork has been laid for using wise compassion as the benchmark for defining intellectual excellences as well, for knowledge, belief formation, and (of course) wisdom are all critical components of wisely compassionate conduct. Indeed, according to an aretaic ethic of compassion, there is no hard and fast distinction to be drawn between ethical and intellectual excellences.

This unity is in keeping with the claim made in chapter 2 that in the classical Daoist tradition, there was no firm division between epistemology and ethics. At a superficial level, this idea seems to resonate quite broadly: Socrates' claim that all wrongdoing arises out of ignorance is a very similar position.[38] But the two traditions diverge as soon as one begins to investigate what sorts of claims might count as knowledge claims. One instructive, if initially perplexing, example can be found in A. C. Graham's analysis of the role of logic and argumentation in Zhuangzian Daoism. According to Graham, "Persuasion by *argumentum ad hominem* [is] the only kind of victory in debate which could have any point for Chuang-tzŭ."[39] Naturally, Aristotle and the logicians that follow him will not find ad hominem attacks convincing and will offer what they take to be very good reasons why this argumentative strategy cannot lead to any definitive conclusions whatsoever. So how is this supposed to work? If Jack is trying to put forth a convincing argument and Jill's counterargument is simply to call him a fool, why should anyone find Jill more persuasive than Jack?

Daoism places a great deal of importance on perspective and on acknowledging that one should never assume one's own perspective to be the most pertinent or most reliable. When Jack makes his argument, he does so assuming his reasons to be universally persuasive, or at the very least persuasive for the one he is attempting to convince. If Jill is a student of the *Zhuangzi,* she will realize that Jack may have things confused—and that she herself may have things confused, for that matter. Thus she will be as willing to adopt Jack's perspective as she is her own. According to Graham, "The crucial point for Chuang-tzǔ is that words have no fixed meanings except in the artificial conditions of intellectual debate, in which one may as well accept the opponent's definitions, since they are no more or less arbitrary than any others."[40] If Jack does not recognize his position is, in the end, dependent upon his perspective, he is indeed a fool.

But this does not make Jill's ad hominem convincing. Presumably, Jack can offer reasons why his perspective is not arbitrary. If Jack truly is a fool, the reasons supporting his perspective are no less foolish than the reasons supporting his argument—but this is question begging. Of course, if Jack is not a fool, then it does not matter what his reasons for anything are, since Jill's assertion is incorrect. But this begs the question in the opposite way. Jill's dubbing Jack a fool is supposed to be convincing *by itself.*

Jill's rebuttal is convincing only if one does not distinguish between knowing and doing, between epistemology and ethics. Jill is making a character judgment, an inference about future conduct based on past and current conduct. In calling him a fool, she is asserting that Jack's argument is not worth listening to because his perspective is one that has led him to conduct himself foolishly. Aristotle and the other logicians will not be any more convinced by this than they were before, but according to Zhuangzian thinking, they are fools as well if they are willing to follow along with a fool's proposal just because of the absence of logically valid counterarguments. This course might be acceptable in purely theoretical terms, but in the *Zhuangzi* no dichotomy is drawn between theory and practice, between philosophy and everyday living, and in life one treats fools with suspicion even if they seem to be voicing good ideas at the moment.

Traditional philosophical divisions mark ethics as a matter of practice, or at least largely as a matter of practice, and epistemology as a matter of theory. The classical Daoists were hardly the only thinkers to reject this classification. A growing trend in contemporary analytical philosophy collapses the distinction between ethics and epistemology, a trend most visible among the works of virtue epistemologists (many of whom are also feminist epistemologists; this is not without significance, as I will argue shortly).

On one end of the spectrum in this trend, ethical excellences and epistemological excellences are identified as being closely connected, as seen in the responsibilist virtue epistemology of Lorraine Code.[41] The intellectual responsibility Code emphasizes is modeled on ethical responsibility, functions in a similar way, and its "jurisdiction," so to speak, will overlap with the "jurisdiction" of ethical responsibility from time to time. (Take William K. Clifford's classic example of the negligent ship owner as a case of this: For the ship owner not to inspect his vessel and then to send it out to sea with passengers aboard is both ethically and epistemologically irresponsible.[42])

On the other end of this spectrum—the end that more closely parallels the present account of compassion—are thinkers such as Linda Trinkhaus Zagzebski, who says, "I argue that intellectual virtues *are* forms of moral virtue."[43] In Zagzebski's view, Clifford's ship owner is ethically irresponsible *because* he is epistemologically irresponsible, and he is epistemologically irresponsible *because of* the ethical ramifications of his intellectual practices. There are not two distinct excellences he lacks here but rather one with both ethical and epistemological jurisdictions.[44]

The present account of compassion entails, as Zagzebski's does and as Dalmiya's seems to, an erasure of the dualism separating cogitation from action, theory from praxis. As Zagzebski puts it,

the kind of thinking that precedes acting is only one of many kinds of thinking, and . . . the acting that follows thinking is only one of many kinds of acting. Thinking is itself a form of acting. . . . There is no special order between thinking and acting. We do both most of the time. It takes tremendous philosophical ingenuity to devise a theory that separates these activities enough to permit a division in normative theory between ethics and normative epistemology. It is my position that this ingenuity is misplaced.[45]

Here one can see the early Buddhists' denial of any absolute separation of *prajñā* from *karuṇā* reflected in twentieth-century analytical epistemology. A compassionate aretaic ethic will echo the sentiment: The philosophical gymnastics needed to separate knowing from doing—and therefore ethical knowing from ethical doing—is nothing but wasted effort.

It should be pointed out that this is hardly the position of all virtue epistemologists. Code intertwines ethical and epistemological excellences but does not identify them. And Ernest Sosa, one of the founding fathers of virtue epistemology and arguably its most renowned proponent, leaves ethics by the wayside. As a case in point, in *Epistemic Justification* Sosa offers a synthesis of his arguments published over of the past twenty-odd years. In one hundred pages describing and defending his reliabilist virtue epistemology, he mentions the word "ethics" not once.[46] That this is even possible marks how starkly Sosa and Zagzebski are set apart.

The difference is important for an ethic of compassion for a couple of reasons. First, "virtue" is a word used by wide range of philosophers on a variety of topics, and by identifying the strong commonality between Zagzebski's epistemology and the present account of wise compassion, the word takes on greater specificity and thereby greater utility. (The fact that I prefer "excellence" in cases where other philosophers write "virtue" does nothing to change this.) Second, it can now be said that an ethic of compassion may also be described as an epistemology of compassion. Both will hinge on excellences (the twin excellences of *prajñā* and *karuṇā,* among others), a fact that would likely have pleased many of the thinkers drawn upon in synthesizing the present account of compassion.

The concept of a compassionate aretaic ethics must now be understood as encompassing compassionate aretaic epistemology as well. It is significant that contemporary feminists such as Dalmiya and Code also push for a close linkage between ethics and epistemology. Compassion as it is being described here is rooted in Confucianism and Buddhism, both the objects of feminist critiques. The cultural histories of Confucianism and Buddhism are at least in part histories of patriarchy, and insofar as patriarchy is not compassionate, an ethic of compassion must demonstrate that it does not follow in all of its forebears' footsteps. This concern will receive further attention in the next chapter, where care ethics (which also sees epistemology and ethics as being indivisible) will come into focus. For now suffice it to say that, perhaps contrary to expectations, the sense of compassion I have drawn out of Confucian and Buddhist traditions is very much in keeping with, not antithetical to, the contemporary feminist conception of excellence as both ethical and epistemological.

OBJECTIONS TO AND A DEFENSE OF
COMPASSIONATE ARETAIC ETHICS

One of the aims of this work as a whole is to demonstrate how compassion can provide constructive moral guidance. In itself, there is a real risk in connecting compassion even loosely with contemporary virtue ethics, for there are philosophers who argue with great conviction against the possibility of a virtue ethic offering useful moral guidance of any kind. Martha Nussbaum argues that there is in fact no such thing as virtue ethics. She argues that virtue ethics "does not demarcate a distinctive approach that can usefully be contrasted with Kantian and Utilitarian ethics," and therefore she "propose[s] that we do away with the category of 'virtue ethics' in teaching and writing."[47]

But one does not need to posit the nonexistence of virtue ethics in order to reject its utility in providing moral guidance. Many philosophers—James Rachels being among the first and Marcia Baron and Philip Pettit being among the more recent—suggest that virtue ethics is better viewed as a description of our moral psychology than as an actual system for resolving moral dilemmas. The core objection has been phrased in any number of ways, but in essence it boils down to the claim that excellences, because they are not and cannot be bound by rules, lack specificity and therefore cannot offer any specific moral guidance.[48]

According to a radical aretaic ethic—that is, an ethic that relies solely on the excellences to determine what is morally right—in any given situation, "morally correct" roughly equals "what an excellent person would do in like circumstances." The most common objection is that this definition lacks substantive guidance. What, for example, does it tell us about whether or not abortion is morally acceptable? Suppose half of a country's population believed abortion ought to be permitted in some cases and the other half believed abortion ought not to be allowed in those cases. It would be both arrogant and naïve for anyone in that country to presume that all those on the opposing side of the issue were vicious people. A more realistic view would dictate that morally upstanding people—that is, excellent people—could be found in either half of the population. There are basically good people to be found on either side of almost any moral issue one chooses to look at, so indexing the morally good position to morally good agents is wholly unenlightening.

Michael Slote makes a distinction between aretaic language (e.g., "morally good," "excellent") and deontic language (e.g., "morally right," "ought").[49] His opponents (Baron and Pettit among them) can grant him this distinction and still claim that deontic language is the surer path to constructive moral guidance.[50] Returning to the hypothetical country in the previous paragraph, one can readily accept two beliefs simultaneously: first, that morally good people live on either half of the population divide; and second, that all of the people on one side of the divide have come to a morally wrong judgment concerning abortion. Indeed, thinkers like Baron and Pettit will say one *has* to believe something like this if one wants to meaningfully address abortion as a moral question. They will also say that the aretaic language Slote prefers is incapable of addressing abortion in the same way.

There are other ways to phrase what amounts to the same kind of objection. Rosalind Hursthouse summarizes another common formulation of the objection:

> The requirements of different virtues, it is said, can point us in opposed directions. Charity prompts me to kill the person who would (truly) be better off dead, but justice forbids it. Honesty points to telling the hurtful truth, kindness and compassion to remaining silent or even lying. . . . So virtue ethics lets us down just at the point where we need it, where we are faced with the really difficult dilemmas and do not know what to do.[51]

The Aristotelian will say this is no objection at all, for Aristotle established *phronēsis* as that excellence that prioritizes the excellences and guides one as to which excellence to act upon (*NE* VI.5, VI.12–13). The objector may reply by positing *phronēsis* as one of the two competing excellences, though it must be observed that examples of such a conflict do not easily spring to mind.

(I can think of none myself, at any rate, and I am inclined to suggest the reason for this is that *phronēsis* is noncompetitive by nature.)

But even if one were to arrive upon a compelling example of such a conflict, it is not clear that the objection specifically targets aretaic ethics at all. Hursthouse argues that this is in fact a much broader moral problem. As she puts it,

> In the mouth of a utilitarian, this may be a comprehensible criticism. . . . But it is strange to find the very same criticism coming from deontologists, who are notoriously faced with the same problem. "Don't kill," "Respect autonomy," "Tell the truth," "Keep promises" may all conflict with "Prevent suffering" or "Do no harm," which is precisely why deontologists so often reject utilitarianism's deliverances on various dilemmas.[52]

Should there ever be a conflict between the obligations of honesty and the obligations of kindness, the utilitarian calculus purports to offer a straightforward solution. (This leaves aside the separate question of how often maximizing utility is a straightforward proposition.) But the conflict problem vexes Kant as sorely as it does Confucius or Aristotle, at least at first glance.

The Kantian solution is to say there is no conflict: "Do not lie" is a perfect duty, "be kind" is an imperfect duty, and perfect duties trump imperfect duties. Is there any reason to think the aretaic ethicist does not also have a ready solution? Hursthouse claims an aretaic ethic is no less capable of normative guidance than is a deontological one. She asks, "Does kindness require not telling hurtful truths? Sometimes, but in *this* case, what has to be understood is that one does people no kindness by concealing this sort of truth from them, hurtful as it may be."[53] Confucius would likely have accused Hursthouse of moving rather too quickly here, generalizing too hastily, but the point is well taken nonetheless. Many putative conflicts between the excellences will turn out not to be conflicts at all.

Yet the objector will still claim that, even if there were never any cases in which the excellences conflicted, an aretaic ethic is still without a formal decision-making procedure to be used in resolving moral dilemmas. But it is not clear that an aretaic ethic necessarily suffers from this deficiency. Elizabeth Anscombe advocates rephrasing all ethical rules in aretaic language, as "do not act wrongly" is hopelessly vague, whereas "do not act unjustly," "do not act dishonestly," and "do not act unkindly" are much more specific in content. Lest "do not act wrongly" seems too general, take a more specific example: "Do not murder." Should one be asked what sorts of killing count as murder, "unjust killing" is at least as good a description as "wrongful killing." Whether one uses aretaic or deontic language, one needs a solid moral grasp on what one means by the addition of the adjective. "Failing to maximize utility" is no clearer a definition of "wrongful" than is "failing to act as an excellent person would" as a definition of "unjust." On both definitions, one must still be able to offer cogent reasons why killing human beings is acceptable in some circumstances (if it ever is) or never acceptable (if it never is). Killing in self-defense or in defense of an innocent is no less worrisome for the deontologist or utilitarian than it is for the aretaic ethicist.

Michael Slote raises another objection concerning the applicability of aretaic ethics: "If someone is faced with a perplexing moral problem, it somehow seems irrelevant and even objectionable for her to examine *her own motives rather than facts about people and the world* in order to solve it. Yet isn't this what agent-basing allows for and even prescribes?"[54] Slote draws a distinction between agent-*based* and agent-*focused* ethics that need not receive much attention here. Suffice it to say that an aretaic ethic of compassion bears at least this much in common with what Slote calls agent-based ethics: It regards the motives, dispositions, or inner lives of moral agents as the basis upon which actions will be evaluated as morally good or bad.[55] This is enough to lay compassionate ethics bare to the potential problem he has introduced.

As it happens, Slote's resolution of the problem parallels a similar solution available to the adherent of a compassionate ethic. To use Slote's example, suppose someone is faced with choosing whether or not to pursue extraordinary medical means to sustain the life of an aged, sickly mother. The moral question at hand is a question of benevolence: Namely, does benevolence prompt me to help her live a greater number of days, or does it prompt me to help her minimize her suffering (though that will cost her some number of days)? If I am to look only to what a benevolent person would do, is it true that I only look inwardly, to the benevolence I have been cultivating in my own person? Certainly not. According to Slote, "An internal state like benevolence focuses on and concerns itself with gathering facts about the world."[56] Compassion has already been defined in a very similar way. Put simply, an aretaic ethic does not imply moral solipsism; on the contrary, it can only reject moral solipsism.

Now, what does all of this do for someone in the hypothetical population described before, one who is wondering what decision to come to regarding abortion? If Anscombe, Hursthouse, Slote, and their ilk are right, an aretaic ethic will have concretely applicable moral guidance to offer. The guidance will take something like the following form. Suppose there are two potential role models, A and B, and that they disagree about the morality of abortion. If I am confused about how to feel about abortion, my first step will be to examine why I take A and B to be morally exemplary. What excellences does each of them display? It is all but certain that the two of them are not equally exemplary in every respect. Realistically speaking, I admire some people for their courage, others for their wisdom, others for their generosity, and so on. I am likely to feel the same way about A and B. I am also likely to find that A and B differ on their opinions about abortion because they are motivated by different excellences. If so, then for me it is a matter of applying something like moral wisdom (it hardly matters whether I name it *prajñā* or *phronēsis*) to decide which of the two excellences takes precedence.

Lest this seems too easy, suppose A and B are both motivated by compassion. (Presumably one of them feels stronger compassion for the fetus, and the other one feels stronger compassion for the pregnant woman.) In that case, my task is just the same as it was before: to use what moral wisdom I have to decide which of my compassionate exemplars is choosing best. Is this any different from how one would make the same decision on utilitarian grounds? Are there not equally valid utilitarian arguments on every side of the abortion issue? On what basis are we to label the aretaic method any less concrete than the utilitarian? (Or the deontological, for that matter; the dictates of Kant's categorical imperative will be hazy at best when evaluating nonrational beings like fetuses.)

This points to a final question. Characteristically speaking, compassion is concerned with the very things utilitarianism is concerned with: satisfaction and suffering. Is there any need for an ethic of compassion when so much work has been done on utilitarianism? If the ultimate mandate of compassion is not "maximize satisfaction and minimize suffering," is it not sufficiently close to this to make any independent ethic of compassion redundant? In short, is an effort to develop compassionate ethics just reinventing the wheel?

Perhaps the most obvious difference between an aretaic ethic of compassion and consequentialism is a difference in moral psychology. For many people, the excellence of compassion is in fact more accurately descriptive of their actions and motivations than is the utilitarian calculus. Philip Pettit points out that consequentialism does not necessarily commit one to what he calls "actuarialism" (what might also be called "ethical bean-counting"). Pettit quotes John Austin's apt defense of the utilitarian: "Though he approves of love because it accords with his principle, he is far from maintaining that the general good ought to be the motive of the lover. It was never contended or conceived by a sound, orthodox utilitarian, that the lover should kiss his mistress with an eye to a common weal."[57] According to Pettit, it is possible to be a nonactuarial consequentialist and therefore to prize the excellences without actually performing any utilitarian calculations regarding them beforehand. One can be motivated by compassion and say upon reflection that it is compassion's tendency to maximize utility that gives it its motivational power.

This misses the inherent attractiveness that the Buddha saw in *karuṇā* and *mettā*. One is led to believe that on the Buddha's view, compassion is good of itself even if it should tend to fail to maximize utility—indeed, even if through its exercise one were consistently miserable and always in the company of miserable others. That this is unlikely makes no difference. The utilitarian is bound to say compassion is an excellence if and only if its practice tends to lead to greater overall utility. It so happens that we tend to be happier insofar as we cultivate compassionate relationships and lead compassionate lives, but consequentialism values this happiness and values the compassion that brings it about only indirectly.

Thus it is not, strictly speaking, true that utilitarianism can avoid

Pettit's actuarialism; it can only choose between direct and indirect actuarialism. Michael Slote draws a distinction between intrinsic and instrumental valuation that follows the same lines: Utilitarianism values utility intrinsically, and consequentialism more generally values favorable consequences intrinsically, whereas on either the utilitarian or the consequentialist view the excellences can only be valued instrumentally.[58] Thinkers like Pettit will want to ask why anyone should have a problem with this view: Why should compassion be valued even when it does not lead to favorable consequences? Indeed, is it not in fact uncompassionate to value compassion intrinsically and without regard for the consequences it brings about?

No adherent of an ethic of compassion will say so. There are people who are so miserable that all a compassionate agent can do is attend to them and suffer with them. Consider a dilemma in "lifeboat ethics": I am drowning beside your lifeboat, which is full to capacity and surrounded by ice-cold water. As a group, we have concluded that should any of us survive, among all of us I am the least capable of maximizing utility. (Suppose everyone in the lifeboat is an HIV researcher on the cusp of a critical breakthrough, while I am a lowly philosopher without future prospects.) If I cling to the side of the boat, that will be enough to sink it, and taking turns treading water is no good, because anyone who enters the water faces the risk of hypothermia. Given our predicament, it is utility maximizing to let me drown and leave all those in the lifeboat where they are, you included. It is also compassionate to do so, since compassion is at least sufficiently oriented toward utility maximization to come to the same conclusion about my future as a philosopher as against a potential vaccine against HIV.

But suppose those of you in the lifeboat are squeamish about watching me die. One of you suggests that you had just as well paddle on, since by all accounts I am going to die anyway, and in fact rumor has it that drowning is not such a bad way to go. I can die in your company—cold comfort at best—whereas all of you will be tormented by nightmares of my death for many nights to come. Should any of you be ridden with guilt at abandoning me, let the nightmares be worse than the guilt. The variables can be set in such a way that you will fail to maximize utility if you choose to wait with me as I die. That said, those in the lifeboat who are compassionate will prefer to stay with me. Even if the best you can do is to suffer with me, it remains quintessentially uncompassionate to turn your back on me. An ethic of compassion places intrinsic value in utility and also in compassion, and it is ultimately because of the intrinsic value of compassion that utility has value. Thus compassionate thinking and utilitarian thinking do give rise to different accounts of moral-psychological motivation, even if the difference between "acting compassionately" and "maximizing utility" is ultimately a slender one.

Conclusion: The Moral Worthiness of Compassion

At the end of chapter 1 was a list of eight necessary conditions for any account of compassion to be a viable source of moral guidance:

1. It must be an ethically primary trait.
2. It must recognize the role of affective as well as cognitive activity in moral decision making.
3. It must be capable of generating personally directed imperatives.
4. It must recognize from its very roots the irreducible relationality of human existence.
5. It must be as concerned with the promotion of satisfaction as it is concerned with the alleviation of suffering.
6. It must not degrade its object.
7. It must not be essentially comparative or competitive in nature.
8. It must not be so narrow in scope that it fails to encompass all those worthy of moral consideration.

The present account of wise compassion has now been developed fully enough that it can be held up to this list for judgment.

Wise compassion is not subordinate to reason or to anything else in the process of ethical evaluation. Indeed, it can serve as the primary moral excellence for two different methods of ethics. It is therefore an ethically primary trait and satisfies the first condition. Because compassion still acknowledges

the need for rationality while at the same time recognizing the necessity
—both psychological and moral—of emotive states in ethical evaluation,
it satisfies the second condition. The account of compassion being developed here includes *autocompasión,* or compassion for oneself, and as such
it can generate personally directed ethical imperatives. It therefore meets
the third condition. Because it is grounded in a relationally constructed,
socially embedded notion of human existence, it satisfies the fourth condition. Grounded as it is in the notion of *jihi,* which includes both *karunā* and
mettā, it focuses on satisfaction as well as suffering, and therefore it meets
the fifth condition. Nothing about the account of compassion developed
here suggests that it must degrade its object or that it is dependent upon
competition and comparison between compassionate agents. Thus there is
no reason to believe that it does not satisfy the sixth and seventh conditions.

The last condition is daunting. "All those worthy of moral consideration"
is a big idea—and a vague one. "Worthy of moral consideration" is a philosophical quagmire of its own. But the purpose of this condition, the reason
it was included on the list, is to respond to the differences in scope seen in
Aristotle's twin concepts of *eleos* and *philia.* Recall that *eleos* was reserved for
strangers and only strangers; friends and loved ones were embraced by *philia.*
Neither *eleos* nor *philia* was deemed to be sufficiently inclusive to serve as the
foundation of an ethic. The present account of compassion is not so exclusive. It includes within its purview the entire relational matrix in which the
ethical agent is embedded. This certainly seems to include all those worthy
of moral consideration. At any rate, it is surely not so exclusive that it fails to
meet the eighth condition.

We have, then, a model of compassion that is capable of providing normative guidance. One can approach this model from a number of possible
avenues. From a religious standpoint, the possibilities are far too many to
number; I drew most heavily on a Buddhist approach because of the notion of the dependently arising ego, but mine is not the only possible Buddhist interpretation, nor is Buddhism the only possible religious approach
to an ethic of compassion. From a secular perspective, compassion is best
explained when it begins with a socially constructed conception of the per-

son, and Confucianism supplied a robust account of this, supplemented by Daoist insights into each person's interconnection with the nonhuman world. Religious and secular models of compassion can both offer constructive moral guidance based upon wise compassion as a guiding excellence and based upon any other excellences that contribute to the cultivation and expression of wise compassion.

CHAPTER FOUR

Objections to an Ethic of Compassion

Is compassion, with all its faults, our best hope as we try to
educate citizens to think well about human relations both inside
the nation and across national boundaries? . . . Or is it a threat to
good political thinking and to the foundations of a truly just world
community? . . . The enemies of compassion hold that we cannot
build a truly wise concern for humanity on the basis of such a
slippery and uneven motive; impartial motives based on ideas of
dignity and respect should take its place. The friends of compassion
reply that without building political morality on what we know
and on what has deep roots in our childhood attachments, we will
be left with a morality that will be empty of urgency—as Aristotle
puts it, a "watery" concern all round.
—Martha C. Nussbaum, "Compassion and Terror"

THERE ARE POTENTIAL objections that apply to any compassionate ethics, for there are objections to compassion itself as a source of moral guidance. The question of partiality has already appeared in previous chapters,
and now it must be directly addressed. Compassion must ultimately reject
impartiality, and if this is not found to be a deficiency, detractors may suggest that a compassionate ethic slips too far in the other direction. In other
words, to be overly partial in one's ethical concerns is to risk being self-
serving, but if selfless compassion avoids this pitfall, it opens itself to the
charge of being self-abusive.

Other objections pertain to the roots of the model of compassion developed over the preceding chapters. The cultural histories of Confucianism
and Buddhism are fraught with racism, sexism, and cultural elitism. If an
ethic of compassion is to get off the ground, it must not be given to the biases

latent in the histories of the traditions that give rise to it. Finally, there is the question of whether an ethic of compassion is too demanding. If moral standards are set so high that virtually no one can reach them, perhaps the moral theory that sets those standards is not worth following. In this chapter, I address each of these potential problems.

Partiality and Nepotism

Impartiality has long been hailed as a hallmark of any reasonable moral philosophy. The standard of impartiality dictates that our ethical thinking is supposed to be grounded in facts, logical principles, and, broadly speaking, objectivity. It pays little heed to personal relationships, emotions, or that which is only contingently true. In his early work, Kant went so far as to say that empirical data itself was too contingent to be relied upon in forming ethical maxims, though he later softened on this position. There is no shortage of ethicists who praise the merits of impartiality nor any dearth of arguments in favor of its necessity. John Rawls' argument stands out among the best of them. His ideas of the veil of ignorance and the original position constitute an excellent summation of the metaethical merits of impartiality.

The "veil of ignorance" is a conceptual shroud in a thought experiment. It masks all the contingent facts one knows about oneself and attempts to strip one's conception of oneself down to its most basic and universal elements. If I don the veil of ignorance, I surrender the knowledge that I am Caucasian, male, a native speaker of English, a U.S. citizen, and so forth. I no longer know my tax bracket, sexual orientation, religious preference, ethnicity, age, health status, educational background, geographic location, or anything else that sets me apart as an individual in a particular time, place, and set of relationships. Nor do I have such knowledge about anyone else; in this thought experiment, all human beings are positioned equally. This is what Rawls refers to as the "original position."

In the original position, behind the veil of ignorance, I am now supposed to think about what sort of civil society would be the most advantageous for me. In present-day American society, I benefit substantially from my status as a straight, white, English-speaking male on the right side of the

poverty line. But the same social forces that benefit my demographic group
cause other groups to suffer. In the original position, I do not know which
demographic group is mine, so if I am smart, I will see those social forces as
potential threats. In the original position, I would rather have a completely
level playing field. All straight, white, wealthy, English-speaking males will
lose certain advantages, but I should gladly surrender those advantages in
order to protect myself from any disadvantages I might inherit should I not
be a member of the favored demographic group.

In Rawls' thought experiment, to demonstrate partiality toward any given
group is to run the risk of undermining one's own chances of leading a desirable life. The veil of ignorance makes gamblers of us all, and smart gamblers will hedge their bets in order to minimize their risks. They will choose
impartiality.

Impartiality ends up leading to such prized ethical concepts as justice and
fairness. Kantian ethics, utilitarian ethics, and casuistic ethics *all* take impartiality as theoretical bedrock. In the face of these, an ethic of partiality
seems very difficult to defend. What role will compassion have in the original position? How can a partialist ethic of compassion contend against these
other giants of moral philosophy?

The differences between the original position and the concentric ring
model of the compassionate self-in-community are immediately apparent.
The original position erases all possible barriers to compassion within the
human community, but at the same time it all but erases the epistemological foundation on which compassion is based. Compassion is based first on
attending and understanding; if the first moment of compassion is rendered
all but impossible, then obviously the second moment will not look quite the
same. In a certain sense, the veil of ignorance liberates one to extend compassion to all human beings (the original position being an exclusively human
position), but this will be an extremely limited form of compassion. To the
extent that one can attend to the most basic needs of human beings—to
only those needs that are apparent in the original position—one can extend
compassion to all human beings. Because one knows so little, one cannot
attend to any great degree, and so compassion at this most abstract level
will also be quite abstract. It will condition the will to alleviate suffering in

a broad and general sense and the will to propagate satisfaction in a broad and general sense. At this level, compassion more closely represents what we usually think of as good will or benevolence, a general well-wishing without much specific content.

But it still makes sense to ask why we are interested in justice at all. Why does anyone want civil rights, impartial treatment, or equal protection before the law? According to Robert Solomon,

> Our celebrated notion of rights, which many theorists take to be the key to justice, is first of all that almost visceral sense of inviolability, the absolute unacceptability of certain intrusions. . . . That is why rights are trump for us, but it is not the having of a right that explains the inviolability; it is the sense of inviolability that accounts for the ascription of rights. . . . Our knowledge of justice begins with our experience of our own place in the world; our sense of justice is first of all our emotional response to a world that does not always meet up with our expectations and demands. Our sense of justice, in other words, has its origins in such emotions as resentment, jealousy, outrage, and revenge as well as in care and compassion.[1]

In sum, we invent rights because of nakedly partial concerns, at least according to Solomon. But even if one does not agree with Solomon's understanding of compassion or his understanding of justice, one can still see that it makes no sense to speak of rights preceding compassion. Rather, it is compassion (among other motivations) that prompts us to be interested in the well-being of others (and ourselves), and it is out of this interest that we posit ideals such as impartial treatment and equal protection.

Rawls' thesis, or the smart gambler's thesis—that in the original position the best choice is to distribute advantages as equally as possible and that when they are distributed unequally it is best to benefit the least advantaged —is therefore compassionate, though at a level so obscured by the thought experiment that it is hardly recognizable as such. The reason for the obfuscation hinges on the difference between politics and ethics. We generally do recognize a boundary between the two (though where it lies is far from clear), inasmuch as we accept the legitimacy of equal treatment of all citizens on the political level while still embracing many instances of preferential treatment on the ethical level. New mothers should not flip coins to decide which of the newborn babies in the maternity ward they will choose to take home, but there is nothing uncompassionate about dispassionately extending equal protection before the law to everyone. Compassion really begins to show its partiality at the personal—that is, the ethical, *not* the political—level.[2]

Yet compassion *is* partial at the ethical level, and to many ethicists this will still sound dangerous. But proponents of an ethic of compassion will challenge the notion that impartiality is possible, and they will also question whether it is in fact ethically desirable. Moreover, there is a sense in which an ethic of compassion is ultimately *more* impartial than the Rawlsian original position.

The first challenge to impartiality raised by an ethic of compassion is to question its very possibility. We are fundamentally subjective beings. This is a psychological, epistemological, and phenomenological truth. It is also an ethical truth. We have no access to an objective point of view. We will never attain omniscience—nor is it guaranteed that even an omniscient being would not also be subjective. Impartiality and objectivity are bound up in each other; insofar as we do not have access to one, we do not have access to the other. In truth, impartiality was never more than a goal; no moral agent can rightly claim to have attained it. In many cases it is a most admirable goal, but one does well to question whether there are not some cases in which the goal of impartiality should be abandoned in favor of something else.

This is the second challenge posed to avowedly impartial ethical theories: Is impartiality always desirable? Arguably it is not. If I see two children drowning in a pool—mine and a stranger's—and I have the opportunity to attempt to save only one, and if at this point I start looking for a coin to flip, I am unquestionably a terrible parent. Moreover, if I appeal solely to an impartial standard as the basis for attempting to rescue my child—for example, my legal obligation stemming from my status as a parent—it is not clear that I am a much better parent than had I flipped a coin. Perhaps I am a better citizen for having recognized my civic duty, but I might have abstained from defacing legal tender from the same motivation. My decision-making process has been wholly "uncontaminated" by partial motivations such as parental love.

An ethic that claims impartiality as the highest standard cannot offer a robust description of some of the most important relationships in our ethical lives. To prize impartiality over all else is to trivialize the ethical worthiness of those relationships. We are ethical beings because we are relational beings. Partialism honors the relationships that make us capable of doing ethics at all. It should not be lightly abandoned, even in the face of such valuable and impartial ethical principles as justice and fairness.

Naturally this can be taken too far. Compassion is partial, but perhaps the purest form of partiality is selfishness. Even if one recognizes the "great self" as an ontological fact, one might still engage in nepotism, seeking to generate maximal advantage for oneself by attending solely to the interests of those who are nearest and dearest. Indeed, this is an apt description of clannish behavior, which has influenced human social interactions for as long as there have been humans.[3] But lest we forget, compassion is opposed to selfishness from its very roots. The wisdom that informs compassion dictates that the surest road toward realizing one's self-interest paradoxically lies in selflessness. Perhaps the principal problem with a partialist ethic is the inherent danger of drifting toward selfishness, but this is the very problem compassion works hardest to fight. When one realizes the "great self," one realizes (or at least one ought to realize) that one must not construe this notion too narrowly.

A third challenge to an impartialist ethic is that there is a very real sense in which an ethic of compassion achieves a greater degree of impartiality than its avowedly objective rivals do. One is best able to extend compassion toward another when one attempts to understand the other as much as possible, to identify with the other as closely as possible, and to see the world from the other's perspective to the greatest degree possible. This includes a sensitivity to social differences, for my existence as a straight, white, natively English-speaking male on the right side of the poverty line renders many forms of suffering invisible to me unless I make the effort to perceive them.

Cultural norms generate forms of suffering that are specific to a given gender, or race, or sexual orientation, or annual income, or combination of any
of these. The nature of compassionate attention is sensitive to all of these.

But consider what happens to these socially specific forms of suffering
in the original position. The veil of ignorance erases all of them. The criticism raised against Rawls is that this erasure amounts to trivializing important social differences.[4] In effect, Rawls treats everyone like straight, white,
property-holding men. This is evident throughout *A Theory of Justice*, for
in the end what Rawls is theorizing about is only distributive justice, not
rectificatory justice or compensatory justice.[5] To be sure, the just distribution
of rights and duties is of concern to people in every level of society, but it only
concerns present distribution, not past harms. The absence of concern for
rectification of or compensation for past harms, the utter blindness of the
thought experiment to actual historical injustices, is glaring. As Charles W.
Mills points out, "Not a single reference to American slavery and its legacy
can be found" in *A Theory of Justice*, despite its having been published just
three years after the assassination of Martin Luther King Jr.[6] By erasing color
lines, gender lines, and so forth, Rawls limits his discussion to a small subset
of ethical concerns, concerns that often dwindle in importance when seen
from the perspective of some of the least advantaged demographic groups
in a society.

By his own admission, Rawls' theory of (distributive) justice as (distributive) fairness is "not a complete contract theory" but only a first step in that
direction.[7] But he says, "It is clear that the contractarian idea can be extended
to the choice of more or less an entire ethical system, that is, a system including principles for all the virtues and not only for justice."[8] Presumably that
system, founded on justice as fairness as derived from the original position,
would be equally as impartial as the theory of justice as fairness. But in the
end, this theory is arguably *less* impartial than an ethic of compassion in
which attention is devoted to social differences. It pretends impartiality but
ends up allowing the interests of the majority to obscure those of minority
groups.

Charles W. Mills describes two divergent approaches with regard to race:
the "color-blind approach" ("Act as if race doesn't exist, and it will cease to

exist") and the "color-sensitive approach" ("[Race] won't go away by pretend-
ing it doesn't exist because social structures will continue to produce that
race-based privilege and disadvantage").[9] An ethic of compassion, being
partial and perspectival, has the color-sensitive approach built into it. Rawlsian justice ends up taking the color-blind approach and effectively rejects
perspectivalism. But in a socially complex environment, the perspectival approach is arguably more likely to lead one toward impartiality than is any
pretense toward color blindness, gender blindness, and so on.

Finally, one would do well to realize that partialism is built into notions of
justice that seek to be impartial. The Fifth Amendment to the U.S. Constitution provides protection from self-incrimination, but the Supreme Court
has ruled that the same protection also extends to married partners; that is,
one is not obliged to offer testimony against one's spouse.[10] Impartiality demands that some spheres of partiality not be infringed. An ethic of compassion will simply assert that our lives are better when we allow those partialist
spheres to encompass more than the impartialist might like them to.

Excesses of Altruism

A critic might still argue that even if compassion does not lead to selfishness,
by embracing partiality it still risks leaning too far in the opposite direction.
Rather than leading to excessive egoism, might it not lead to excessive altruism? That is, might it not lead one to self-abusive behavior in promotion of
the interests of others?

Take as an example the famous story in early Indian Buddhism of
Śākyamuni and the tiger. In an earlier incarnation, Śākyamuni is said to have
been walking in a forest when he came across a starving tiger. Because of his
supreme compassion, he gave his own body to the tiger to satisfy its hunger.
The tiger, of course, ripped Śākyamuni limb from limb and devoured him,
but Śākyamuni was willing to undergo such horrible suffering to alleviate
the suffering of another sentient being.

Let us bring the problem into the modern day. Suppose I go to the hospital for a routine physical. The doctor who is examining me notices my blood
is B-negative and therefore rather rare. It so happens that in the next wing

the doctor has five other patients, all of whom have B-negative blood, and all of whom are in desperate need of a pint of blood. It is easily within the hospital's technological means and the doctor's technical abilities to transplant the five needed pints from my body into the five other patients—at the cost of my life. Suppose the doctor informs me of all of this: Does an ethic of compassion bind me to offer up my organs to save the other five?

We can let Śākyamuni off the hook by adding two other details to his story: that he was very close to realizing enlightenment in this former life and that he believed in reincarnation. If he is convinced he is coming back, his decision to sacrifice himself is a bit easier. Not so for me; sitting on my hospital bed, I remain an agnostic regarding past and future lives. But we can add facts to influence my decision, too. Suppose I have neither friends nor family, and suppose the other five have rich and healthy social lives. Suppose the reason I have no friends or family is because all of them just died tragically; suppose I am terribly depressed by this, and by surrendering my blood I can bring an end to my own suffering while prolonging the lives of the other five. Suppose further that the other five are all brilliant researchers on cures for cancer or Alzheimer's disease, whereas my future as a philosopher portends nothing so glamorous. Factors like these, and indeed problems like this one, are usually raised to question the reliability of act utilitarianism, but they are no less relevant here. Does compassion demand that I effectively commit suicide to save them, as Śākyamuni did for the tiger?

Scheler writes of the "true and authentic *transcendence* of one's self" (TNS 45–46) by which one may make supremely self-sacrificial acts in the interest of another. Images of the samurai may come to mind, charging headlong into battle without fear or performing ritual disembowelment as a form of political protest.[11] Think also of a G.I. in a trench throwing himself on a grenade to save the rest of his platoon, or a mother pushing her child out of the path of a speeding bus only to be hit herself. Robert Trivers has argued that, from a biological point of view, this latter case does not constitute altruism (but rather a contribution to the survival of the mother's genetic information), and of course the psychological egoist will hold not only that none of the above examples are instances of altruism but that true altruism is a psychological impossibility.[12] Sociobiologist E. O. Wilson pushes still further, holding that pure altruism is in fact a biological impossibility—in other words, that no living being is ultimately capable of anything other than the egoistic pursuit of the survival of its genes. For Wilson, what we call altruism is just "the mechanism by which DNA multiplies itself through a network of relatives."[13] In response, Peter Singer observes that "sociobiologists often sound like psychological egoists." But like psychological egoism, the sociobiological theory of altruism is fraught with problems, both empirical and philosophical.[14] If those who argue against psychological egoism and sociobiology are right, then self-sacrificial altruism—true and authentic *transcendence* of the self, to use Scheler's words—is a possibility. But to what extent does compassion demand it of us? Will it demand self-sacrifice that is self-abusive?

Scheler himself provides reasons to believe otherwise. He writes of the "abnormally *vain* man" and the "mental parasite," individuals who are "utterly in thrall to the notice and opinion of other people" and who will do almost anything—including suicide—to gain the approval of their spectators (TNS 42–43). Of course, altruistic behavior may never enter the abnormally vain man's head, and the mental parasite may be too sick to truly engage in such behavior. Scheler does not bring up these unhealthy individuals to discuss altruism but rather to discuss self-respect. For him, "Without a certain self-awareness and self-respect, acquired at first hand, and not derived from the effect produced on others, it is not possible to live morally" (44). This idea can be incorporated into an ethic of compassion to ensure it does not demand self-abusive acts of altruism.

Compassion began with the idea that we are all socially constituted, embedded in inescapable networks of relationships. Any course of action that is self-abusive also has the potential to abuse those other beings to which one is relationally bound. If I sacrifice my blood so that five other patients might live, my death will have social consequences. Even if all of my friends and family members are dead, I still exist in a social matrix. Zhuangzi, the great venerator of the maimed and crippled, would have pointed out that, as the survivor of a tragedy (namely, the deaths of all who were close to me), I have knowledge and experience that most others do not have—and I am therefore possessed of wisdom inaccessible to most people. I still have gifts to offer. I still have the potential to build new relationships. In any event, even if I decide to sacrifice my life, my example will live on. What will the rest of society think of the patient who was drained to have his blood distributed among the other patients? And what of the attending surgeons: Will they be thought of as vampires or as heroes? What of the recipients of my blood, or the hospital where the operations took place? Socially embedded beings leave ripples in their relationships even after their deaths.[15]

Thus self-respect can be justified in an ethic of compassion because of its broader social effects. These effects can be measured in a number of ways. First, as in the above case, one can recognize the compassionate self-in-community as a "great self," incorporating not only the agent but those with whom the agent interacts as well. Seen from the standpoint of the great self, self-respect and self-abuse take on a much wider scope.

A second approach is to recognize that compassion extends inward as well as outward. If I am a compassionate person, I am concerned for my own well-being as well as for that of others. This does not allow me to ignore others' interests in favor of my own, but by the same token it also does not justify letting others' interests run roughshod over mine. As with the *nin* (人, individual) and *gen* (間, social) aspects of Watsuji Tetsurō's *ningen* model of human existence, one must attempt to find parity between the two. According to Watsuji, a crucial part of human ethical life is wrapped up in finding and maintaining this parity. An ethic of compassion will recognize the need for a similar kind of parity.

Another justification for compassionate self-respect will closely resemble a utilitarian justification. The utilitarian might argue that a society whose members exhibit and value self-respect is more likely to maximize utility than is a society in which self-respect makes no appearance. A widespread absence of self-respect would very likely lead to widespread fear. If neither my doctor nor I respect me, there is no apparent reason why I should not sacrifice my life for five other patients. But just because I have no self-respect does not mean that I do not fear death. If I both fear death and live in a society that does not honor self-respect, going to the hospital is a very bad idea for me: I may not walk out with all the organs I entered with (and that is assuming I walk back out at all). Intelligent utility maximizing agents in such a society will fear doctors and hospitals—and rightly so. A society whose members honor and exhibit self-respect is much more likely to maximize utility.

According to a compassionate aretaic ethic, the same observations may be used to justify self-respect as an excellence (i.e., a trait that facilitates the cultivation and exercise of compassion). Agents will arguably be better able to conduct themselves compassionately if they exhibit self-respect than if they do not. Moreover, because the best of us serve as role models to others in society, self-abusive behavior on the part of those who achieve the highest excellence would be supposed to lead to widespread self-abusive behavior on the part of those who aspire to similar achievement. Truly excellent agents will behave selflessly without behaving self-abusively.

Watsuji's philosophy of *ningen* is a useful one for thinking about self-respect and compassion. If private (*nin*, 人) and public (*gen*, 間) concerns are inextricably intertwined in the human being and if both must be respected in order to live authentically, then self-respect is in essence a balancing of these concerns. The hazy border between selflessness and self-abuse is always in the background of Watsuji's discussion of *ningen*'s often conflicting sides. But for *ningen*, self-abuse is abusive of both sides, for both sides constitute the self. This, I think, is the most appropriate way to think of compassionate self-respect and self-abuse: Because the self is socially constituted, to respect or abuse it is to respect or abuse an entire relational matrix.

Hierarchies of Power

Because an ethic of compassion will be a perspectivalist ethic, it will be sensitive to differences in social power. Compassionate agents will attempt to adopt the perspectives of parties on both sides of a hierarchical relationship, examining ethical issues from the standpoints of the empowered and the disempowered alike. This, at least, is the ideal. But some might object that the account of compassion presented here has been developed out of traditions that have been used to reinforce significant social inequalities. History supplies feminists with a great deal of ammunition to attack Confucianism as a misogynistic tradition, and Buddhism's historical treatment of women is also tarnished. Proponents of Buddhism or Confucianism may offer their retorts, of course, but even if the two traditions should be wholly exonerated of chauvinism—a task many feminists will likely deem impossible—it remains true that gender inequalities have persisted throughout the cultural history of those traditions and that historically the adherents of the traditions have not done enough to combat such inequalities.

Gender inequalities are not the only social power relations in question. The story of Japanese Buddhism is intermeshed with stories of thriving cultural elitism and racism. To the extent that the popular culture perceived no contradiction between Buddhist beliefs and racist beliefs, institutionalized Buddhism is arguably guilty of promoting racism. This need not be confined to racist beliefs nor to Buddhism; to the extent that the laity in any tradition does not commonly perceive a conflict between their tradition's precepts and the basic precepts of any given form of prejudicial discrimination, that tradition is arguably guilty of promoting that particular form of prejudice. And people will argue, with greater or lesser degrees of justification, that the traditions upon which the present account of compassion is founded are guilty of promoting various kinds of prejudice. This model of compassion needs to show that it is not similarly guilty of embracing racism, misogyny, homophobia, cultural elitism, or any other form of social injustice.

This is particularly difficult to do for an admittedly partialist philosophy, for traditionally the impartialist has simply appealed to impartiality itself to be exonerated of such charges. We have already seen how arguments of this kind may be criticized from minority perspectives (Charles W. Mills' critique of John Rawls being a good example), but partiality is not relieved of its burden simply because impartiality fails in what it purports to accomplish. The model of compassion developed here must be free of any abusive hierarchies that may exist in the philosophies that underlie it.

It should be noted from the outset that not all hierarchies are ethically problematic. In terms of social power, parents do not and should not operate on equal terms with their small children. Nobody would be better off if six-year-olds were granted autonomy equal to that of their legal guardians. Of course, some parents and guardians are abusive, but it is the abuse that we find morally objectionable, not the inequality of the hierarchical relationship. It is explicitly prejudicial to say that no six-year-olds should wield the same degree of social power as the adults who care for them, but most of us are content to say it nonetheless. Indeed, it is *compassionate* to acknowledge an inequality between parents and children, for such an inequality accurately identifies the needs of both sides and works to ensure the well-being of both sides.

Hence compassion can recognize some hierarchical social institutions as morally acceptable while condemning others. This is one of Confucianism's basic insights: We seek not *equality* in our relationships but *parity,* even if this parity can only be achieved over the course of a lifetime. Had I lived in Confucius' day, as a child I would have owed my parents deference and my younger siblings would have owed me deference. Were I to grow up and become a parent myself, my children would owe me deference and I would owe them the same care and guidance my parents once owed me. Then, as my parents grew old, as the eldest son it would have fallen to me to take care of them—and they, taking residence with my family and me, would owe me a degree of deference as the head of the household. All of these relationships are unequal, but I experience all sides of the inequalities: The deference I show is later shown to me.

But no such lifelong parity is possible for gays in a homophobic society, women in a misogynistic society, and so on. They are bound to show deference where none is shown in return. Such hierarchies cannot be deemed compassionate forms of inequality. Thus the ethic of compassion I have developed here has some basis for distinguishing between compassionate and uncompassionate forms of inequality.

Another point to be noted is that it is generally considered fair play to divorce a philosophical idea or ideal from the philosopher or school of philosophers that gave birth to it. Kant, for example, established the theory of race upon which modern racism is founded,[16] and there is little doubt that in his personal life he was what we today would call a racist,[17] but one would hope that today we might recognize Kant's important contributions to modern philosophy without subscribing to his racist beliefs. By the same token, we need not disregard the worthwhile insights of Confucianism, Buddhism, or Daoism just because they thrived in less than egalitarian cultures: To do so is to throw out the baby with the bathwater. Just as one can theoretically be a Kantian deontologist without being a racist, so too can one practice compassion as I have described it without simultaneously putting into practice the social inequalities Dōgen or Confucius would have observed in the Kamakura period or the Eastern Zhou dynasty.

That said, the specter of those inequalities still haunts the model of compassion being developed here. Rawls' original position turns a blind eye to all past injustices, but this, it was argued, is uncompassionate. It may not be sufficiently convincing to claim that the past inequalities were simply uncompassionate and that, had the Confucians *really* expressed Confucian compassion, and had the Buddhists *really* expressed Buddhist compassion, those transgressions never would have taken place. An ethic of compassion should have internal safeguards against such harmful inequalities.

To discover what these are, I will compare compassion to the account of care developed by recent care ethicists. Nel Noddings first qualified care in the technical sense as being an engrossment with another, an apprehension of the other's reality, a moving away from self-interest to the interests of the other.[18] The similarities to compassion should already be apparent: "An apprehension of the other's reality" corresponds to the moment of attentiveness, and "an engrossment with another" and "a moving away from self-interest to the interests of the other" are both suggestive of the relational model of the compassionate self-in-community.

Noddings says care is "largely reactive and responsive,"[19] demanding participation by both the one who cares (the "one-caring") and the one who receives care (the "cared-for"). As an ethical ideal, it is that which provides us with the motivation to be moral. It is ethically basic, preceding rational judgments and evaluations, and it is grounded in our relationality, which Noddings holds to be ontologically basic.[20] Again, the similarities to the compassion I am describing are readily apparent.

Care also exists only in particular relations between the one-caring and the cared-for, and it is therefore not universalizable in the usual ethical sense. Care is not universally applicable, nor is there some abstract universalized care that can be applied to everyone. The only sense of care that is universal is that care that arises from the relationality that is basic to our existence.

We exist in relationships, and so we have the capacity to exist in caring relationships, but this is a *natural* care, not the *ethical* sense of care developed by Noddings. Natural care is universalizable, but ethical care will not admit of such a high degree of abstraction. It is, in effect, avowedly partial, just as compassion is.

Building upon Noddings' work, Joan C. Tronto identifies four elements of an ethic of care: attentiveness (the recognition of a need); responsibility (the analogue of "obligation" in care ethics[21]); competence (the ability of the one-caring to administer care); and responsiveness (the cared-for's recognition of having received care and the one-caring's attentiveness to that recognition). The cycle of care begins and ends with attentiveness, and while attentiveness as I have defined it is not identical to Tronto's usage of the term, there are certainly important commonalities between caring attentiveness and compassionate attentiveness.

There are other ways in which compassion is similar to care, but this cycle of attentiveness ranks among the highest in importance. Care ethics was first developed by feminist thinkers who were sensitive to political and social inequalities and who sought a way of thinking about ethics that would display a similar sensitivity. The inclusion of what Tronto calls responsiveness —also called the reciprocity condition—is an important safeguard in care ethics against abusive hierarchies of power. One cannot legitimately claim to care for another while paying no attention to the other's responses to one's attempts at caring. There is a vitally important feedback loop that cycles between the cared-for's responses to care and the one-caring's reactions to the cared-for's responses. In short, true care hinges upon attending to the cared-for.

Compassion also hinges upon attending to the object of compassion, and this points to another important feature common to an ethic of care and an ethic of compassion. Both of them locate ethical evaluation similarly, and neither of them will locate ethical evaluation in actions nor even in individuals. The classical bifurcation between act-based and agent-based approaches to ethical evaluation is not robust enough to incorporate care ethics, nor an ethic of compassion, nor some of the traditions I have drawn upon to flesh out the ethics of compassion. Watsuji Tetsurō, for instance, holds that for *ningen,* a being with both private and public interests, ethics is located not in the individual but in the betweenness (*aida,* 間) existing between person and person or person and world (*seken,* 世間). We can only speculate as to how Watsuji would have performed ethical evaluations (his concern in the *Rinrigaku* was with metaethics), but I think it is safe to conclude that he would have been less inclined to say "that act is good" and more inclined to say "that relationship is working well."

This inclination is Confucian in origin—the *Rinrigaku* was informed through and through by Watsuji's previous monograph on Confucianism —and is arguably equally true of Confucian moral evaluation. Little attention is devoted to the individual action, and indeed the individual agent receives attention only insofar as that agent is located in a network of social relationships. (To be sure, it makes little sense to speak of an "individual" agent in a Confucian or Watsujian context except as a convenient linguistic device; persons are always persons-in-context.) The same is true in care ethics: Ethical evaluation is an evaluation of ongoing caring relationships, not of individual acts or agents. It follows that all parties involved in the relationships are always a part of moral evaluation, and when one party is systematically oppressed, this will be reflected in the evaluation of the relationship.

This serves as a safeguard within care ethics, protecting against abusively hierarchical social institutions. The same kind of internal safeguard arguably exists in an ethic of compassion as well. Because it is best understood when grounded in an irreducibly social understanding of human existence and because it begins with attentiveness, if compassion does not attend to the social imbalances that exist in the social matrix in which it finds itself, then to that extent we must deem it a failure. Put the other way, compassion will be deemed effective to the extent that it attends to and seeks to alleviate the harms caused by social imbalances that exist in the social matrix in which it finds itself. Of course, this does not guarantee that all compassionate agents will be wholly free of prejudice; no theory can promise that. But it does mean that to the extent that one is unjustifiably prejudiced, one cannot be considered compassionate, and it echoes something already suggested in chapter 3: Namely, that to extinguish unjustifiably prejudicial thinking is to help break down the barriers to compassion.

Important similarities notwithstanding, there are significant differences between compassion and care that must not be overlooked. First, although an ethic of compassion will mimic some of the effects of the reciprocity condition, there is no reciprocity condition built into compassion. The reciprocity condition represents a built-in desire for criticism in the caring relationship, which is supposed to help maintain healthy caring relations. If this is built into an ethic of compassion, it exists in the habituation of proper attentiveness and the genuine will to attend to needs, and it is therefore largely an internal process (as opposed to care's dyadic process). On the other hand, the reciprocity condition exposes care ethics to certain problems—for instance, there is an element of moral luck involved, since the cared-for *must* be able to respond, either personally or by proxy, in order for true care to take place—that an ethic of compassion avoids by not requiring the condition. And it remains that compassion is not wholly an internal process; it does require regular input from the world.

Second, the "great self" of compassion is not the "great self" of care, and the partiality of compassion is not the partiality of care. These two claims are tightly intertwined. There is a kind of impartiality built into the model of compassion I have been describing—not a Rawlsian impartiality but a Buddhist one. I am still a particular agent embedded in and constituted by particular relationships, but if I slough off the ego entirely, I will see that I should be willing to step beyond those relationships and care for all sentient beings as my brothers and sisters. This, at least, is what Dōgen would have me do,[22] but care ethicists will have none of this. According to them, it is uncaring for me to cast off my personal relationships. Obviously there is a lot more that might be said—Dōgen did not counsel brutality in cutting off one's ties, and care ethicists do not recommend clinging fiercely to one's relationships no matter the cost to others—but the general idea is there. Care's particularity will, in the end, reject the Buddhist sense of egoless particularity and have much more in common with Confucian particularity.

This distinction draws attention to a certain tension between the Buddhist and Confucian philosophies of human relationality, both of which were helpful in developing the present model of compassion. I suggested in the concluding paragraph of chapter 3 that there are at least two possible approaches to an ethic of compassion: one religious and the other secular. I have drawn upon Sōtō Zen Buddhism to develop an account of the former and Confucianism to describe the latter. To the extent that the two disagree, it will be the Confucian account that care ethicists will likely find most appealing.

This section began with the suggestion that there are cogent feminist objections to a model of compassion grounded in traditions such as Confucianism and Buddhism, whose histories have not been devoid of misogynistic practices to say the least. It is remarkable, then, that this account of compassion should bear so many important similarities to care ethics, which arose out of explicitly feminist philosophical concerns. Care ethics was developed in response to the predominant social inequalities that obtained (and still obtain) when the theory of care came into being. An ethic of compassion is concerned with all of those inequalities as well and indeed with any form of social inequality that is insensitive to the needs of one side or abusively preferential toward the needs of the other side. Perhaps "conservative Confucians" or "conservative Buddhists" would object to this bastardization of their philosophical beliefs. That criticism is worth sustaining if by sustaining it one secures protection against abusive social hierarchies.

Conclusion

I have now proposed a normative aretaic ethic by which compassion can offer constructive moral guidance and defended it against several philosophical objections to compassion as a source of moral guidance. Compassion runs the double risks of being either overly nepotistic or overly self-sacrificial, but it can walk the razor's edge between these two. Though an ethic of compassion will openly reject impartiality, this is not nearly as objectionable as one might think; indeed, partiality is arguably of vital importance to an ethical life. But partiality does not amount to unfairness, and indeed an ethic of compassion will reject abusive social biases and hierarchies.

This chapter and the previous chapter constitute a theoretical foundation for the ethics of compassion. In the following chapter, my focus will shift from theory to practice, as I analyze how compassion is put into effect in everyday life.

CHAPTER FIVE

Compassion in Action

It is then certain that compassion is a natural feeling, which, by
moderating the violence of love of self in each individual, contributes
to the preservation of the whole species. It is this compassion that
hurries us without reflection to the relief of those who are in distress:
it is this which in a state of nature supplies the place of laws, morals and
virtues, with the advantage that none are tempted to disobey its gentle
voice.... In a word, it is rather in this natural feeling than in any subtle
arguments that we must look for the cause of that repugnance, which
every man would experience in doing evil, even independently of the
maxims of education. Although it might belong to Socrates and other
minds of the like craft to acquire virtue by reason, the human race
would long have ceased to be, had its preservation depended only on
the reasonings of the individuals composing it.
—Rousseau, "Discourse on the Origin of Inequality"

KANT SAYS THE following of the good will:

> Even if, by some especially unfortunate fate or by the niggardly provi-
> sion of stepmotherly nature, this will should be wholly lacking in the
> power to accomplish its purpose; if with the greatest effort it should yet
> achieve nothing, and only the good will should remain ... yet would it,
> like a jewel, still shine by its own light as something which has full value
> in itself. Its usefulness or fruitlessness can neither augment nor diminish
> its value.[1]

Perhaps compassion is like the Kantian good will—admirable in and of
itself—but this will not satisfy the compassionate agent. Compassionate
disposition demands compassionate praxis; it demands results. The same

might be said of one with a Kantian good will—if I were such a one, surely I
would be frustrated if I were wholly incapable of *doing* anything good—but
it remains that Kant's definition of the good will is by his own description
one "in which no account is taken of any useful results."[2]

This suggests a kind of moral solipsism in which one's conduct is regarded
as moral or immoral independently of the existence of any other thing. According to Kant's view, in theory I could be nothing other than an instan-
tiation of Descartes' *cogito*—a solitary, disembodied, thinking entity—and
still lead a moral life. An ethic of compassion, originating out of a socially
constructed account of existence, will regard the idea of moral solipsism as
nonsense.[3] True compassion will always seek out practical application and
will take as given the social field in which that focused application takes
place.

Because of compassion's persistent drive to be applied, the distinction
drawn between "applied ethics" and "theoretical ethics" in contemporary
academic ethical discourse will take on a different character in the context
of an ethic of compassion, as will the two terms themselves. Theoretical ethics, or philosophical ethics, is the study of ethical theories or styles of ethical
reasoning, and it is not to be confused with applied ethics, which is the "solv-
ing" of ethical issues such as abortion, stem cell research, same-sex marriage,
and so on. Applied ethics, in turn, is not to be confused with one's daily life:
These "problems" are typically presented in purely theoretical terms, issues
that one may encounter someday and that one probably ought to have an
opinion about, but not the stuff of day-to-day living. The same is true of theoretical ethics, which is typically taught as being only of academic interest.

On the other hand, Rousseau maintains that were it not for an innate
sense of compassion, human beings would never have survived long enough
to develop ethical theories of any stripe. This chapter's epigraph speaks to his
faith in the constancy of compassion, "the pure emotion of nature," which he
finds to be "so much the more universal and useful to mankind, as it comes
before any kind of reflection."[4] If Rousseau is right, compassion precedes
philosophy. Purely academic compassion is no compassion at all.

Generally speaking, accounting classes are supposed to turn out better

accountants, anatomy classes are designed to train better nurses and physical therapists, and so forth, but the aim of ethics classes is not to produce
better people or better behavior. Many ethics professors will readily confess
that their sole goal is to present information, and that they have no intention of changing their students' ethical conduct. An adherent of an ethic
of compassion will be puzzled by this approach. True compassion is never
purely theoretical, never of academic interest alone. Neither is compassionate practice without theoretical backing; *karuṇā* and *prajñā* are indivisible.
The distinction between "theoretical" and "applied" ethics points to nothing in this view and should therefore be discarded.

Of course, one can still speak theoretically about compassion—this book
constitutes just such an exercise—but truly compassionate discourse will
always have some practical application as its end. And an ethic of compassion will naturally be equipped to respond to the issues of applied ethics—if
it were not, it should hardly be worth discussing—but its approach will
diverge significantly from the kind of dialogue that currently holds sway
regarding those issues.

The instinct in applied ethics as a discipline seems to be to dissect problems into two opposing sides, one of permission ("people ought to be allowed to do X") and one of prohibition ("people ought not be allowed to do
X"). This is all the more accurate a description of contemporary American
culture. It has become nearly impossible to have a public discussion of the
issues of applied ethics. The debate over abortion quickly becomes a shout-
ing match, one group yelling about the rights of fetuses while another yells
about the rights of women, neither side capable of hearing the other. The
debate over same-sex marriage has been, if anything, even worse. Some opponents object not to homosexual marriage but to homosexuality itself, their
objection being formed on what they take to be sound moral grounds, and
in rare cases some opponents perceive a moral risk in even speaking with a
homosexual person. At the same time, it is all too easy for gays to equate
opposing gay marriage with endorsing divestiture of their basic civil rights,
and so some foreclose the possibility of open dialogue from that side as well.

At the same time that the two dominant sides (on any one of these issues) cannot hear each other, their clamoring drowns out all other voices. One feminist critique of the abortion debate, though virtually no one has heard it, is that there can be no legitimate discussion of abortion at all until men and women are made equals in the society.[5] There is a movement opposed to same-sex marriage within the gay community, though again virtually no one takes it into account.[6] For the most part, contemporary debate over such critical ethical issues is consumed by a Manichean brand of dualism, each side seeing itself as good and the other as anathema. The ethical dualist becomes an ethical duelist, with applied ethics being a venue for philosophical swordplay. The goal is victory; agreement, harmony, and compromise fall by the wayside.[7]

Dueling is a sort of relationship, but it is not the sort an ethic of compassion seeks to foster. In ethical debate, including debates over the issues of applied ethics, an ethic of compassion will seek to move beyond dualistic and antagonistic thinking, first by recognizing that none of these issues is so simple that there are only two sides to take on it, and second by realizing that what is central to all of these issues is suffering in one form or another. As Śāntideva said, suffering is bad by definition; there is no dueling to be done, no argument to be had on this point. A compassionate approach to the issues of applied ethics will begin with the assumption that everyone on every side ought to be united in minimizing suffering and that differences of opinion arise only on the nature and location of the suffering.

But this is a vague prescription. I shall take up two classical issues of applied ethics — capital punishment and physician-assisted suicide — and show how an ethic of compassion will address them. In the case of capital punishment, I rely heavily on the work of Helen Prejean, a Jesuit nun who has dedicated her life to the abolition of the death penalty. Prejean's approach meshes tightly with the account of compassion developed over the previous chapters, and her treatment of capital punishment will serve as the model for the subsequent analysis of euthanasia and physician-assisted suicide. Following these two analyses will come a conclusion concerning what "applied ethics" means in an ethic of compassion and what sorts of issues will count as issues of applied ethics.

Compassion in Activism: Helen Prejean and Death Row

"When Chava Colon from the Prison Coalition asks me one January day in 1982 to become a pen pal to a death-row inmate, I say, Sure." Thus opens Sister Helen Prejean's book, *Dead Man Walking.* On the day she agreed to exchange letters with an inmate, she was teaching high school dropouts in a housing project called St. Thomas in the inner city of New Orleans. She had already dedicated her life to assisting the indigent and the socially oppressed, but by beginning correspondence with Elmo Patrick Sonnier, a multiple murderer, kidnapper, and rapist, her life of service underwent a radical transformation. *Dead Man Walking* is the Pulitzer-nominated account of how she began to work for the abolition of the death penalty, both in the United States and abroad. She is now internationally renowned as an opponent of capital punishment, the subject of the Academy Award–winning film *Dead Man Walking,* the author of two best-selling books on capital punishment, and a person who continues to stand out as an exemplary model of compassion.[8]

The word "compassion" appears from time to time throughout her book, but it is in her conduct that it is expressed most loudly. She begins by recognizing Pat Sonnier, one of the most heinous criminals in the Louisiana penitentiary system, as a human being worthy of dignity and respect. She serves as his spiritual adviser up until the night of his electrocution—which she witnesses, horrifying as it is, because she "can't bear the thought that [he] would die without seeing one loving face" (DMW 47). She later reaches out to his incarcerated brother (who is serving a life sentence for the same crimes for which Pat was executed), their mother, the families of their victims, and eventually to other death row inmates, to the families of their victims, and to the families of inmates and victims more generally through the organization of advocacy groups and support circles. Prejean even extends her compassion to the prison officials who will carry out the execution of the man she has befriended. Few groups are more opposed to each other than those she attends to and seeks to help.

The first inmate for whom she serves as a spiritual adviser is Pat Sonnier, and it is significant that she refers to him as "Pat." Virtually all of the staff at

Angola Prison, where he is incarcerated and where he will be executed, refer to him only as "Sonnier." The lone exception is the priest who offers him his last sacraments, who calls him "Elmo," Pat's legal first name and one he hates to be called (DMW 117). "Pat" is what his family calls him, and Prejean does the same. This is important because to name is to humanize; by using his last name, the prison staff shield themselves from the reality of what they do with the electric chair. While Prejean refers to all those incarcerated on death row as "inmates," the prison chaplain refers to them as "these people"—in other words, not "us"—and "scum of the earth" (31). The first rule the guards are taught at Angola is "never relate on a *personal* level with the inmates," and one guard even told an inmate as he was being strapped into the electric chair, "You gotta understand, Tim, this is nothing personal" (230, 129). The constant depersonalization of the inmates is very clearly a deliberate defensive mechanism; the aim is to erect an impenetrable barrier to compassion, so that it is psychologically acceptable not to contemplate what happens in the death house.

But Prejean does the opposite: She breaks down all the commonly existing barriers that would have ordinarily separated a nun and schoolteacher from a murderer, rapist, and kidnapper who is about to die. As the two of them exchange letters, she says, "I begin to think of him as a human being" (DMW 15). This is an important step, though she admits it surprises her: "Despite his friendly letters I had half expected Charles Manson—brutish, self-absorbed, paranoid, incapable of human encounter" (40). At no point does she forget the horrific crimes committed by Sonnier, nor by Robert Lee Willie (the second inmate to whom she comes to serve as a spiritual adviser), nor does she let them forget what they did,[9] but she does recognize them as moral beings like her.

Lest one think that this observation is an obvious one, consider the legal environment in which she finds herself situated: one where lawyers must persuade jurors to see their defendants as human beings if their clients are to escape death (60) and in which prosecutors need not establish that capital punishment has any deterrent effect since, in the words of one district attorney, "If it doesn't, all we've lost is the life of a convicted criminal" (145). When the common consensus is that the basic compassion one extends to all human beings need not include those convicted of heinous crimes, Prejean's interaction with the inmates as equals is an exceptional example of compassionate conduct.

What enables her to identify with condemned criminals as fellow human beings is her persistent drive to adopt their perspectives in order to understand their plight. When she learns of periodic strip searches in Angola, she says, "I shudder to think of myself in this type of situation" (DMW 43). Seeing Pat Sonnier's attempts at bravado before the warden, she says, "I wonder what kind of dignity I would muster if I were facing my executioners" (47). When he muses on his last words, she tells him "how his anger at a time like this is understandable and how it would be understandable too if he chose to make his last words . . . a hateful attack on people who have come to watch him suffer and die, and maybe if I were in his place I would want to do the same thing—at least a part of me would" (108).

But then she urges him to take the compassionate steps she takes, to imagine himself in the position of those who want to see him dead, "to think about the parents of David and Loretta [his murder victims] and how they have already suffered torments and whether he wants to add to their grief" (DMW 108). She uses this tactic frequently, inviting the inmates to adopt the perspectives of their victims and the victims' families. To Robert Willie, she says, "Look what these parents are going through. . . . Their daughter raped and stabbed and left to die in the woods. What if someone did that to your mother? What would you want to do to them?" (189). Regarding Faith Hathaway, the woman he raped and murdered, she asks him, "Have you ever really faced her pain, felt it, taken it inside yourself?" (229).

This last phrase is metaphorical to be sure, but the message is clear: The inmates she counsels tend not to consider the experiences of the people they hurt unless they are guided to do so. Robert even overlooks his own mother's suffering in the face of his imminent execution. He wants her not to speak at his pardon board hearing, but Prejean tells him, "I know it's bound to be upsetting for her, and you'd like to save her from it, but if you die, after you're gone, it may be bad for her if she didn't have the chance to speak for you" (DMW 208). Here she adopts his perspective and his mother's; she shows compassion for him while inviting him to show compassion himself.

Prejean's book is replete with examples of adopting multiple perspectives. She attempts to identify with virtually everyone she encounters, including those who are diametrically opposed to her own values and political goals. She readily and repeatedly identifies with the families of the murder victims, a particularly challenging task given that they often "think that compassion toward the murderer means betrayal of the victim" (DMW 292). Her driving concern throughout the book is that she has not done enough to comfort the families or that she has added to their pain.[10] Even when the parent of a victim is particularly vociferous about wanting vengeance, even when the desired revenge is described in the most gruesome terms, Prejean does not hold back. She goes so far as to express respect for one such parent, Vernon Harvey, though she finds his position morally abhorrent (169). Indeed, she does more than respect him: She comes to console him in his home; she bakes him pies; she helps restore him to health after heart surgery; most significant of all, she gives his opinions a voice in her book. That, some would say, is no way to write a manifesto for the abolition of capital punishment, but Prejean airs opinions on all sides of the issue. This includes prison guards (98, 231), the priest at Angola (104), and the chair of the pardoning board (216ff.), all of whom are complicit in or responsible for the executions she fights to abolish, and all of whom become the objects of her compassion.

The thoroughness with which she expresses her compassion is striking. At one point, Pat tells her about hunting rabbits as a youth, about carrying them in a sack and clubbing the sack if his bullets failed to kill one of the rabbits. The difference between her reaction and his is quite distinct: "I am thinking of the clobbered rabbits. He is thinking of the food" (DMW 38). When Prejean arranges for a plot for Pat in a Catholic cemetery, she even thinks of what the nun buried next to him might have felt about the prospect of lying next to a man when in life she never wanted to share her bed with one (127). One might say one cannot show compassion for corpses, but Prejean's instinct is to consider the interests of all parties involved, no matter how tertiary.

Even when she speaks of her own stress and suffering, she typically describes it not as her own but rather as an experience others would have in her situation. When a prison official asks her whether she was distraught seeing

Pat Sonnier die, she says, "Who wouldn't be" (DMW 156)?[11] When considering the patent vengefulness of the parents of Faith Hathaway, she asks, "Who can blame them for wanting to see her murderer executed?" (181). One might think these rhetorical questions are just a manner of speech, but there is a difference between "I don't blame them" and "Who can blame them?" The former comes from the ego; the latter is an appeal to a communal perspective.

Even when Prejean describes her distress directly, it is frequently described in a remote sort of way: "I realize that I am very, very tired"; or "The relief I feel in seeing [a colleague] makes me realize how close the terror is" (DMW 100, 108). She does not describe feeling the strain but rather realizes that she has been feeling it. Typically this is how we become aware of the distress of other people, not our own, but Prejean puts the suffering of her inmates first and tends to notice her own discomfort only when she is not ministering to them.

Prejean's selflessness and willingness to recognize others' perspectives as legitimate and valuable—no matter how different they may be from her own—have remarkable effects on other people. Though neither Pat nor Robert is forthcoming about his crimes with others, they both come to confess the truth to Prejean. In her first meetings with each of them, she notices that neither man talks about what brought him to death row. But Prejean says, "I have no right to demand that he confess to me his terrible sin. That kind of revelation demands trust and should be freely given. I respect that" (DMW 39). This stands in stark contrast to the attitude of Angola's resident priest, whose sole goal seems to be to extract confessions from the inmates in order to perform rites of absolution. Because of the respect she shows to them, the inmates she befriends open up to her. Pat Sonnier's brother Eddie, whom she also counsels, takes to calling her "Sis." To this she says, "It fits. I know I'm family to him" (161). Because she is accepting of them, others are accepting of her; by allowing her compassion to flow freely to others, she encourages others to break down their own barriers to compassion.

She has the same opening effect on those who look forward to the execution of prisoners. A counterdemonstrator against Prejean's abolitionist demonstration—a mother whose child was murdered—snaps at Prejean, and Prejean responds, "I'm sorry about your daughter." Elizabeth Harvey, wife of Vernon Harvey and another one of the counterdemonstrators, tells the mother Prejean is "all right" and that she doesn't try to "change" people (DMW 291). This could hardly be more wrong; Prejean is constantly working to change people's attitude toward the death penalty. Her book is full of evidence to this effect. At one point, even the governor of Louisiana is afraid to meet with her because he worries she might change his position (106). But her strategy is not to missionize but rather to lead by example. Prejean listens and cares and gives freely of herself, and only afterward does she speak of what she holds to be the truth of the matter. She seeks to change compassionately: that is, by attending to others, respecting their points of view, and doing what she can to alleviate their suffering and bring about their happiness.

And in the course of doing this, she sacrifices. The physical suffering she willingly undergoes is bad enough: Over the course of Pat Sonnier's last weeks, she contracts a bronchial infection (he smokes constantly in the death house, and she is allergic to cigarette smoke), has a fainting spell, and experiences sleepless nights and almost chronic fatigue. This is to say nothing of the hours and dollars she spends coming to his aid, her stress, personal attacks directed against her mother, her horror at watching a man burned to death by electrical current—and Pat is only the first of three condemned prisoners she befriends through the course of the book, the first three in a career of similar work that now spans three decades.[12] Her description of her own feelings when, as the last of his appeals are rejected, Pat's execution becomes a certainty, is particularly evocative of the theoretical aspects of compassion laid out earlier:

> Warden Maggio tells Pat in a matter-of-fact voice: "Sonnier, the Fifth Circuit turned you down."
> I do not give any outward sign, but inside I fall headlong down a chasm. . . . I feel unreal. . . .
> . . . [Pat] looks up at me. "Sister Helen, I'm going to die."
> My soul rushes toward him. I am standing with my hands against the mesh screen, as close as I can get to him. I pray and ask God to comfort

him, cushion him, wrap him round, give him courage to face death, to step across the river, to die with love. The words are pouring from me (DMW 111–13).

Notice how closely her sense of self is tied to his. When his appeal is turned down, she experiences psychological vertigo; she loses a sense of her own reality. Then, when he verbally acknowledges his imminent death, she describes her feelings and actions as "rushing" and "pouring," language evocative of compassion's flow. Her need to be as physically close to him as possible mirrors a moral, emotional, and psychological closeness to him. It is not surprising that she prays for him; she is a nun, after all, and she does for him exactly what she would do for herself. The boundary between his needs and her needs fades away, and she is only left with the experience of suffering and the desire to bring about its cessation.

What is remarkable about Prejean is her capacity to show compassion to so many opposed groups and factions surrounding her. Indeed, she repeatedly problematizes the idea of "taking sides" on the issue of capital punishment.[13] Killers and victims are not on different sides to her, nor are death row convicts and those who will execute them, nor are the members of the legal team who defend the rights of the convicts and the victims' parents who want to see those rights erased. Capital punishment is in large part a race issue,[14] and many of the groups Prejean interacts with throughout the course of her narrative are starkly racially divided. The overwhelming majority of St. Thomas' population is black, and this is also true of death row; Parents of Murdered Children, a victims support group, is entirely white; Survive, another victims support group, is mostly black. Prejean moves easily between all these groups, a significant accomplishment given the tension that exists between them with such a highly charged issue as capital punishment. She refuses to take sides in any case, allying herself only with the alleviation of suffering for everyone involved.

Her accomplishments to this end are extraordinary. Throughout the course of the book, she assists in bringing about all of the following: an annual special Mass for the victims of violent crime; two separate support groups for victims of violent crime; training sessions and recruiting for

would-be spiritual advisers to death row inmates; multiple Pilgrimage for
Life walks (multiday walking demonstrations for the abolition of capital
punishment); the first full-time position in the state of Louisiana devoted to
speaking out against the death penalty; numerous demonstrations, lectures,
workshops, and weekend seminars on the death penalty; and an organized
opposition to cuts in victims' assistance programs. In the fourteen years that
have passed since *Dead Man Walking* was published, she has been giving an
average of 140 lectures a year on abolishing the death penalty and has published a second book, this one focusing on the executions of demonstrably
innocent convicts.

With all her activism, she has many opportunities to offer arguments
against the institution of capital punishment. She has many at her disposal,
but she says she always saves one in particular for last: "I end by challenging
people to ask themselves whether we can continue to allow the government,
subject as it is to every imaginable form of inefficiency and corruption, to
have such power to kill. 'It's not a marginal issue,' I say. 'We're all complicit.
Government can only continue killing if we give it the power. It's time to
take that power back'" (DMW 166–167). Her ultimate argument against the
death penalty hinges upon a sense of communal responsibility that points
to a notion of a "great self." Of course, she is partly referring to the political
structure of a democracy, but more than this, she is pointing to a communal
sense of responsibility.

Indeed, communal responsibility is arguably a better paradigm than individual responsibility for discussing institutionalized practices like capital
punishment. Throughout the course of an inmate's execution, everyone
involved has the opportunity to claim absolution from responsibility. The
members of the Pardon Board are "just upholding the decision of the court";
the guards who strap down the prisoner are "just doing their jobs"; the governor is "just carrying out the laws of the state." But of course all of these are
just excuses. Pardon Board members and death chamber guards are arguably obliged to quit their jobs if those jobs are immoral. And for the governors, Prejean says there can be no excuse. In *The Death of Innocents,* she
says, "In the twenty-first century, the investiture of absolute power over life
and death in an individual governor represents the last vestige of the 'divine

right of kings.' No power on earth is greater. Or scarier. Especially when such power is entrusted to politicians, motivated more by 'expediency' than by conscience."[15]

The governor she has in mind is George W. Bush, whose administration executed 152 prisoners in six years—"more than any other governor in the recent history of the United States," Prejean observes. This is putting it mildly: These executions make up roughly one-sixth of all executions carried out in the United States since the reinstitution of the death penalty in 1976. In fact, 152 executions not only surpasses any governor in recent history but also any *state* in recent history, with the lone exception of Texas.[16] Prejean quotes Bush as saying, "I take every death penalty case seriously and review each case carefully. . . . Each case is major because each case is life or death."[17] Yet, "By the time Bush left the governor's office, he had denied clemency in *all cases*," making a point of spending thirty minutes or less on each clemency petition.[18]

According to Prejean, "To distance himself from his legal and moral responsibility for executions, Bush often cited a Texas statue that says a governor may do nothing more than grant a thirty-day reprieve to an inmate unless the Texas Board of Pardons and Paroles has recommended a broader grant of clemency."[19] One might find this explanation more convincing but for two salient facts: Bush appointed all eighteen members of the pardons board, and the pardons board *never* meets in full to review a capital sentence. Phone calls are exchanged among some of them, and according to Prejean, "no one knows if the clemency appeals are even read."[20] In short, "The Texas Pardons Board is a farce," a smokescreen employed by the governor to obscure his moral connection to the executions.

What is particularly egregious about these executions is that a self-described "compassionate conservative" carried them out. Prejean points out that "Unlike the courts, [Bush] was not restricted to pure legalities. As far back as 1855, the Supreme Court saw compassion and mercy as central to the exercise of gubernatorial clemency. This means that governors and their boards are free to consider *any basis for mercy*."[21]

Yet, as Prejean explains, Bush was unwilling to consider such mitigating circumstances as a history of abuse as a child, a history of prostitution as a child, or even developmental disability in granting clemency.[22] In one case he even mocked the prisoner that was about to be executed: When asked what he thought Karla Fay Tucker would say to him before her execution, in a mocking, whimpering tone he said, "Please, please, don't kill me!"[23]

Compare the then-governor of Texas with the former governor of Illinois, George Ryan. Ryan initiated a moratorium on capital punishment after it became clear that too many death row convicts were being exonerated based on DNA evidence. After 13 exonerations, Ryan ordered an unprecedented 142 clemency hearings in two weeks.[24] Finally, deeming the risk of executing an innocent to be too great to run, Ryan commuted the sentences of all of Illinois' condemned prisoners—164 in all—to life imprisonment. "There is no honorable way to kill," Ryan said. "Because the Illinois death penalty system is arbitrary and capricious—and therefore immoral—I no longer shall tinker with the machinery of death."[25] The commutation of the prisoners' sentences and the moratorium on executions earned Ryan a Nobel Peace Prize nomination in 2003. It certainly does not follow that Ryan is a paragon of virtue—in 2003 he was also indicted in federal court on eighteen counts of corruption[26]—but his position on capital punishment is markedly different from that of Bush, who famously maintains that the state of Texas has never executed an innocent and insists that his thirty-minute method for verifying guilt and ensuring due process is "fail-safe."[27]

If the governors who oversee executions cannot hide behind the legal barriers they erect for themselves, neither can the citizens of the states that allow executions, at least on Prejean's view. For her communal responsibility extends to all of us, no matter how the process is crafted to distance us from it. Executions typically take place in the middle of the night, deep within a prison complex, concealed from the public eye. Individual voters cannot feel real power over such a practice, whether they support it or not. But for Prejean this does not excuse any of us. For her we are all responsible for the injustice that openly persists in our communities. She finds it revealing that on the death certificates of executed criminals the cause of death is listed as "homicide."[28] It is a crime, and the great selves in which we find ourselves are the guilty parties.[29]

Communal responsibility receives some attention in the philosophical community, but Prejean is speaking of activism, not academia.[30] She is speaking of communal action to rectify communal wrongdoing, a great self taking care of itself. Her political activism is therefore an expression of her compassion on multiple levels: It suggests our connection to a great self, it is motivated by an attentiveness to those who are marginalized and wronged, and it expresses a will to bring an end to their suffering.

Some detractors may respond to this by saying that an ethic of compassion is too demanding. Śākyamuni feeds himself to the starving tiger, but I will freely admit that I would never do such a thing. The problem is not even that I would be too scared to sacrifice myself; to be honest, it would never occur to me that I ought to feed myself to a tiger. Prejean's sacrifice is not as extreme as Śākyamuni's, but she has still given up much more than most of us are willing to part with: her leisure time; freedom from excessive stress; a normal sex life and romantic life; the convenience of a regular job close to home; the comfort of knowing no one close to me is likely to be killed by the state. None of these is trivial to me. If an ethic of compassion obliges us to surrender all of these things and more, it arguably asks too much of us. What will Prejean or Śākyamuni say to this?

Both Buddhism and Christianity have a long-standing tradition of separating the laity from monks and nuns. It is true that any one of us may don the cloth, so to speak, but it is also recognized that not all of us are cut out for that sort of life. Just as some of us are not born to be linebackers, some of us are not born to give ourselves over to the well-being of others. Moral philosophy should not only be for moral superheroes, but for those of us who are not heroic, the heroes give us role models to emulate.

Having recognized natural propensities, though, it remains that very few of us are living up to our moral potential. We know the ten dollars we spend at the movie theater would be better spent at Oxfam, and we see the movie anyway—or if not Oxfam, some other organization. However we frame it, however we justify our expenditures to ourselves, we have the ability to help and we routinely choose not to.

Prejean asks more of us. Compassion asks more of us. But compassion does not seem to be any more demanding than any other school of moral philosophy. A long-standing critique against Kant's ethics is that no reasonable person can live up to his standards. (He famously demands, as noted earlier, that one refrain from lying even when the life of an innocent is at stake and even when that lie is told to the would-be killer.[31]) Equally venerated by history is the objection against utilitarianism that no one can maximize utility all the time and also maintain anything like an ordinary life. (Every moment I spend cleaning my house or walking my dogs is a moment not spent in the service of those who are worse off than I am.)

To this the ethicist may simply say, so what? Ordinary life has little to recommend it. In my neighborhood, ordinary life includes recognizing the fact that while about a third of the world's human population goes to bed hungry every night, my dogs never go to bed hungry. What I spend on their food would purchase a much greater volume of food for the needy if I were to donate it to Oxfam. Kant will be unhappy with my prioritizing two rescued Labrador retrievers over two billion rational beings. Utilitarians will be unhappy with my decision to fill two bellies when I could fill four, or ten, or twenty. Compassion is left unsated whenever famine could have been alleviated and wasn't. All of these moral philosophies ask more of me, and indeed they should: I am capable of doing better than I have been doing thus far.

But this is no shortcoming of the ethics of compassion if it is true of every moral philosophy. Anything that is true of all alternatives cannot be a weakness or strength of any of them. Even if I am incapable of throwing myself before a starving tiger, at least I am capable of leading a better life today than I did yesterday. This too is a feature of ordinary life.

That said, we may shift from ordinary lives to a different kind of extraordinary ones. I have in mind the lives that are wracked with extraordinary degrees of pain. These are the lives it seems compassion might bid us to end.

Compassionate Killing? Euthanasia and Physician-Assisted Suicide

Among all the topics in applied ethics, euthanasia and physician-assisted suicide (PAS) stand out as having a particularly obvious and immediate connection to compassion, for it is the awareness of a patient's suffering and the concomitant desire to alleviate that suffering that motivate philosophical analysis of the issue. But though it begins with compassion, as it moves forward the discourse frequently confuses compassion's directives or even ignores them. This is true even in seminal works on the topic. In this section, I analyze some of those works and show how compassion can lend focus and clarity to the debate.

A compassionate analysis of the issue will begin with pulling apart the two central terms: euthanasia and PAS. These two are so frequently linked in the literature that they are easily mistaken to be identical, but there is an important distinction between the two. Euthanasia is prima facie a merciful act, and therefore a good one, as indicated by the prefix *eu*. Of course, opponents argue that euthanasia is not to be allowed, but this argument stands against the prima facie assumption that one's intent is merciful when one intends to euthanize. In other words, the opponents' argument has it that in spite of the fact that one intends to do good by them, acts of euthanasia are nevertheless wrong (or harmful, or sinful, or nonuniversalizable—the exact definition of the wrongdoing varies depending on who motivates the argument). Suicide, when not qualified as being physician-assisted, is prima facie an unfortunate event, possibly immoral but possibly noble. (A samurai committing seppuku in protest of an immoral order was held among the most honored of selfless deeds.) To call a suicide "physician-assisted" gives it a clinical connotation (like just about anything else that is physician-assisted), which tends to offset the negative connotations of the word "suicide." As such, PAS has the connotation of being morally neutral, with open possibilities of its being good or bad.

So as not to presume anything about its moral status, I will use the term "PAS" instead of "euthanasia." In my discussions of other scholars, however, I will use whatever terms they prefer. This is because to do otherwise would be cumbersome and confusing and also because compassion demands it: Any who are sensitive to the difference in terminology will have chosen vocabulary because of its moral connotations, and those choices will be respected here.

James Rachels is credited with first prompting philosophers to address PAS as a moral issue. In his "Active and Passive Euthanasia," he argues that the distinction between active euthanasia (in which a physician takes an active role in bringing about the death of a patient) and passive euthanasia (in which the physician withholds vital care) is morally irrelevant at best and that the American Medical Association (AMA) should lift its ban on the former.[32] According to his argument, if there is any moral distinction to be drawn between killing and letting die, there is good reason to believe that in some cases, killing is actually preferable to letting die. In both active and passive euthanasia, the final result is the same, and given that one route to that end can promise less suffering than the other, Rachels argues that there is no reason the AMA should deny its members that option. Governments may maintain their own prohibitions against active euthanasia, but according to Rachels the AMA should not do so.

Rachels' argument is deemed a landmark in the literature, as evidenced by its appearance in a huge number of introductory ethics textbooks and anthologies of applied ethics and biomedical ethics. Another common entry in the ethics anthologies—often appearing coupled with Rachels'—is Thomas D. Sullivan's "Active and Passive Euthanasia: An Impertinent Distinction?" Sullivan's thesis (an almost immediate response to Rachels' article) is that Rachels' distinction between active and passive euthanasia is nonsensical. Sullivan favors instead the language used by physicians themselves.

The 1973 AMA resolution on euthanasia, to which both Sullivan and Rachels are responding, uses the language of "extraordinary means" of preserving life as opposed to "ordinary means." For Sullivan, ordinary means are those procedures and medications that "offer reasonable hope of benefit for the patient and which can be obtained and used without excessive expense, pain, and other inconveniences"; extraordinary means, then, are those medicines and procedures that do not offer reasonable hope of benefit or those that are accompanied by excessive pain, expense, or other inconvenience.[33] According to Sullivan, the doctrine "is not a doctrine that rests on some supposed distinction between 'active' and 'passive' euthanasia, whatever those words are supposed to mean. . . . It is simply a prohibition against intentional killing, which includes direct actions and malevolent omissions."[34]

I focus on the Rachels and Sullivan articles because both are widely regarded to be well-reasoned, well-argued works of applied ethics, and because for all of that, both overlook some of the most important aspects of the issue of assisted suicide. Sullivan's argument rests on the distinction between ordinary and extraordinary medical means, these being defined with reference to what is beneficial for the patient, but at no point does he question what we might mean by "benefit" for an individual in the end stages of a terminal disease. A crucial point of Rachels' article—one that seems to pass by Sullivan unnoticed—is that for some patients the only reasonable hope of benefit may lie in a quick, painless death. Given that Sullivan's argument turns on the notion of benefit, it is hard to see what any of his ruminations come to.

Rachels stands in no better stead. The central example used in his article is that of babies born with both Down syndrome and some other congenital defect—say, an intestinal blockage—that simple surgery can remove but that will result in the death of the infant if not removed. Most infants born with such defects undergo the required surgical procedures, but in the case of Down syndrome babies, parents and physicians sometimes agree not to operate. "The reason why such operations are not performed in these cases," says Rachels, "is, clearly, that the child has Down's and the parents and doctor judge that because of that fact it is better for the child to die."[35]

There is no mention of the fact that many people with Down syndrome are entirely capable of leading happy, fulfilled lives. They hold jobs, attend college classes, and enjoy spending time with their friends and families. In Rachels' defense, he does say it is absurd to base the decision to euthanize on an irrelevant congenital defect, "no matter what view one takes of the lives and potentials of [Down's] babies,"[36] but this half-sentence is all he has to say about Down's patients' prospects. It is true that their families must often care for them in many ways—care that demands money, time, and effort—and that these demands may well be at the heart of the decision to let the Down's babies die. However, if parents ever chose to forego a simple operation for their infant because they did not want to be burdened with raising a child with exceptional needs, their choice would more accurately be described as infanticide than euthanasia.

Clearly Rachels is not advocating infanticide, but his mention of the Down's infants' suffering is brief. Indeed, a good deal more of his article is devoted to a lengthy quote from a doctor who oversees some of these babies' deaths: "As a surgeon whose natural inclination is to use the scalpel to fight off death, standing by and watching a baby die is the most emotionally exhausting experience I know. . . . This is a terrible ordeal for me and the hospital staff—much more so than for the parents who never set foot in the nursery."[37] That the suffering of the hospital staff should outrank the suffering of bereaved parents will strike many as objectionable, to say the least. That the hospital staff's suffering is described in any detail at all when the dying infant's suffering receives no real description is beyond objectionable.

Sullivan is guilty of the same offense: He refers to the patient's suffering in only one paragraph, his last. I cite it in full because it is so telling:

> I fully realize that there are times when those who have the noble duty to tend the sick and the dying are deeply moved by the sufferings of their patients, especially of the very young and the very old, and desperately wish they could do more than comfort and companion them. Then, perhaps, it seems that universal moral principles are mere abstractions having little to do with the agony of the dying. But of course we do not see best when our eyes are filled with tears.[38]

Notice first that the primary subject of the paragraph is not the patients but their attending physicians and other health care providers. Also notice that Sullivan admits that appeals to universal moral principles appear to be irrelevant, and yet he suggests that the morally correct thing to do is to try to see through our tears and (presumably) reacquire those universal principles. That is to say, we are to reject the response that is immediate and clearly relevant—the tears; the emotional, personal, relational attachments—and seek to put in its stead one that is obscured and seemingly irrelevant. In direst times of need, we are to treat our loved ones as universal principles would treat them: as placeholders.

The heart of the problem is that neither Rachels nor Sullivan puts the well-being of the patient to be euthanized at the center of his analysis. This is a grave mistake, for if there is any line between euthanasia and murder it is a hazy one, and at least in their initial articles on the subject, Rachels and Sullivan have done more to obscure the line than to help us find it.[39] Moreover, their mutual failure to put the well-being of the patients at the center of their discussion is paradigmatically uncompassionate. They have both lost sight of the suffering of the very ones whose suffering is most at issue.

It hardly needs to be said that an ethic of compassion will take more than a passing glance at the suffering of the sick and the dying. It will set their plight at the center of any meaningful discussion of assisted suicide, and it will not dismiss the tears that come with the discussion as morally irrelevant. There will certainly be a place in the discussion for universal principles (or at least guidelines), for in the end there must be *some* hope for an applicable resolution. But with regard to assisted suicide, attempts at universal principles are all too often overly simplistic (as we have already seen)—and divisive as well. Rachels, the utilitarian, has chosen his side of the issue, and Sullivan, the Kantian, chooses the other. For the compassionate agent, the goal is to not take sides and by so doing to diffuse the dualistic thinking that allows for the possibility of there being sides.

Philippa Foot's article "Euthanasia" makes progress toward this end, and though her article is of roughly the same vintage as Rachels' and Sullivan's, her approach is notably different. She does not earnestly begin her analysis of euthanasia itself until roughly halfway into her piece. The opening pages are dedicated to dictionary definitions of euthanasia, anecdotes from survivors of Hitler's and Stalin's concentration camps, and what counts as a good life for plants and animals. Perhaps this seems like philosophical wandering, and one might be more inclined to say so were one to note that, by word count, Foot's article is triple the length of Rachels' or Sullivan's. But in her introductory ruminations, she points out that Hitler claimed to be euthanizing the Jews. Literally, "euthanasia" means only "good death"; it does not specify *for whom* the death must be good. Unsurprisingly, Foot specifies that the death must be good for the one who is to die, but lest this seem too obvious to warrant mention, remember that neither Rachels nor Sullivan focuses primarily (to say nothing of solely) on the dying patient.

According to Foot, "We shall literally not know what we are talking about if we ask whether acts of euthanasia defined as we have defined them [i.e., as deaths that are good for the one who is to die] are ever morally permissible without first understanding better the reason for saying that life is a good, and the possibility that it is not always so."[40] This should have been the central issue of Sullivan's analysis, if only he had raised it. The stories of the concentration camps contribute to Foot's investigation of a critically important question: "Is there a conceptual connection between *life* and *good?*"[41] Is the life of a concentration camp internee a good for that person? If a doctor were able to prolong such a life, would the doctor be providing a benefit?

According to Dmitri Panin, a former internee in Stalin's Sologdin camp, "Death from a bullet would have been bliss compared with what many millions had to endure dying from hunger."[42] Those of us who were not there should respect Panin enough to take him at his word, but does it follow from this that the camp officers who shot their prisoners were euthanizing them? Or, supposing this is still murder, suppose a prisoner were able to obtain a guard's pistol. Would it be euthanasia if this prisoner were to go on a shooting spree? The most unambiguous case would be if this prisoner were to use the gun to commit suicide, but on this subject Panin's memoir is quite contrary to what many would expect: "I should like to pass on my observations concerning the absence of suicides under the extremely severe conditions of our concentration camps. The more that life became desperate, the more a prisoner seemed determined to hold onto it."[43]

The lives of the concentration camp prisoners under Hitler and Stalin surely stand out among some of the worst that human beings have ever lived. If even that kind of existence does not warrant suicide, then it is not the balance of pains versus pleasures in a life that make it a good. Instead, Foot finds the conceptual connection between *life* and *good* in what she calls "a minimum of basic human goods": "What is ordinary in a human life—even in very hard lives—is that a man is not driven to work beyond his capacity; that he has the support of a family or community; that he can more or less satisfy his hunger; that he has hopes for the future; that he can lie down to rest at night."[44] This list of basic goods applies to concentration camp prisoners and patients of certain illnesses alike. It hardly matters if the reason one cannot sleep is the nausea induced by chemotherapy or the bedbugs of a filthy mattress in a freezing barrack.

The connection to basic human goods allows Foot to understand what constitutes (at least in part) a good human life and therefore to understand what might constitute a good death: "An act of euthanasia, whether literally act or rather omission, is attributed to an agent who opts for the death of another because in his case life seems to be an evil rather than a good."[45] The next question, then, is whether or not such acts are morally justifiable. A straightforward act-utilitarian analysis will make this appear to be an open-and-shut case, but Foot sees two sorts of obligations at play here: obligations of justice and obligations of charity.

The justice she has in mind is Aristotelian, not Rawlsian: It is the excellence that governs the fair treatment of others. Euthanasia is tied up with claims to a right to life, and Foot maintains that the rights question must be answered before taking up the concerns of kindness. It is only merciful to kill, she says, if the one to be killed has granted consent. To kill someone who has not surrendered the right to life is not to euthanize but to murder.

According to this line of reasoning, rights trump kindness, or to use Foot's vocabulary, justice trumps charity. Here "charity" is used in its original sense—*caritas*, or love—and it seems to follow from Foot's argument that one cannot properly claim to treat the other lovingly if one is willing to violate the other's rights. In this analysis, the details do not matter much. Rachels' distinction between active and passive euthanasia is irrelevant, as is Sullivan's distinction between ordinary and extraordinary means. Provided that the patient requests assistance in dying, and if kindness dictates that one gives that assistance, why should it matter whether this is done through extubation or lethal injection?

But for Foot, the issue is not yet closed. Just because it may sometimes be morally acceptable to euthanize, it does not follow that euthanasia ought to be legalized. Legalization is the mutual concern of both Rachels and Sullivan, for both of their arguments concern what the American Medical Association ought to do about its position on euthanasia, and the law of the land will be decided at least in part on what doctors as a group suggest it ought to be. But Foot sees a danger in shifting from individual cases to universalized rules:

For it is one thing to say that some acts of euthanasia considered only in themselves and their results are morally unobjectionable, and another to say that it would be all right to legalize them. Perhaps the practice of euthanasia would allow too many abuses, and perhaps there would be too many mistakes. Moreover, the practice could have very important and highly undesirable side effects, because it is unlikely that we could change our principles about the treatment of the old and the ill without changing fundamental emotional attitudes and social relations.[46]

Foot shows remarkable foresight here, at least in comparison to her contemporaries. Writing in 1977, she anticipates the issues raised by Diane Coleman and Carol Gill in the 1990s and later, issues that are still generally overlooked (despite Coleman and Gill's efforts) in contemporary discussions of physician-assisted suicide.[47] Coleman and Gill are not philosophers by training (Coleman is a lawyer, Gill a psychologist), but their work on PAS is perhaps more relevant than that of any philosopher cited thus far. Both Coleman and Gill use motorized wheelchairs and also ventilators to assist with breathing while they sleep. Both consider themselves to be at risk of being euthanized against their will. Their most important work on euthanasia and PAS comes in the form of testimony offered to such influential bodies as the House of Representatives' Judiciary Committee. This was of particular importance in 1996, for earlier in that year the Ninth Circuit Court of Appeals ruled that assisted suicide was acceptable as a financial solution for the poor or uninsured.[48]

Coleman and Gill argue that in a growing number of cases, U.S. courts have been ruling against respecting the lives of the sick or disabled.[49] For example, in one case a mother "killed her brain-injured non-verbal teenaged daughter. The judge said her actions were understandable, and that other parents could be expected to react in the same way. He sentenced her to community service."[50] If Coleman and Gill have represented the case accurately, the judge's sympathy extends not to the murdered daughter but to the mother. It should hardly be necessary to mention that a discussion of assisted suicide ought to focus on the one who is to die, but as evidenced by Rachels, Sullivan, and the presiding judge in this case, it is all too easy to focus on everyone but the one who is to die. This is also evidenced by the most well-known physician to assist in suicides in the United States, Jack Kevorkian, who wrote, "The voluntary self-elimination of individual and mortally diseased or crippled lives taken collectively can only enhance the preservation of public health and welfare."[51]

Table 5.1. Dr. Jack Kevorkian's assisted suicides, June 1990–September 1996

	MALE	FEMALE
Terminal	5	4
Not terminal	4	21
Unclear whether terminal	2	1
Age range	27–82	39–76
Average age	57	63

By now the connection to compassion should be clear. Genuine acts of assisted suicide are presumed to be compassionate acts. I take it that no further argument is necessary to prove that the primary focus ought to be on the patient's suffering, though a properly compassionate approach will also take all other relevant suffering into account. What should not be taken for granted is how dangerous PAS can become when this primary focus is lost.

An examination of those whom Kevorkian assisted in committing suicide can reveal some of this danger. Between 1990 and 1996, Kevorkian assisted in the suicides of eleven men and twenty-six women.[52] Some statistics about them, presented in Table 5.1, may prove enlightening.

Forty-five percent of the men were clearly terminal as opposed to just fifteen percent of the women, and among those who were clearly not terminal the women outnumber the men by more than five to one. One must wonder why women are so disproportionately represented among Kevorkian's patients, most particularly since the majority of them were not terminal when they requested his involvement. Coleman and Gill address this question directly:

If anyone doubts that women will be exploited and endangered by assisted suicide, that doubter should study Kevorkian's "clients." The first eight were all middle-aged or elderly women with chronic illnesses and disabilities. Many said they feared being a burden on others. An autopsy on one of them revealed no evidence of any physical illness. Women with disabilities are going to be the first to feel a "duty to die."[53]

It is not irrelevant that most of the twenty-six women were in their fifties, sixties, and seventies when they died. Women of their generation were ste-

reotypically given the role of the homemaker and caretaker. Cooking, cleaning, and changing diapers were chores attributed to them, and for many of
them, their disabilities and diseases would require that someone else would
need to change their diapers and cook their meals. In many cases, these duties would fall to their husbands (men of the same generation, with very
different household responsibilities ascribed to them) or to their children
(the very ones for whom these women had served as caretaker and protector).
One can see how easily the feeling of being a burden could become a heavy
burden itself.[54]

Coleman continues to lead Not Dead Yet today, and in April of 2005
—another important time in the PAS debate in the United States, for Terri
Schiavo's much-publicized death was imminent—she spoke to Congress
again: "Here's how I'm beginning to look at things. The far right wants to
kill us slowly and painfully by cutting the things we need to live: health care,
public housing and transportation, etc. The far left wants to kill us quickly
and call it compassion, while also saving money for others perhaps deemed
more worthy."[55] Coleman suggests that the PAS debate has been following
a script that, like so many other moral debates in contemporary American
politics, tends toward Manichean oversimplification. "Concerned disability
groups," she says, "don't fit the script and so we have been marginalized or
ignored entirely."[56]

Coleman argued with Gill in 1996 that if PAS were to be legalized, what
euthanasia advocates call "the right to die" would quickly become a duty to
die, and this duty would weigh most heavily on members of marginalized
groups: women, the disabled, and the poor (or more specifically, those who
cannot afford health care). Indeed, they found this trend had already begun:

> Assisted suicide is not a free choice as long as people with disabilities
> are denied adequate healthcare, affordable personal assistance in our
> own homes, assistive technology, equal education, nondiscriminatory
> employment, and free access to our communities' structures and trans-
> portation systems. Based on recent developments in both public and pri-
> vate managed care, it is already possible in some states for impoverished,
> disabled, elderly and chronically ill people to get assistance to die, but
> impossible for them to get shoes, eyeglasses, and tooth repair.[57]

In her 2005 testimony before the House and her 2006 testimony before the Senate, Coleman contended that the situation had not improved, and that if anything it had grown worse since the state of Oregon legalized lethal prescriptions.

For Foot and for contemporary disability rights advocates, it is clear that being sensitive to the prevailing attitudes concerning death, disease, and disability is an indispensable part of any analysis of euthanasia and PAS. But what help will this be in arriving at a universal principle concerning PAS? The AMA will stand by its current policy or it will adopt a new one; it must do one or the other. If the AMA lifts its ban on PAS, patients will be exposed to potential abuse. If the AMA does not lift the ban, terminal patients must endure preventable agony for untold days and weeks before they die.

A third alternative is to change the nature of the ban and to change the nature of what legalized PAS will look like should it ever be allowed. Clearly, there are patients who perceive death to be a preferable alternative to living. It is equally clear that those patients are as deserving as any other of the psychological counseling, pain medication, or depression medication that will help them see life as a boon again. And finally, it is clear that for some patients no amount of medication or counseling will cure their diseases or alleviate their pains and that some of them could reasonably wish to die without suffering from depression or any other psychological malady. Even the staunchest opponents of PAS will accede to this. What must be eliminated is the inherent danger in lifting the ban.

The first step might be the implementation of universal health insurance, for surely no society should facilitate dying without first doing its best to facilitate living. A second step might be to recognize that even with free access to health care, some patients will not receive equal treatment. Coleman and Gill cite studies reporting that "quadriplegics and other significantly disabled people are dying wrongfully in increasing numbers because emergency room physicians judge their quality of life as low and, therefore, withhold aggressive treatment."[58] They also report that "Dutch physicians follow a practice not to offer assisted ventilation to quadriplegics,"[59] demonstrating that the same problem holds even in countries that do provide universal health care. Whatever policy the AMA adopts concerning PAS, it should at the same time adopt a policy requiring that all patients have access to routine health care. The AMA could arguably follow Sullivan at least this far: It is wrong prima facie for a physician to deny or withhold routine treatment.

But the policy on PAS needs further support. There must also be a policy demanding adequate training in the medical and psychological needs of patients with disabilities and terminal diseases. This policy would have to be a part of a much larger project, for at present those who are disabled or suffer from chronic or terminal illness do not have the full support of the medical professions, the legal system, or in many cases even their own families. Without widespread change in our attitudes concerning disease, disability, and dying, legalizing PAS will always constitute a threat.

This overarching project must also address attitudes toward gender if women are to be relieved of any perceived duty to die. Universal health care would relieve the uninsured of that duty and would therefore be a necessary protection for the poor as well as for the disabled. One can see already that a universalizable principle concerning PAS will be far reaching indeed if it comes from an ethic of compassion. Is it so far reaching as to be unattainable and therefore useless? I do not think so. An ethic of compassion can give the AMA very concrete guidance: Physicians need better training concerning the needs of the disabled and the dying, and no policy on PAS—whether for or against—will make much sense without this. It gives the rest of us concrete guidance as well. It tells us to extend compassion in ways we may not have thought about before, and it tells us that whatever our position on PAS is to be, it must always be based on compassion for the one who is to die.

Some will say this is still too vague, for it does not hand down a decision on one side or the other. In response, it might be pointed out that utilitarianism is equally vague inasmuch as one can come up with utilitarian arguments in favor of and against legalizing PAS. But this approach is indicative of the very kind of dualistic reasoning an ethic of compassion seeks to leave behind. A better response is to say that for an ethic of compassion, it is only natural *not* to hand down a decision on this side or that. The goal is not to take sides but rather to jettison the idea of there being "both" sides (that is, two and only two sides), to see what is useful on every side and then to seek out a new position.

Conclusion: Applied Compassion

In the end, where an ethic of compassion strays from the beaten path is in how it will categorize what counts among the issues of applied ethics. Consider the sorts of things that have been taken into account as compassion has been discussed through the previous chapters. Family relationships frequently make up the core of the compassionate self-in-community. Other relationships are encompassed as well, be they with coworkers, neighbors, strangers, or even animals and plants. An ethic of compassion is an ethic about relationships, and it is in the context of relationships that it will situate the traditional issues of applied ethics.

Seen in this way, the issue of abortion amounts to the question of how best to conduct the relationships between women, fetuses, and the state. Same-sex marriage, dietary ethics, and all the rest can be viewed in a similar light. But everyday relationships will count as matters of applied ethics, too. Maintaining a stable and healthy relationship with a partner or spouse is, according to an ethic of compassion, an ethical matter. Right-thinking people agree that spousal abuse is morally wrong, but people often stop thinking about ethics as soon as all evidence of maltreatment is absent. We do not commonly think of a happy partnership as a morally laudable achievement; we usually just say something like, "those two are really great together."

Praising a solid marriage or a good friendship in moral terms comes naturally to a thinker like Elizabeth Anscombe, who urges us to jettison oppositional pairs like "right" and "wrong" in favor of more descriptive labels appealing to specific virtues and vices (e.g., "just" and "unjust").[60] We do use words such as "loving," "caring," and "steadfast" to describe people in their relationships, and according to Anscombe and the virtue ethicists these are all morally positive evaluations. Compassionate ethics will take a similar tack. When we speak of good mothers, good husbands, or good bosses, according to an ethic of compassion there is potentially a moral goodness latent in these descriptions.

When a person is described as "good," it is typically in the context of that person's virtues (and hence "excellent" is a better descriptor than "good" here). An excellent shortstop does not display the same virtues as an excellent teacher or an excellent prime minister. Some of their excellences are measures of skill—the shortstop's accuracy in throwing, for instance—while some are moral measures—for example, the prime minister's integrity. Others are both: According to an ethic of compassion, the teacher's skill in connecting with students and teaching to different learning styles is a skill in building lasting interpersonal connections. This contributes to the students' flourishing and is therefore to be counted among the moral excellences. To call someone an "excellent teacher," then, is potentially a moral evaluation.

This is important because an ethic of compassion will include our interpersonal affairs as matters of applied ethics. This is a rather Confucian position to take. (Think of the "five cardinal relationships"—perfectly ordinary relationships that in Confucianism receive the closest moral scrutiny.) Given its Confucian underpinnings, it should be no surprise that this account of compassion should arrive at a Confucian conclusion. To the classical Confucians, the idea of drawing a conceptual barrier between applied ethics and day-to-day living would have seemed very strange indeed. The existence of specialists and journals dedicated to applied ethics is indicative of just such a barrier within contemporary academic philosophy.

Not all contemporary ethicists subscribe to this division, of course. Care ethics, for example, explicitly recognizes mothering as an ethically significant undertaking. Like care ethics, compassionate ethics will reject the separation of applied ethics and daily life. It will reject the criteria (never overtly laid out by applied ethicists themselves) according to which the "problems" of applied ethics are chosen. Abortion is a medical procedure tied up in moral controversy, but it is only one among many. Doctors and families make complex moral decisions when considering chemotherapy versus palliative care, for instance, but this sort of issue does not appear next to the articles on abortion and euthanasia in introductory philosophy texts. Capital punishment receives ethicists' attention, but legalized slavery in the form of prison labor programs passes largely unnoticed. Because such programs are pervasive in southern American states and because blacks are represented in disproportionately inflated numbers in the inmate populations in those states, the institution of American slavery abolished in the nineteenth century persists in the twenty-first. Should this not dominate the pages of applied ethics journals? Social and political philosophers, feminist philosophers, and critical race theorists have generally been the ones in philosophical academia to address institutionalized prejudice on this scale, but is there anything to be gained by drawing such boundaries between fields? Whatever "applied ethics" is, surely these academics are engaging in it.

According to an ethic of compassion, the designation "applied ethics" is both arbitrary and redundant. One can still usefully employ metaethics to talk *about* compassion, and one can still talk about a compassionate *approach* to the traditional questions of theoretical and applied ethics, but compassion itself goes beyond the dualistic thinking separating theory from practice and ethics from life.

What all of this amounts to is a broadened sense of moral responsibility. Whether we have any moral responsibility at all, or whether in truth we lack the free will needed to have responsibility of any kind, is, of course, a philosophical quagmire unto itself. I leave it to others to solve those sorts of puzzles. For the present, suffice it to say that if we do have moral responsibility, an ethic of compassion will regard it as being rather broader than it is often thought to be (and, of course, if we do not have moral responsibility, then it hardly matters what an ethic of compassion has to say about it).

The difference between the scope of responsibility as found in an ethic of compassion as opposed to that found in many other approaches to ethics—most particularly in what are called "act-based" approaches—can be seen in the dilemmas of applied ethics. These are traditionally treated as special problems that impose themselves on people who would otherwise have gone about leading their normal lives. But normal life is nothing but interactions in various relationships, and according to an ethic of compassion all of these bear ethical significance to greater or lesser degrees. Ethics is not something one steps outside of the daily routine to do; it *is* the daily routine. The Confucians understood this, as evidenced by their great concern with ritual propriety in everyday life. The Buddhists also understood this, as evidenced by their admonitions to always live fully in the present moment. The compassionate agent will approach every relationship with the same sense of gravity.

A widely shared intuition in ethics is that, if ethical responsibility exists at all, it resides in particular decisions. One may be faced with a hundred ethically relevant decisions throughout the course of a day, but in each case one's responsibility is only to make the right decision *now*. An ethic of compassion rejects this common intuition, holding that if ethical responsibility exists, it is located not in decisions but in relationships. Unlike decisions, relationships do not have clear beginnings and endings. And not only are they ongoing, they are also self-definitive and self-transformative. On this view, then, if one has ethical responsibility at all, that responsibility is radically expanded to include almost every aspect of one's waking life. Lest this burden be deemed too heavy, it must be pointed out that as the scope of responsibility expands, the possibility for praise expands as well. If the burden is greater under this account of responsibility, so too is the possibility for reward and fulfillment.

Chapter 1: What Is Compassion, and What Is It Not?

1. Robert C. Solomon describes compassion in similar terms (*A Passion for Justice,* 233), though my conception of compassion is very different from his. The linkage of feeling to action is not unique to compassion, of course. Vrinda Dalmiya says of care that "claims like 'I care for you but I will not *do* anything' are contradictory" ("Why Should a Knower Care?" 37). Further comparisons between compassion and the care of care ethics will be drawn in later chapters.

2. Max Scheler, *Nature of Sympathy.* (Hereafter cited in text as NS.)

3. In the English translation, the German *Erbarmen* is rendered as "compassion." I will employ the original German in my discussion of Scheler because his understanding and usage of "compassion" differs significantly from my own.

4. Cf. Mercer, *Sympathy and Ethics.*

5. German is not the only language to identify both of these as separate phenomena and to recognize the relationship between the two. Pāli does so as well, as observed by S. Tachibana: "According to the Buddhist psychology, as we have the feeling of Anukampā or commiseration, so we have the feeling of Anumodana or *Mitfreude*" (*The Ethics of Buddhism,* 273). Tachibana also notes the absence of a single English term capturing the idea of *Mitfreude.*

6. The divine origins of love and of compassion (which originates in love) are clear in *The Nature of Sympathy.* Cf. NS 142, "Love is an emotional gesture and a spiritual act," and NS 39, "compassion, which is a heightened commiseration bestowed from above."

7. Brown, "Compassion and Societal Well-Being," 216.

8. Why Brown cites *Politics* 1252a24–1253b22 is unclear to me, since neither compassion nor anything closely resembling it is mentioned in those lines.

9. All citations from the *Rhetoric* are drawn from W. Rhys Roberts' translation appearing in McKeon, *Basic Works of Aristotle.*

10. In fact, the two concepts have still more in common, for both Aristotle and Scheler speak of their respective concepts in the context of theatrical performance. Scheler's projective empathy helps actors understand the feelings of the characters they play, and Aristotle's *eleos* is what puts audience members in touch with tragedy-stricken characters on stage.

11. See chapter 3, "Defining Compassion," for elaboration on this preference.

12. All quotations from the *Nichomachean Ethics* (NE) are drawn from the Hackett translation by Terence Irwin.

13. See NE 1166a27 and 1166a7–8. Cf. David Konstan, "Altruism"; "Ancient Pity"; "Pity and Self-Pity."

14. Konstan argues that given this conception of pity, the Greeks did not have the notion of self-pity. However, there is a sense in which the Greeks could recognize one's friendship with oneself: What was said earlier about friends could also apply to the self. See Konstan, "Pity and Self-Pity," and also his *Friendship in the Classical World,* 77–78. Konstan admits that he is in the minority on this interpretation of Greek friendship. Cf. Julia Annas, *The Morality of Happiness,* 223.

15. It is important to note that this is just one of five possible "features" by which Aristotle says friendship can be defined.

16. Cf. NE 1158b12–1159a14, 1162a4–34, 1163a24–1163b30.

17. Cf. NE 1156a12–1156b6, 1157a4–1157b5, 1158a2–1158b12, 1162b1–1163a21.

18. Cf. NE 1156b7–32, 1157b5–1158a1, 1159b3–12, 1164a34–36.

19. Cf. NE 1168a27–1169a7.

20. Cf. NE 1156b25.

21. Respectively, II Corinthians 13:13, II Corinthians 14:1, and John 3:16.

22. For a comparison of *agapē* and *erōs,* see the Nygren book of that title (1953). For *agapē* and *koinonia,* see Post, *A Theory of Agape,* 13, 91ff. For *agapē* and "Medieval Caritas," see AE 55, 609ff. For *caritas* and *cupiditas,* see Arendt, *Love and St. Augustine,* 17, 18ff., 77ff. Arendt recognizes the distinction between *caritas, dilectio,* and *amor* (and recognizes that Augustine himself sometimes elides them; cf. pp. 38–39). In *The Four Loves,* C. S. Lewis elucidates the differences between *storge, philia, erōs,* and "charity," the latter of which is undoubtedly *caritas* or *agapē.* J. Bruce Long equates *agapē* and *caritas* with *karunā* (see Eliade, *The Encyclopedia of Religion,* vol. 9: 31), surely a mistake, for even if Augustine himself sometimes identifies *amor* and *caritas,* the Buddhist sense of *karunā* cannot have been available to early Christian thinkers.

23. Lewis, *The Four Loves,* 146.

24. Ibid.

25. Arendt, *Love and St. Augustine,* 19. Arendt says this is as true of *caritas*—that is, *agapē*—as it is of *cupiditas.*

26. À Kempis, *The Imitation of Christ,* 83, 84.

27. Post, *A Theory of Agape,* 12.

28. Ibid.

29. Heschel, *Between God and Man,* 144.

30. Post, *A Theory of Agape,* 59.

31. Ibid.

32. Post, *A Theory of Agape,* 106ff.; Nygren, AE 61ff.

33. Post, *A Theory of Agape,* 60.

34. Augustine, *Confessions,* IV, 10.

35. Ibid.

36. Ibid., 7.

37. Ibid.

38. Lewis, *Four Loves,* 137–138; Arendt, *Love and St. Augustine,* 13–14.

39. Arendt, *Love and St. Augustine,* 10.

40. Lewis, *Four Loves,* 137.

41. Ibid., 137–138.

42. Ibid., 137.

43. Ibid., 138.

44. Ibid.

45. Lee Brown says the same of compassion, maintaining that both love and compassion are feelings, and that it is incoherent to think that one can be ethically required to feel a particular feeling. According to Brown, "One cannot be held accountable for the feelings that one has. Feelings and emotions are involuntary responses" (Brown, "Compassion and Societal Well-Being," 222). More will be said on this later in the survey.

46. As the foundation of religious morality, of course there is no problem. The religion may simply hold that *agapē* is in accordance with divine will, that it demands only as much love toward oneself and others as is in accordance with divine will, and that to fulfill the will of the divine is by definition ethically right. But to fully articulate such an account is beyond the purview of this book.

47. Here Baier cites Hume, THN, 320.

48. Cf. Baier, APS 149–150.

49. Rousseau, *Social Contract and Discourses,* 197.

50. Ibid., 200.

51. Singer, *The Expanding Circle,* 3.

52. Reisert, *Jean-Jacques Rousseau,* 16.

53. Rousseau, *Discourses,* fn 15. The translation here is Allan Bloom's, as taken from *Emile* (E) 484 fn 17.

54. Cf. the associations made at E 67: "pride, the spirit of domination, *amour-propre,* the wickedness of man." Cff. Rousseau's description of *amour-propre* at E 68: "Dominion awakens and flatters *amour-propre,* and habit strengthens it." Reisert describes the role of *amour-propre* in the development of conscience in *Rousseau: Friend of Virtue,* 19–22.

55. Cf. Hobbes, *Human Nature,* chapter 9, §10: "Pity is imagination or fiction of

186 Notes to Pages 32–40

future calamity to ourselves, proceeding from the sense of another man's present calamity; but when it lighteth on such as we think have not deserved the same, the compassion is the greater, because there then appeareth the more probability that the same may happen to us. For the evil that happeneth to an innocent man, may happen to every man."

56. Aristotle's thoughts on friendship and justice are relevant here: "If people are friends, they have no need of justice, but if they are just they need friendship in addition; and the justice that is most just seems to belong to friendship" (NE 1155a27–29). Thus in a sense, Aristotle prefers the ethics of friendship—and by extension the ethics of compassion, inasmuch as friends have compassion for each other—to the ethics of justice, whereas Rousseau does precisely the opposite. This is particularly interesting given that both Rousseau and Aristotle agree that the strength of friendship lies in the fact that it operates wholly independently of duty but rather out of heartfelt inclination. The advantages of this from a standpoint of moral psychology are readily apparent, but while Aristotle sees this as a selling point for the ethics of friendship, Rousseau sees this as a weakness of compassion, because it is given to abuse and moral hypocrisy.

57. Berkowitz, *Nietzsche,* 105.

58. For the former, see TSZ 218, 265. For a sampling of the latter, see TSZ 13–14, 46, 260–261, 265–267.

59. Berkowitz, *Nietzsche,* 105. Berkowitz's use of the word "compassion" here is not compatible with my own.

60. Indeed, it is even possible for one to deliberately use another's pity to deceive him, as Zarathustra does to the "grudge-joys and drudge-boys" (TSZ, 174–175).

61. Cf. TSZ 264.

62. Cf. TSZ 13–14, 260, 261, 266–267.

63. Cf. TSZ, 159, 264.

64. Notice that deception has once again crept into the picture: Love of the neighbor can be just as deceptive as pity was shown to be.

65. TSZ 9. For a form of pity that Nietzsche apparently embraces, see Zarathustra's "pity for all that is past" (TSZ, 203).

66. Brown makes a similar observation in "Compassion and Societal Well-being," 218, 219, 222.

67. Solomon, *A Passion for Justice,* 225 (hereafter cited in text).

68. Snow, "Compassion," 195.

69. Ibid.

70. Indeed, according to historian Tony Ashworth, in the trench warfare of World War I British and German troops commonly forged illicit truces, "a process of reciprocal exchange among antagonists, where each diminished the other's risk of death,

discomfort and injury by a deliberate restriction of aggressive activity, but only on the condition that the other requited the restraint" (Ashworth, *Trench Warfare, 1914–1918,* 19). These went beyond trading fire with one another; they even agreed to let each other eat breakfast in peace, "since like us they are hungry" (ibid., 30).

71. Snow, "Compassion," 197 (hereafter cited in text).

72. Ibid., 202.

73. Ibid. There is a worthwhile comparison to be made between Snow's view of humans as always potentially vulnerable and Alasdair MacIntyre's theory of human beings as dependent rational animals. Cf. MacIntyre, *Dependent Rational Animals,* in which MacIntyre's vision of our dependency hinges on our vulnerability.

74. Snow, "Compassion," 204.

75. Brown, "Compassion and Societal Well-being," 218.

76. Not only does Brown problematize examples of irrational compassion when the subject at hand, properly speaking, is rational compassion; he also appears to adopt a Hobbesian understanding of rationality that Snow explicitly challenges. Snow's model of rational compassion will fail by Hobbesian standards because it rejects those very standards, but somehow Brown has missed this point. Indeed, the cases in which the compassion he writes of corresponds to Snow's conception of compassion are few in the extreme; in any event, they are greatly outnumbered by the cases in which he writes on something very different from what Snow has in mind.

77. Solomon, *A Passion for Justice,* 235. Solomon also links compassion with fair-mindedness (245), which is often taken to be a hallmark of rationality (and also, in some cases, opposed to compassion, as will be discussed in chapter 4). In any case, unlike Brown, Solomon does *not* link compassion with injustice (246ff.).

78. Brown, "Compassion," 219.

79. Ibid., 220.

80. Ibid., 218.

81. Cf. Brown, 218.

82. Ibid., 222.

83. Incidentally, it is not incontestably clear that a state can legislate justice any more than it can compassion, at least on a personal level. It can certainly legislate just practices for institutions, and it can certainly legislate punishments for injustice, but these differ from the personal excellence of justice. It is not at all obvious that one's ability to follow rules in order to avoid punishment is a sufficient condition for being a just person, and in any case, this is not *necessarily* a sufficient condition.

84. Snow, "Compassion," 204.

85. Nussbaum, "Compassion and Terror," 943.

86. Ibid., 945.

87. Ibid.

88. Ibid., 943.

89. Solomon, *A Passion for Justice*, 230.

90. Ibid., 225.

91. Philosophers who explicitly define compassion as being responsive to happiness as well as suffering are few in the extreme. The only one I know of is Julian H. Franklin, who defines compassion as "the capacity to share the suffering of others and hope for its removal, or to share the joy of others and help to see it last" (*Animal Rights and Moral Philosophy*, 78). But Franklin rejects compassion as being "subject to caprice and extremism," holding that "the project of an ethics based on compassion and sympathy is deeply flawed" because compassion is "entirely concrete" and "requires an abstract basis of comparison" for making moral judgments (ibid., 87, 81).

Chapter 2: What Is the *Com-* of Compassion?

1. From Paul Williams' introduction to Śāntideva's *Bodhicaryāvatāra* (BCV viii).

2. Tachibana, *Ethics of Buddhism*, 185.

3. Ibid., 272.

4. Ibid.

5. Tachibana recognizes the latter similarity himself on page 273.

6. Tachibana, *Ethics of Buddhism*, 185.

7. Nakamura has devoted an entire book to the philosophical and religious importance of *jihi*. Cf. the first chapter of his *Jihi*, which is devoted to the meanings of the characters *ji* and *hi*.

8. Cook, "Dōgen's View of Authentic Selfhood," 146.

9. There are people who, due to neurological dysfunction, are actually incapable of feeling pain. They typically die prematurely because their brains never register pain, so they often fail to do even the simplest self-preserving things like removing their hands from hot pots. Cf. Ronald Melzack's *The Challenge of Pain* and *The Puzzle of Pain*.

10. Walpola Rahula's exegesis of the *skandhas* is better than any I might offer; see his *What the Buddha Taught*, 20–26.

11. Of course, Śāntideva is hardly alone in making such observations; mereological problems of this sort pervade Indian philosophy. For a handful of salient examples from the Buddhist tradition, cf. *Milindapanha* 25 and 40; *Visuddhi-Magga* chapter 18; and *Mūlamadhyamakakārikā* chapter 14.

12. Cf. BCV 8/121.

13. I follow David Kalupahana's translation of *pratītyasamutpāda* in his *History of Buddhist Philosophy*, as he offers what I take to be the best analysis of this pivotally important term.

14. Incidentally, one can glean a hint here of why *prajñā* and *karuṇā* are one in Buddhist philosophy. Suffering arises from delusion. *Prajñā* seeks the clear sight that frees one from delusion. *Karuṇā* seeks to alleviate all suffering regardless of its location. Hence both *prajñā* and *karuṇā* seek an end to suffering.

15. Of course, the meditation in BCV 8/90 ("All equally experience suffering and happiness") is not unique to Śāntideva. This theme pervades virtually every school of Buddhism from Śāntideva's day up until modern times. Contemporary Tibetan Buddhism as shaped by the Dalai Lama is one good example in which the equality of suffering is heavily emphasized. Cf. Jeffrey Hopkins, *Cultivating Compassion,* passim, especially chapter 2.

16. According to the Dōgen scholar Bokuzen Nishiari, "This fascicle is the skin, flesh, bones, and marrow of the Founder. The fundamental teaching of the Founder's lifetime is expounded in this fascicle." "The ninety-five fascicles of the *Treasury of the True Dharma Eye* [*Shōbōgenzō*] are offshoots of this fascicle" (quoted in Tanahashi, *Moon in a Dewdrop,* 245).

17. Abe and Waddell, trans., "Shōbōgenzō genjōkōan," 130.

18. Cross and Nishijima, trans., *Master Dōgen's Shōbōgenzō,* vol. 1, 33.

19. Jaffe, "Shōbōgenzō Genjō Kōan," 4.

20. Kim, *Dōgen Kigen: Mystical Realist,* 61ff.

21. Kasulis, *Zen Action: Zen Person,* 83. According to Kasulis, Abe Masao and Norman Waddell follow this interpretation of *kōan* in their translation of *genjōkōan* as "manifest absolute reality" (Dōgen, "Shōbōgenzō genjōkōan," 129–140).

22. Kasulis translates *genjōkōan* as "presencing of things as they are" (*Zen Action: Zen Person,* 83ff.). Cook renders it as "presencing absolute reality" ("Dōgen's View of Authentic Selfhood," 137). Both of these are deliberately broad in scope, as is Kim's "*kōan* realized in life." I take it that all three of these translators recognize the same all-inclusiveness that Suzuki acknowledges when he defines *genjō* as "everything."

23. Jaffe, "Shōbōgenzō Genjō Kōan," 4.

24. Translation mine, from Dōgen, *Dōgen Zenji Zenshū.* I have, of course, borrowed Kasulis' "presencing things as they are" in my translation.

25. This is the central message of the *Tenzo-kyōkun* ("Instructions for the Cook"). See Tanahashi, *Moon in a Dewdrop,* 53–66.

26. Cook, "Dōgen's View of Authentic Selfhood," 131.

27. Ibid., 138.

28. Cf. *Sansuigyō* and *Bendōwa* for two of his best discussions of this idea. See also Graham Parkes, "Voices of Mountains," for a detailed philosophical analysis of them.

29. DZZ, *Yuibutsu Yobutsu,* translation mine. For alternative translations, cf. Cook, "Dōgen's View of Authentic Selfhood," 139, and MDS4, 216.

30. DZZ, *Genjōkōan,* translation mine.

31. The translation of *dukkha* as "suffering" has met with criticism (cf. Kalupahana, *History of Buddhist Philosophy,* 87–88; and Williams, *Buddhist Thought,* 42–43), but I would suggest that however *dukkha* is translated, compassion is still concerned with dissolving it.

32. Cf. *Shoaku-Makusa:* "When we cause even the mountains, rivers, and the Earth and the sun, moon, and stars to do practice, the mountains, rivers, and the Earth and the sun, moon, and stars, in their turn, make us practice.... We cause right and wrong, cause-and-effect, to practice" (MDS 1, 100–101). Our practice is entwined with the practice of nature, and both of these are tied up in ethical practice.

33. Cf. Kalupahana, *History of Buddhist Philosophy,* 88: "Very often, the reason for considering an object unsatisfactory (*dukkha*) is that it is impermanent (*anicca*) and subject to transformation or change (*viparināma-dhamma*)."

34. Cook, "Dōgen's View of Authentic Selfhood," 140.

35. Ibid.

36. Indeed, Francis H. Cook says this is true of the entire Mahāyāna tradition: "In Mahāyāna thinking authentic selfhood is the necessary foundation for true compassion.... Compassion in Mahāyāna Buddhism is defined as the dynamic expression of enlightened understanding, or the treatment of other beings in accordance with reality (Sanskrit *tathatā*)" ("Dōgen's View of Authentic Selfhood," 145).

37. Cf. *Mencius* II.A.6 for his catalog of the *tuan* and the incipient tendencies from which they arise.

38. From Lau's introduction to his translation of the *Mencius,* 11, 12.

39. *Mencius,* 18.

40. According to Philip J. Ivanhoe, "From the time of Mencius until the resurrection of his theory by Ch'eng Yi in the eleventh century, almost no thinker in China advocated any version of the theory that human nature is good. And there is little reason to believe such a theory was proposed prior to Mencius' statement of it" (*Ethics in the Confucian Tradition,* 29). Cf. also D. C. Lau, "Theories of Human Nature"; A. C. Graham, "Background of the Mencian Theory"; and A. C. Graham, *Two Chinese Philosophers,* 44–60 and 131–137, as per Ivanhoe's footnote. For a different perspective on Mencius' view of human nature, cf. Irene Bloom, "Fundamental Intuitions and Consensus Statements," 97–110. Bloom also comments on Mencian compassion (101–102).

41. Burton Watson, trans., *Basic Writings of Mo Tzu, Hsün Tzu, and Han Fei Tzu,* Hsün Tzu 157.

42. D. C. Lau discusses this difference in philosophical emphasis in his introduction to his translation of the *Mencius* (12 ff.).

43. Unless otherwise noted, all citations from the *Analects* are taken from Ames

and Rosemont's translation of *The Analects of Confucius*. "LY" denotes D. C. Lau's translation of the text.

44. Herbert Fingarette seconds this observation, noting that if my desires differ from yours, it is not enough for me to gauge my conduct toward you according to what I do and do not want ("Following the 'One Thread'").

45. There are, of course, other interpretations of *shu*. David S. Nivison suggests that *shu* and *zhong* (忠) have a hierarchical structure, *shu* being a kind of reciprocity extended to those of equal or lower social standing than oneself, and *zhong* a correlative sort of reciprocity and loyalty shown to social superiors ("Golden Rule Arguments," 41). Bryan Van Norden argues that this interpretation is unsupported by the text (Nivison, "Unweaving the 'One Thread,'" 228, 230). Whatever *shu's* relationship to *zhong*, there is general consensus that *shu* itself affords an understanding of the other by using oneself as a mirror, so to speak—that is, by putting oneself in the other's place. For my purposes here, this is enough.

46. The notion of the discrete, atomic self is arguably the foundation of the notion of human rights as well, and therefore the source of ongoing political tension between China and governments in Europe and North America. William Theodore deBary and Tu Weiming's edited volume, *Confucianism and Human Rights,* is an extended commentary on the problems inherent in attempting to apply the rights of an individuated conception of self onto a notion of selfhood that is socially and relationally constructed.

47. Ames, "The Focus-Field Self," 206.

48. See Ames, "The Focus-Field Self," 188–204 passim. Also cf. Hegel, *Philosophy of History,* and Hansen, "Individualism in Chinese Thought."

49. Ames, "The Focus-Field Self," 206, emphasis mine. Ames includes a helpful quote from Ambrose King on the articulation of family as *lun* 倫: "The individual's behavior is supposed to be *lun*-oriented; the *lun*-oriented role relations, however, are seen as personal, concrete, and particularistic" (Ames, 206, from Ambrose King, "Individual and Group in Confucianism," 58).

50. Ames, "The Focus-Field Self," 208 (from Arnheim, *Power of the Center,* vii).

51. Cf. also Ames, "The Focus-Field Self," 212n, and Ames and Hall's translation of Laozi's *Daodejing,* 11ff., passim.

52. Ames, "The Focus-Field Self," 212n.

53. Cf. *Analects* 6/7, where Confucius speaks of his disciple Yan Hui, who "could go for several months without departing from authoritative thoughts and feelings."

54. Cf. Śāntideva, BCV 8/129, 8/130, 8/136, 8/141.

55. Fingarette, "The Music of Humanity," 217.

56. Confucius, *The Analects of Confucius,* 20ff.

57. Cf. Kasulis, *Intimacy or Integrity*, 37, 57–63, 72–77, 86–96, 108–116.

58. By "diminished," I do not mean to imply a value judgment, for there are good losses as well as bad ones. A woman who escapes an abusive marriage is diminished, for the part of her that is defined by her relationship with her spouse is lost, though the loss is a benefit to her (just as the loss of a tumor is a benefit).

59. Plato, *The Symposium*, 188e–190b.

60. For other examples, cf. 15/33 and 17/8.

61. Laozi, *Daodejing*, 183.

62. Ibid.

63. Laozi (Lao Tzu), *Tao Te Ching*, 129. I shift to the Lau translation only for readability in the present context; philosophically speaking, the two translations are arguably quite compatible in this instance.

64. Laozi, *Daodejing*, 183.

65. Ibid., 184.

66. Kirkland, "'Responsible Non-Action,'" 294.

67. Ibid.

68. Laozi, *Daodejing*, 184, emphasis mine.

69. Zhuangzi, *Chuang-tzǔ: The Inner Chapters*, 51, 52, 53.

70. Ibid., 45.

71. Properly speaking, the term "Buddhist" may be too encompassing in this context, given that Buddhism undergoes important changes as one tracks it from India through China to Japan and beyond. I use it here with caution and with the thought that every form of Buddhism will take *karunā* and *anātman* as philosophical bedrock.

72. Zhuangzi, *Chuang-tzǔ: The Inner Chapters*, 4.

73. Creel, *What Is Taoism*, 3.

74. Kirkland, "'Responsible Non-Action,'" 297. The James Rachels quote is from Rachels, *Elements of Moral Philosophy*, 11.

75. Welch, *Taoism*, 165.

76. See James Legge, who uses both of these (*The Texts of Taoism: The Tao Te Ching and the Writings of Chuang-tzǔ*, 498–500, 508–509), and A. C. Graham, who uses "Donothing Saynothing" (albeit with considerably deeper philosophical reflection) (Zhuangzi, *Chuang-tzǔ: The Inner Chapters*, 159–160).

77. Chan, *Source Book in Chinese Philosophy*, 791.

78. Laozi, *Daodejing*, 38.

79. "Taking no unnatural action" and "doing things noncoercively" are also translations that reject Russell Kirkland's translation of *wei* as "human action intended to achieve results" ("'Responsible Non-Action,'" 295). This is a rejection that should be made; Kirkland's reading of *wei*—and therefore of *wu wei*—is suspect at best.

80. Laozi, *Daodejing*, 81–82, emphasis mine.

81. Ibid., 175, emphasis mine.

82. Indeed, the following line of *Daodejing* 63 reads, "Be non-interfering in going about your business."

83. Laozi, *Daodejing*, 183.

84. Clarke, *Tao of the West*, 93 and 95, respectively.

85. Zhuangzi, *Chuang-tzŭ: The Inner Chapters*, 89.

86. In all fairness to the Confucian, *Analects* 3.4 does state that "in mourning, it is better to express real grief than to worry over formal details" (*The Analects of Confucius*, 82–83). And in *Analects* 19.1, praise is given to those who "in participating in a funeral concern themselves with grief" (ibid., 218). Thus the remarks of Master Sanghu's friends disparage not Confucianism but only those who behave like Zigong.

87. Zhuangzi, *Chuang-tzŭ: The Inner Chapters*, 105.

88. Ibid.

89. Clarke, *Tao of the West*, 95.

90. "'Responsible Non-Action,'" 294. The "elsewhere" to which Kirkland refers is *Daodejing* 5, which D. C. Lau and Ames and Hall translate using "straw dogs." Though Kirkland's "straw and dogs" is highly suspect, I will make use of his translation since his is the one I wish to engage. However, for a more detailed philosophical explanation of the meaning of "straw dogs" in *Daodejing* 5 (and through it a convincing case against Kirkland's translation), see Laozi, *Daodejing*, 84–85. See also the footnote in D. C. Lau's translation (Laozi [Lao Tzu], *Tao Te Ching*, 61).

91. Laozi, *Daodejing*, 84–85.

92. Ibid., 85. It is worth noting that Confucius would be unlikely to make the same concession in the same way; Daoism's rejection of human exceptionalism is, in part, a rejection of anthropocentric tendencies the classical Daoists saw in Confucian thinking.

93. Danto, *Mysticism and Morality*, 118.

94. Zhuangzi, *Chuang-tzŭ: The Inner Chapters*, 51.

95. Ibid., 4.

96. Creel, *What Is Taoism*, 3.

97. By "relativism" I mean the belief that moral "truths" are not absolute. By "pluralism" I mean the belief that while there are absolute moral truths, there is a plurality of morally viable ways to interpret them, discover them, and arrive at them. By "perspectivalism" I mean the epistemic position holding that in order to arrive at moral truth or make a moral judgment, one must first draw information from as broad a spectrum of relevant perspectives as possible. (I do *not* mean Ernest Sosa's virtue perspectivism.) To my knowledge, the term "moral perspectivalism" was coined by Julie McDonald in her epilogue to *Contemporary Moral Issues in a Diverse Society*. I follow McDonald's usage of this term.

98. Indeed, it seems Daoism will have to reject relativism, for the two are in fundamental disagreement over the possibility of there being a Way. Daoism holds that there is a kind of proper Way-making and that one can lose one's Way and find it again. Even given the possibilities of multiple Ways, the possibility of losing and finding one's Way still amounts to a rejection of relativism.

99. For an example of this phenomenon, see Leonard Harris' idea of the "serial agent"—that is, a group that acts with an agency not attributable to any one of its members—in "Agency and the Concept of the Underclass" (in particular, pp. 35–38). See also Larry May's discussion of the "social existentialist account of responsibility" in his *Sharing Responsibility* (18–24). Cheshire Calhoun addresses some of the same questions May raises in her "Responsibility and Reproach," where she examines how responsibility for sexist behavior works in a predominantly sexist society, and who in such a society may be reproached. I do not include the American pragmatists among the ranks of analytic philosophers, but John Dewey, George Herbert Mead, and others did devote their attention to the difference between "I" and "we" as loci of moral responsibility; an analysis of them can be found in Steve Odin's *Social Self in Zen and American Pragmatism*.

100. The child displays filial responsibility (*xiao,* 孝) to the extent that the parent instills it and then earns it by acting authoritatively (*ren,* 仁). If the child misbehaves, the parent is at least partly to blame. Cf. *Analects* 4/20: "The Master said, 'A person who for three years refrains from reforming the ways (*dao* 道) of his late father can be called a filial son (*xiao* 孝).'" If a son quickly reforms the ways of his late father, there are two possible explanations: Either the son is not filial or the father was not authoritative.

101. Cf. *Analects* 13/18.

102. Watsuji, *Watsuji Tetsurō's* Rinrigaku, passim. For an alternative translation containing many of the same key concepts, see Dilworth's translation of Watsuji's "The Significance of Ethics."

Chapter 3: Defining Compassion

1. Sidgwick's conceit is not that whites may not be bound to show the same level of kindness to nonwhites; indeed, this is only a hypothetical claim anyhow, tempered by the word "perhaps." The conceit is that, by including the reader within "our own race," he overlooks the possibility that any nonwhite might be included among his readership. This is surely a failure to take nonwhites seriously as pursuers of such academic interests as philosophy.

2. Here compassion has much in common with care, as can be seen in Joy Kroeger-Mappes' description of care: "The ideal of care is an activity of relationship, of seeing

and responding to need. The moral imperative is to care, namely to discern and alleviate trouble in the world" (Kroeger-Mappes, "The Ethic of Care," 110).

3. Of course, Aristotle emphasized wisdom as well, but despite his relevance I hesitate to draw upon him here, because neither *theōria* nor *phronēsis* is equivalent to Buddhist *prajñā* or the Confucian or Daoist understanding of *zhi* (知).

4. Martha Nussbaum calls this "empathetic imagining" and discusses its role in ethical reasoning, including a discussion of how one might develop one's capacity for empathetic imagining. Cf. Nussbaum, *Poetic Justice*.

5. Kant, *Grounding for the Metaphysics of Morals*, Ak. 389.

6. Kant, *The Metaphysics of Morals*, Ak. 6: 216.

7. The problem with the inclinations for Kant is that they are not a priori but mediated by experience, and they are therefore unfree. Kant describes compassion (*Mitleidungschaft*) as being "unfree" and "communicable"—in this sense like a "contagious disease"—as opposed to the freely chosen "*will* to *share in others' feelings*," which he recognizes as a duty, albeit only an indirect and conditional one (*The Metaphysics of Morals* 6: 456–457).

8. Goleman, *Emotional Intelligence*, 52–55.

9. Ibid., 52–53.

10. Elliot's impairment was so bad that he could not make even simple preferences such as when to schedule a doctor's appointment. Without any rational basis to choose to set the appointment for one free day rather than another, he became completely intellectually paralyzed, unable to make a decision. Goleman concluded that even the choice of Tuesday or Wednesday required an emotional impetus, however tiny, that Elliot was unable to generate.

11. Warren, *Ecofeminist Philosophy*, 110, emphasis mine.

12. Goleman, *Emotional Intelligence*, 53.

13. Anthony Kenny explores the relationships between concern, motivation, and action in his *Action, Emotion and Will*. As I understand him, if I have any differences with his conception of these connections, they are not significant enough to the present project to warrant discussion of them here.

14. Kant, *On a Supposed Right to Lie*, 427.

15. Laurence Thomas makes a convincing case for this in his book, *Vessels of Evil*.

16. From "Turning Point," in *Selected Poetry of Rainer Maria Rilke*.

17. Cf. Kant, *Grounding for the Metaphysics of Morals*, Ak. 394.

18. Eliot Deutsch draws distinctions between "individuals," "selves," and "persons." For Deutsch, an individual is "all the conditions and materials, both particular (the natural color of one's hair) and universal (the central nervous system of the body), of our individual being." A self is "that spontaneous vitality, the essential spirituality, which is the ground of our being." A person is "not a given, but an achievement.

A person is a creative articulation, in varying degrees of rightness, of his/her indi-viduality within the enduring reality of the self" (Deutsch, *Personhood, Creativity and Freedom,* 1). On Deutsch's analysis, the being at the center of the diagram is an individual and possibly a self (depending on what is meant by "essential spirituality" and whether such a thing exists).

19. Should the reader require further persuasion, consider that even in everyday conversation we describe ourselves as being divided ("She's just not the same person around her parents"; "I'm not myself today"; "I'm beside myself with anger"). Bud-dhist philosophy naturally springs to mind in such a context, but in the contem-porary analytic tradition the same issues arise in the work of Derek Parfit, whose writings have spawned no shortage of commentary and discussion. (Parfit's "Personal Identity" and "Divided Minds and the Nature of Persons" are representative of his works on the subject.) In the continental tradition, Nietzsche wrote, "It is always as if I were a multiplicity," and Graham Parkes suggests that Nietzsche sees the self as being an ongoing composition (Parkes, *Composing the Soul,* 1). If the self is conceived of as divisible, there seems to be no reason why one part of the self could not feel compassion for another part of the self.

20. Of course, these are rarer in some philosophical traditions than in others. Ben-tham is the first figure I can think of in Anglo-European philosophy who explicitly highlights the inherent moral worthiness of nonhuman animals, while Dōgen is sim-ply rephrasing in his own terms the Buddhist injunction, in his day already well over a thousand years old, against harming animals.

21. Zhu Xi, *Focusing the Familiar,* Ames and Hall, trans., 68.

22. Watsuji, *Rinrigaku,* 15, 17.

23. I am indebted to Peter Singer, who presented a similar argument to me in conversation.

24. Cf. O'Neill, *Towards Justice and Virtue.*

25. Thomas P. Kasulis models this differently (*Intimacy or Integrity,* 63). His dis-cussion of what he calls "The Buddhist Self" is instructive.

26. Peter Singer argues that physical proximity is of no concern when speaking of moral obligation (cf. "Famine, Affluence, and Morality"). Singer's moral obligation is very different from the sense of moral obligation I have in mind, but he does have a point: The demands of compassion are no less obligating for two identically suffering people, even if one of them is next door and the other is across the ocean. My point here is not that compassion impresses a lesser obligation with regard to the suffering person across the ocean but rather that simple epistemological and phenomenological limitations make it more difficult to perceive that person's need.

27. Watsuji Tetsurō says of Dōgen's Zen that "in the moment of enlightenment the self and the cosmos become one" (*Shamon Dōgen,* in *Watsuji Tetsurō Zenshū,* vol. 4,

176). Cf. Dōgen, *Bendōwa*: "If a human being, even for a single moment, manifests the Buddha's posture . . . the entire world of Dharma assumes the Buddha's posture and the whole of space becomes the state of realization" (MDS I: 4–5); and later in the same fascicle: "Zazen, even if it is only one human being sitting for one moment, thus enters into mystical co-operation with all dharmas, and completely penetrates all times" (MDS I: 6).

28. Indeed, Dōgen was angered by those who claimed one could gain powers such as clairvoyance, telepathy, or levitation through Buddhist meditation. Cf. *Fukanza-zengi* (*Shikantaza*, 43). Cf. Hee-jin Kim, *Dōgen Kigen*, where Kim compares Dōgen's approach to *zazen* with that of Tsung-che, who "entertained the idea that zazen was a means to the attainment of magical yogic powers" (Kim, 58).

29. Cf. Dōgen, *Bendōwa*: "Everything in the Universe in ten directions—soil, earth, grass and trees; fences, walls, tiles, and pebbles—performs the Buddha's work" (MDS I: 5).

30. Graham Parkes raised these latter two questions and a host of others in his essays on Buddhism and environmentalism. Cf. Parkes, "Voices of Mountains, Trees, and Rivers."

31. Kant, *Metaphysics of Morals*, Ak. 6: 456–457.

32. Ibid., Ak. 6: 280.

33. Kant, *On a Supposed Right to Lie,* Ak. 427.

34. Both quotes taken from John McCain, *Why Courage Matters* (39, ix).

35. Cf. Rousseau's "Discourse on the Origin of Inequality," where he describes compassion as "the only natural virtue" and says that "from this quality alone flow all those social virtues. . . . What is generosity, clemency or humanity but compassion applied to the weak, to the guilty, or to mankind in general? Even benevolence and friendship are, if we judge rightly, only the effects of compassion" (in *Social Contract and Discourses*, 197–198).

36. James Rachels' discussion of virtue ethics in *Elements of Moral Philosophy* offers perhaps the most widely read summary of this argument. More recently, in her "Normative Virtue Ethics," Rosalind Hursthouse argues against this position, suggesting that virtue ethics is no more susceptible to this problem than any other school of ethical thought. (Supposing that one must choose between being forthright and being kind, for instance, neither Kantian thinking nor utilitarian thinking is better equipped than a virtue ethic to offer conclusive and compelling guidance on the choice.)

37. Cf. NE 1097b10ff., and indeed all of NE Book VIII, for the importance of friendship in Aristotelian ethics. Human *eudaimonia* involves social life, and so any pursuit of *eudaimonia* will entail the pursuit of friendships and other social relationships.

38. Cf. Plato, "Apology," 25d–26b.

39. Graham, *The Inner Chapters*, 25–26. Graham writes of Zhuangzi as if there were an actual historical person of this name, but even if no such person existed, the point can just as easily be attributed to the author or authors of the *Zhuangzi*.

40. Ibid., 26.

41. Cf. Code, *Epistemic Responsibility*, and Code, "Toward a 'Responsibilist' Epistemology."

42. See Clifford, *Lectures and Essays* vol. 2, 177–188, for the original instance of this example.

43. Zagzebski, *Virtues of the Mind*, 77, emphasis mine.

44. Vrinda Dalmiya describes care in similar terms in "Why Should a Knower Care?" According to her, care can be thought of as a "knowledge saturated skill," in that "caring is as much a cognitive disposition as an ethical virtue" (50, 42). Dalmiya argues for a care-based epistemology (46–50) that bears some similarities to the compassionate ethico-epistemology I propose here. For instance, Dalmiya says, "It is certainly not hard to imagine a community and situation where, in response to the query 'How do you know that Uma hates her job?' it is quite acceptable for someone to reply simply, 'Because I care for her'" (45). I envision wise compassion as having a similar kind of application and explanatory power.

45. Zagzebski, *Virtues of the Mind*, 231.

46. *Epistemic Justification*, coauthored by Sosa and Laurence BonJour, represents each philosopher's efforts to defend his position against the critiques of the other. The volume provides a synthesis of Sosa's numerous publications on virtue epistemology.

47. Nussbaum, "Virtue Ethics: A Misleading Category?" 168, 201.

48. Cf. Rachels, *Elements of Moral Philosophy*, 159–179; Marcia Baron, "Kantian Ethics," in Baron, Pettit and Slote, *Three Methods of Ethics*, 5–6, 54–64; and Philip Pettit, "The Consequentialist Perspective," ibid., 139–141.

49. Cf. Slote, *From Morality to Virtue*, 89.

50. Marcia Baron argues that there is not a substantive difference between deontic and aretaic language; cf. Baron, Pettit, and Slote, *Three Methods of Ethics*, 49–56.

51. Hursthouse, "Normative Virtue Ethics," in Stephen Darwall, ed., *Virtue Ethics*, 192. (The original appearance of Hursthouse's article was in Roger Crisp, ed., *How Should One Live?*)

52. Ibid.

53. Ibid.

54. Slote, "Agent-Based Virtue Ethics," in Darwall, *Virtue Ethics*, 221. (The original appearance of Slote's article was in *Midwest Studies in Philosophy* 20.)

55. I paraphrase Slote's phraseology here. According to Slote, "Agent-based views . . . treat the moral or ethical status of actions as entirely derivative from independent and fundamental ethical aretaic facts (or claims) about the motives, disposi-

tions, or inner life of the individuals who perform them" (ibid., 204). On the other hand, an agent-focused ethic "focuses more on virtuous individuals and individual traits than on actions" (ibid.). Neither of these adequately describes the aretaic compassionate ethic being developed here, in part because of the metaphysical assumptions underlying the words "agent" and "individual." But the relevant similarity with regard to the potential problem Slote raises is all that is necessary in the present context.

56. Ibid., 221.

57. Austin, *The Province of Jurisprudence*, 108, from Pettit in Baron, Pettit, and Slote, *Three Methods of Ethics*, 102. For Pettit's discussion of "non-actuarialism," cf. *Three Methods of Ethics*, 99–102.

58. Cf. Slote, *From Morality to Virtue*, 228.

Chapter 4: Objections to an Ethic of Compassion

1. Solomon, *A Passion for Justice*, 244.

2. Whether there is necessarily tension between something like compassion (a principle or excellence of ethics) and something like justice (a principle or excellence of politics) is beyond the scope of this book, but what Allison M. Jaggar says about the ethics of care may prove instructive here: "If care and justice are construed as values or ideals, there seems no reason to doubt that both may be part of the same value system and compatibility in this sense is not threatened by occasional uncertainty over which ideal should take precedence" ("Caring as a Feminist Practice," 184).

3. "We were social before we were human," says Peter Singer (*The Expanding Circle*, 3). Primatologists and sociobiologists alike affirm that no primate species—the human species included—could have survived long without sophisticated social behavior. (However, to be fair to Singer, he would strongly object to the partialist ethic I am defending here. Cf. Singer, "Famine, Affluence, and Morality.")

4. Cf. Charles W. Mills, *The Racial Contract*, 120ff.; Mills argues that raceless social contract theories lack important explanatory power. Also cf. Carole Pateman, *The Sexual Contract*, especially her analysis of Rawls beginning on p. 42, which culminates in her claim that "Rawls' participants in the original contract are, simultaneously, mere reasoning entities, and 'heads of families,' or men who represent their wives" (43).

5. For an analysis of compensatory justice, see Robert Nozick, *Anarchy, State and Utopia*. For an analysis of rectificatory justice, see Rodney C. Roberts, *Injustice and Rectification*. There is far more to be said about the various "species" of justice, but my concern here is with impartiality, not justice per se.

6. It should be noted that Mills is not a fan of Nozick either; in the same sentence

in which he highlights the total absence of any reference to American slavery in *A Theory of Justice,* he says Nozick's theory of justice in *Anarchy, State and Utopia* is just as blind to "the utter divergence of U.S. history" from the ideals of his theory.

7. Rawls, *A Theory of Justice,* 17.

8. Ibid.

9. Mills, "White Being Black Being," 9.

10. Cf. *Blau v. United States,* 340 U.S. 332; *Wolfe v. United States,* 291 U.S. 7.

11. Mishima Yukio's short story, *"Yūkoku"* ("Patriotism"), offers a gripping (if gruesome) portrayal of the blending of loyalty and self-sacrifice—to say nothing of a darkly prescient glimpse of what was to come in his own tragic life. Suzuki Shōsan is the other figure whose name springs to mind when scholars of *bushidō* think of *seppuku.* Cf. Suzuki's *Warrior of Zen* and Winston L. King's *Death Was His Kōan.* Graham Parkes offers further insights on Suzuki in his "Death and Detachment." See also Yamamoto Tsunetomo's *Hagakure,* passim, especially the analects on 55, 158, and 164.

12. Trivers, "Evolution of Reciprocal Altruism," 35. For a thorough treatment of psychological egoism, cf. Feinberg, *Reason and Responsibility,* 529–539.

13. Wilson, *Sociobiology: The New Synthesis,* 120. Wilson's position does allow for the possibility that a being may secure greater selective advantage by *mimicking* altruistic behavior and perhaps even fooling itself into believing that it acts altruistically; hence the existence of what appear to be altruistic behaviors in nature.

14. See Singer, *The Expanding Circle;* the book is essentially an extended argument against the sociobiological positions put forth by figures such as Wilson and Richard Dawkins (*The Selfish Gene*).

15. Cf. *Analects* 1.11, where Confucius emphasizes a son's loyalty to his father's posthumous legacy. See also the second chapter of Watsuji Tetsurō's *Shamon Dōgen,* where Dōgen's teacher Myōzen wrestles with the problem of whether or not to venture on a pilgrimage to China, leaving his master Meiyū alone on his deathbed. (*Watsuji Tetsurō Zenshū,* vol. 4, 169–171.)

16. See Kant's "On the Different Races," where he affirms "the immutability and permanence of race," and also his *Observations on the Feeling,* in which he holds that "So fundamental is the difference between [the black and white] races of man ... it appears to be as great in regard to mental capacities as in color." See also Mills for a critique of these passages (*The Racial Contract,* 70), and see Emmanuel Eze for an extended indictment of Kant as the father of modern race theory ("The Color of Reason").

17. Kant could not have been called a racist in his own time, for the term "racism" was coined by the French some sixty years or so after Kant's death in 1804.

18. Nel Noddings, *Caring*, 9–16.

19. Ibid., 19.

20. Ibid., 4.

21. Selma Sevenhuijsen describes this well, borrowing from Joan Tronto and Carol Gilligan: "The ethics of care involves different moral concepts: responsibilities and relationships rather than rules and rights" (Sevenhuisjen, *Citizenship and the Ethics of Care*, 107).

22. Cf. *Shōbōgenzō Zuimonki*, third fascicle, or *Shamon Dōgen*, chapter 6, where a conflicted monk asks Dōgen whether he ought to continue in the monastery or go home to take care of his sick, aging mother. Dōgen suggests that if he were to stay the course as a monk, and if she were willing to die alone so that he could stay on, both of them would be following the Buddha-way.

Chapter 5: Compassion in Action

Epigraph: In *Social Contract and Discourses*, 199–200. See footnote 4 of this chapter for more on Rousseau's compassion as developed in the "Discourse."

1. Kant, *Grounding for the Metaphysics of Morals*, Ak. 394.

2. Ibid.

3. Naturally, this is not peculiar to an ethic of compassion. Care ethics also takes communal existence to be ontologically primary and sees individual existence as an intellectual abstraction. Eve Browning Cole's *Philosophy and Feminist Criticism* is not itself a work of care ethics, but there she does offer a feminist critique of the *cogito* and an argument for the ontological primacy of the community (cf. chapter 3).

4. Rousseau, *Social Contract and Discourses*, 198, 197. The compassion (*pitié*) Rousseau speaks of here is of the most primitive kind, not the more robust version of it one finds in *Emile*. Allan Bloom distinguishes between the two of them as "animal compassion" and "active human compassion" (E 18). But this distinction does not detract in any way from the primacy of compassion, for the "animal" compassion of the "Discourse on the Origin of Inequality" is a necessary precondition for philosophy and is ultimately the motivation for allowing justice to trump the "human" compassion of *Emile*, for "of all the virtues justice is the one that contributes most to the common good of men" (E 253).

5. For an argument along these lines, cf. Sally Markowitz, "Feminism and Abortion."

6. For a few examples of arguments for this position, cf. Cheshire Calhoun, "Family's Outlaws," Nitya Duclos, "Some Complicating Thoughts," and Andrew Sullivan, *Virtually Normal*.

7. Joy Kroeger-Mappes suggests that this preference of victory over compromise is a natural by-product of adherence to an ethic of rights as opposed to an ethic of care. Cf. "The Ethic of Care."

8. Prejean's second book, *The Death of Innocents,* focuses on those who are wrongly convicted and executed. If anything, her second book advocates her cause more forcefully than the first; nevertheless, I shall devote more attention to the first book than the second. To have compassion for innocents facing wrongful death is easy—even instinctual. The compassion Prejean shows for murderers and rapists in *Dead Man Walking,* men who were clearly guilty of their crimes, is rare and difficult to come by.

9. Cf. DMW 14, 15, 83–84, 203–204, 228. At DMW 185, seeing Robert Willie's arrogance and defiance, Prejean says she will "challenge him to take responsibility for his crime and to ask forgiveness of the Harveys [the family of his murder victim, Faith Hathaway]."

10. Cf. DMW 14, 26, 139, 224, 286.

11. The response Prejean gets from the warden of Angola is instructive: "We can't let our feelings dominate our actions or we couldn't carry out our responsibilities" (DMW 156). This removal of emotion from moral responsibility is exactly the kind of Kantian reasoning Karen Warren problematized in her analysis of the case of Elliot (chapter 3). The difference between the warden's "emotion-free" approach to moral decision making and Prejean's approach is significant: The warden and those who work for him speak of being able to carry out executions only by suppressing their thoughts about it, both emotionally and intellectually. (Indeed, the warden confesses, "Never thought about it too much, really" [DMW 157].)

12. The third inmate she serves as spiritual adviser was Willie Lawrence Celestine; he is mentioned as her book comes to a close (DMW 343).

13. Cf. DMW 25–26, 81, 209.

14. Prejean cites evidence throughout her book demonstrating that death sentencing is heavily dependent on the race of the victim and the defendant (blacks frequently receive death sentences for killing whites but almost never for killing blacks) and on the defendant's income (which in Louisiana and the other so-called "Death Belt" states is divided along racial lines). Even the U.S. Supreme Court has declared that racism in death sentences is "inevitable" (*McClesky v. Kemp,* 107 S. Ct. 1756 [1987]).

15. *The Death of Innocents,* 241.

16. In the eighteen years from the time the death penalty was reinstated until the time Bush became governor, Texas executed 174 prisoners (a total Bush would come close to doubling in his six years). Runner-up is West Virginia, with 91 executions from 1976 until 2004. In all, the United States has executed 929 prisoners since 1976, 16.3 percent of those being performed during Bush's tenure. My source for these fig-

ures is Prejean's *The Death of Innocents;* Prejean frequently cites www.deathpenalty info.org as her source.

17. Prejean, *Death of Innocents,* 241.

18. Ibid., 245, and ibid., 241–245.

19. Ibid., 243.

20. Ibid. If Prejean is implying that the appeals are not read, then one might suggest that by not giving Bush the benefit of the doubt she is not showing him compassion. If so, the next charge would be hypocrisy: She extends her compassion to murderers but not to those who execute murderers. Though Prejean does confess to feeling anger and outrage toward Bush, it is not clear that calling someone out for being uncompassionate is itself uncompassionate. Being intolerant of intolerance is arguably a necessary condition of tolerance. Similarly, it may well be the case that being tolerant of someone's lack of compassion signals a deficit in one's own compassion. As Robert C. Solomon argues (cf. chapter 1), sometimes the appropriate moral response is outrage. Whether or not that is true of Prejean's reaction in this case is not obvious (or at least not obvious to me).

21. Prejean *Death of Innocents,* 244.

22. Ibid., 241–249.

23. Ibid., 248. See also Mark Crispin Miller, *The Bush Dyslexicon,* 121.

24. "Clemency hearings end," *Chicago Tribune,* October 29, 2002.

25. "Clemency for all," *Chicago Tribune,* January 13, 2003.

26. "George Ryan indicted," *Chicago Tribune,* December 18, 2003.

27. Cf. Prejean, *Death of Innocents,* 241. Cff. Miller, *The Bush Dyslexicon,* 245, and also 243, where Miller quotes Bush in a telling Freudian slip: "The only thing I can tell you is that every case I have reviewed, I have been comfortable with the innocence or guilt of the person that I've looked at. I do not believe we've put a guilty—I mean, innocent person to death in the state of Texas."

28. Prejean, *Death of Innocents,* 7.

29. Homicide is (obviously) criminal by definition, but it is not immoral by definition, and thus there is an open question as to whether an ethic of compassion must define all instances of capital punishment as immoral. For an execution to be morally permissible, it would have to be done as an expression of compassionate will, arising out of compassionate attendance to the needs of the prisoner to be executed (and also to the needs of the state, the victims or their families, the families of the prisoner, etc.). Some criminals have asked to be executed for their own good as well as for the good of potential future victims. In such cases one must ask whether the individuals making the requests are of sound mind, but if these people are neither suicidal nor otherwise chronically depressed, then in theory it is possible to execute them for their own good—that is, to execute them out of compassion. But such cases will be so few

and far between that for all practical purposes, compassionate ethics must counsel that all executions be regarded with suspicion, at least prima facie.

30. Leonard Harris' concept of serial agency is particularly relevant here. (See Harris, "Agency and the Concept of the Underclass.") See also Laurence Thomas' *Vessels of Evil*, where he suggests that the Holocaust and the institution of American slavery could not have happened without the communal endorsement of everyday German and (white) American citizens.

31. Cf. "On a Supposed Right to Lie."

32. The AMA's 1973 resolution to oppose assisted suicide still stands, reiterated more recently in *Compassion in Dying v. Washington,* where it filed an amicus brief stating that "physician-assisted suicide should not be legalized, at least as of this time." Cf. 1996 WL 94848 (9th Cir. [Wash.]).

33. Sullivan is employing definitions laid out by Paul Ramsey in his book *The Patient as Person,* 122. Ramsey's definitions, in turn, are abbreviated versions of definitions offered in Gerald Kelly's *Medico-Moral Problems,* 129.

34. Sullivan, "Active and Passive Euthanasia," 45.

35. Rachels, "Active and Passive Euthanasia," 79.

36. Ibid.

37. Ibid., 78, from Shaw, "Doctor, Do We Have a Choice?" 54.

38. Sullivan, "Active and Passive Euthanasia," 45–46.

39. I say "initial articles" because Rachels refines his position significantly in his later work, voicing a much greater regard for the well-being of the patient in his later essays on PAS.

40. Foot, "Euthanasia," 88.

41. Ibid., 90.

42. Panin, *The Notebooks of Sologdin,* 66–67. From Foot, "Euthanasia," 88.

43. Ibid., 85. From Foot, "Euthanasia," 90.

44. Foot, "Euthanasia," 95.

45. Ibid, 96.

46. Ibid.

47. Even as I write this, in the current legislative session the House and Senate of the state of California are scheduled to decide whether or not PAS is to be legalized there. The international organization Death With Dignity is predicted to be successful in its lobbying efforts to persuade the California legislature to legalize PAS.

48. Cf. *Compassion in Dying v. Washington,* 79 F.3d 790 (9th Cir. 1996). Though this decision was overturned by the U.S. Supreme Court in *Washington v. Glucksberg,* the idea of euthanasia as a solution to economic troubles has not disappeared. In 1999 then-governor George W. Bush signed a Texas law allowing doctors to override the will of a patient's family and remove vital care such as feeding tubes or assisted

ventilation. Among opponents of the bill, it was widely believed that the motivation behind the bill was to save hospitals money. Cf. *Miller v. HCA* and Holly O'Neal Rumbaugh's case comment in *41 Houston Law Review 675* (Summer 2004).

49. Coleman's disability rights organization, Not Dead Yet, catalogs articles, court cases, and briefs of amici curiae at its Web site, www.notdeadyet.org.

50. Diane Coleman and Carol Gill, "Disability Rights Opposition," as read before the Constitution Subcommittee of the Judiciary Committee of the U.S. House of Representatives on April 29, 1996.

51. Ibid. For Kevorkian's views on PAS (what he calls "medicide" or "obitiatry"), cf. his *Prescription: Medicide.* There Kevorkian argues that assisted suicide should be an elective option not only for the terminally ill, but also for the disabled and for death row prisoners. (Kevorkian's term for execution is "obligatory assisted suicide" [195].) He also contends that medical research could be greatly advanced if the disabled, terminally ill, and legally condemned could also volunteer for human medical experimentation (132, 202, 241).

52. Appendix to Coleman and Gill, "Disability Rights Opposition" (in McDonald, *Contemporary Moral Issues,* 202–203). I have been unable to establish the gender of two people listed, Ali Khalili and Pat Digangl. Neither Khalili nor Digangl were terminal cases.

53. Coleman and Gill, "Disability Rights Opposition," 201.

54. Indeed, according to Coleman's 2006 testimony before the U.S. Senate ("Consequences of Legalized Assisted Suicide and Euthanasia"), 37 percent of the doctors who issued lethal prescriptions since Oregon legalized the procedure cited "feelings of being a burden" as the reason for issuing the prescriptions.

55. Coleman, "Testimony before the Subcommittee," April 19, 2005.

56. Ibid.

57. Coleman and Gill, "Disability Rights Opposition," as read before the Constitution Subcommittee of the Judiciary Committee of the U.S. House of Representatives on April 29, 1996.

58. Ibid. Coleman and Gill cite many more examples than this: "Disabled people who need ventilators are often not offered assisted breathing as an option. Those who already use ventilators report that they are increasingly asked by medical personnel to consider 'do not resuscitate' orders and withdrawal of life support. Children with non-terminal diseases who never asked to die are killed 'gently' by the denial of routine treatment. People with relatively mild disabilities are routinely denied life saving organ transplants," and the list goes on.

59. Ibid.

60. Cf. G. E. M. Anscombe, "Modern Moral Philosophy," 8–9.

Author's note: In cases in which the author of a text is unknown or unnamed (e.g., the *Daodejing*), I have chosen to list the name of the author conventionally attributed to the work (e.g., Laozi in the case of the *Daodejing*), despite the likelihood that no such individual existed. This seems preferable to listing the work by the translator's name(s), since in some cases I have used multiple translations of the same text, and it may prove helpful to the reader to see all cited translations grouped together rather than scattered throughout the bibliography.

Ames, Roger T. "The Focus-Field Self in Classical Confucianism." In *Self as Person in Asian Theory and Practice*, eds. Roger T. Ames, Wimal Dissanayake, and Thomas P. Kasulis. Albany: State University of New York Press, 1994.

Annas, Julia. *The Morality of Happiness.* New York: Oxford University Press, 1993.

Anscombe, G. E. M. "Modern Moral Philosophy." *Philosophy* 33, no. 124 (January 1958): 1–19.

Arendt, Hannah. *Love and Saint Augustine.* Chicago: University of Chicago Press, 1996.

Aristotle. *Nichomachean Ethics.* Trans. Terence Irwin. Indianapolis: Hackett Publishing, 1999.

Arnheim, Rudolph. *The Power of the Center: A Study in the Visual Arts.* Berkeley: University of California Press, 1982.

Ashworth, Tony. *Trench Warfare 1914–1918: The Live and Let Live System.* London: Macmillan, 1980.

Augustine. *Confessions.* Trans. R. S. Pine-Coffin. London: Penguin Books, 1961.

Austin, John. *The Province of Jurisprudence Determined.* London: Weidenfeld and Nicolson, 1832 (new edition 1954, intro. by H. L. A. Hart).

Baier, Annette. *A Progress of Sentiments: Reflections on Hume's Treatise.* Cambridge, MA: Harvard University Press, 1991.

Baron, Marcia, Philip Pettit, and Michael Slote. *Three Methods of Ethics: A Debate.* Oxford: Blackwell, 1997.

Bedau, Hugo Adam. "Capital Punishment." In *Matters of Life and Death,* ed. Tom Regan. Philadelphia: Temple University Press, 1980.

Berkowitz, Peter. *Nietzsche: The Ethics of an Immoralist.* London: Harvard University Press, 1995.

Bloom, Irene. "Fundamental Intuitions and Consensus Statements: Mencian Confucianism and Human Rights." In *Confucianism and Human Rights,* eds. William Theodore de Bary and Tu Weiming. New York: Columbia University Press, 1998: 94–116.

Blum, Lawrence. "Compassion." In *The Virtues: Contemporary Essays in Moral Character,* eds. Robert B. Kruschwitz and Robert C. Roberts. Belmont, CA: Wadsworth, 1987.

BonJour, Laurence, and Ernest Sosa. *Epistemic Justification: Internalism vs. Externalism, Foundations vs. Virtues.* Oxford: Blackwell Publishing, 2003.

Brown, Lee M. "Compassion and Societal Well-Being." *Pacific Philosophical Quarterly* 77 (1996): 216–224.

Calhoun, Cheshire. "Family's Outlaws: Rethinking the Connections between Feminism, Marriage, and the Family." In *Feminism and Families,* ed. Hilde Lindemann Nelson. New York: Routledge, 1997.

———. "Responsibility and Reproach." *Ethics* 99 (January 1989): 389–406.

Chan, Wing-tsit. *A Source Book in Chinese Philosophy.* Princeton, NJ: Princeton University Press, 1963.

Clarke, J. J. *The Tao of the West: Western Transformations of Taoist Thought.* London: Routledge, 2000.

Clifford, William K. *Lectures and Essays,* vol. 2. London: Macmillan, 1897.

Code, Lorraine. *Epistemic Responsibility.* Hanover, NH: University Press of New England for Brown University Press, 1987.

———. "Toward a 'Responsibilist' Epistemology." *Philosophy and Phenomenological Research* 45 (September 1984): 29–50.

Cole, Eve Browning. *Philosophy and Feminist Criticism: An Introduction.* New York: Paragon Press, 1993.

Coleman, Diane. "The Consequences of Legalized Assisted Suicide and Euthanasia," May 25, 2006. http://judiciary.senate.gov/testimony.cfm?id=1916&wit_id=5379.

———. "Testimony before the Subcommittee on Criminal Justice, Drug Policy and Human Resources of the Committee on Government Reform of the U.S. House of Representatives," April 19, 2005. http://www.notdeadyet.org/docs/ColemanCongTestmy041905.html.

Coleman, Diane, and Carol Gill. "The Disability Rights Opposition to Physician-Assisted Suicide." www.notdeadyet.org/house1a.html.

Confucius. *The Analects of Confucius: A Philosophical Translation.* Trans. Roger T. Ames and Henry Rosemont Jr. New York: Ballantine Books, 1998.

———. *The Analects (Lun Yü).* Trans. D. C. Lau. New York: Penguin Classics, 1979.

Cook, Francis H. "Dōgen's View of Authentic Selfhood and Its Socio-ethical Implications." In *Dōgen Studies,* ed. William R. LaFleur. Honolulu: University of Hawai'i Press, 1985.

Creel, Herrlee. *What Is Taoism, and Other Studies in Chinese Cultural History.* Chicago: University of Chicago Press, 1970.

Crisp, Roger, ed. *How Should One Live?* Oxford: Clarendon Press, 1996.

Dalmiya, Vrinda. "Why Should a Knower Care?" *Hypatia* 17, no. 1 (winter 2002): 34–52.

Danto, Arthur C. *Mysticism and Morality: Oriental Thought and Philosophy.* Harmondsworth, UK: Penguin, 1976.

Dawkins, Richard. *The Selfish Gene.* Oxford: Oxford University Press, 1976 (30th anniversary ed., 2006).

DeBary, William Theodore, and Tu Weiming, eds. *Confucianism and Human Rights.* New York: Columbia University Press, 1998.

Deutsch, Eliot. *Personhood, Creativity and Freedom.* Honolulu: University of Hawai'i Press, 1982.

Dickinson, G. Lowe. *An Essay on the Civilizations of India, China, and Japan.* Garden City, NY: Doubleday, Page and Company, 1915.

Dōgen Kigen. *Dōgen's Pure Standards for the Zen Community.* Trans. Taigen Daniel Leighton and Shohaku Okumura. Albany: State University of New York Press, 1996.

———. *Dōgen Zenji Zenshū.* Tokyo: Shunjūsha, 1988–1993.

———. "Genjō Kōan: Realization of Truth: A Portion of the Shōbōgenzō, by Dōgen Zenji." Trans. Tanahashi Kazuaki and Robert Aitken. *Diamond Sangha* 5, no. 3 (1965): 1–4.

———. *Master Dōgen's Shōbōgenzō,* vols. 1–4. Trans. Gudo Nishijima and Chodo Cross. London: Windbell Publications, 1996.

———. *Moon in a Dewdrop: Writings of Zen Master Dōgen.* Ed. Kazuaki Tanahashi. New York: North Point Press, 1985.

———. *Shikantaza: An Introduction to Zazen.* Trans. Shōhaku Okumura. Kyoto: Kyoto Sōtō Zen Center, 1985.

———. *Shōbōgenzō: Zen Essays by Dōgen.* Trans. Thomas Cleary. Honolulu: University of Hawai'i Press, 1986.

———. "Shōbōgenzō genjōkōan." Trans. Abe Masao and Norman Waddell. *Eastern Buddhist* 5, no. 2 (October 1972): 129–140.

Duclos, Nitya. "Some Complicating Thoughts on Same Sex Marriage." *Law & Sexuality* 1 (1991): 31–61.

Eliade, Mircea, ed. *The Encyclopedia of Religion,* vols. 2, 8, 9. New York: Macmillan, 1987.

Eze, Emmanuel. "The Color of Reason: The Idea of 'Race' in Kant's Anthropology." In *Anthropology and the German Enlightenment,* ed. Katherine Faull. Lewisburg, PA: Bucknell University Press, 1995.

Feinberg, Joel. *Reason and Responsibility.* Belmont, CA: Wadsworth, 1978.

Fingarette, Herbert. "Following the 'One Thread' of the *Analects.*" *Journal of the American Academy of Religion Thematic Issue S* (September 1980): 373–405.

———. "The Music of Humanity in the Conversations of Confucius." *Journal of Chinese Philosophy* 10 (1983).

Fisher, Berenice, and Joan C. Tronto. "Toward a Feminist Theory of Care." In *Circles of Care: Work and Identity in Women's Lives,* eds. Emily Abel and Margaret Nelson. Albany: State University of New York Press, 1991.

Foot, Philippa. "Euthanasia." *Philosophy and Public Affairs* 9 no. 2, (1977): 85–112.

Franklin, Julian H. *Animal Rights and Moral Philosophy.* New York: Columbia University Press, 2005.

Goleman, Daniel. *Emotional Intelligence.* New York: Bantam Books, 1995.

Graham, A. C. "The Background of the Mencian Theory." *Tsing Hua Journal of Chinese Studies* n.s. 6, 1–2 (1967): 215–274.

———. *Two Chinese Philosophers: Ch'eng Ming-tao and Ch'eng Yi-chu'an.* London: Lund Humphries, 1958.

Hall, David L., and Roger T. Ames. *Thinking Through Confucius.* Albany: State University of New York Press, 1987.

Hansen, Chad. "Individualism in Chinese Thought." In *Individualism and Holism: Studies in Confucian and Taoist Values,* ed. Donald Munro. Ann Arbor: University of Michigan Press, 1985.

Harris, Leonard. "Agency and the Concept of the Underclass." In Bill E. Lawson, *The Underclass Question.* Philadelphia: Temple University Press, 1992.

Harrison, E. J. *The Fighting Spirit of Japan.* London: W. Foulsham and Company, 1955.

Hegel, Georg Wilhelm Friedrich. *Philosophy of History.* Trans. J. Sibree. New York: Dover, 1956.

Heschel, Abraham J. *Between God and Man.* Ed. F. A. Rothschild. New York: Free Press, 1959.

Hobbes, Thomas. "Human Nature." Part 1 of Hobbes, *The Elements of Law Natural and Politic,* ed. J. C. A. Gaskin. Oxford: Oxford University Press, 1994.

Hopkins, Jeffrey. *Cultivating Compassion: A Buddhist Perspective.* New York: Broadway Books, 2001.

Hume, David. *A Treatise of Human Nature.* Oxford: Oxford University Press, 1960.

Hursthouse, Rosalind. "Normative Virtue Ethics." In *Virtue Ethics,* ed. Stephen Darwall. Oxford: Blackwell Publishing, 2003.

Ivanhoe, Philip J. *Ethics in the Confucian Tradition: The Thought of Mencius and Wang Yang-ming.* Atlanta: Scholars Press, 1990.

Jaffe, Paul, ed. "Shōbōgenzō Genjō Kōan: An Analytic Study." Unpublished compilation.

Jaggar, Allison M. "Caring as a Feminist Practice." In *Justice and Care: Essential Readings in Feminist Ethics,* ed. Virginia Held. Boulder, CO: Westview, 1995.

Kalupahana, David J. *A History of Buddhist Philosophy: Continuities and Discontinuities.* Honolulu: University of Hawai'i Press, 1992.

Kant, Immanuel. *Grounding for the Metaphysics of Morals* and *On a Supposed Right to Lie because of Philanthropic Concerns.* Trans. James W. Ellington. Indianapolis: Hackett Publishing, 1993.

———. *The Metaphysics of Morals.* Ed. Mary Gregor. Cambridge, UK: Cambridge University Press, 1996.

———. *Observations on the Feeling of the Beautiful and Sublime.* Trans. John T. Goldthwait. Berkeley: University of California Press, 1960.

———. "On the Different Races of Humankind" ("Von den Verschiedenen Rassen der Menschen"). Trans. Jon Mark Mikkelsen. Indianapolis: Hackett Publishing, 1999.

Kasulis, Thomas P. *Intimacy or Integrity: Philosophy and Cultural Difference.* Honolulu: University of Hawai'i Press, 2002.

———. *Zen Action: Zen Person.* Honolulu: University of Hawai'i Press, 1989.

Kelly, Gerald, S. J. *Medico-Moral Problems.* St. Louis: Catholic Hospital Association, 1958.

Kempis, Thomas à. *The Imitation of Christ.* Trans. L. Sherley-Price. Harmondsworth, UK: Penguin Books, 1952.

Kennett, Roshi Jiyu. *Zen Is Eternal Life.* Emeryville, CA: Dharma Publishing, 1976.

Kenny, Anthony. *Action, Emotion and Will.* London: Routledge and Kegan Paul, 1963.

Kevorkian, Jack. *Prescription: Medicide: The Goodness of Planned Death.* Buffalo, NY: Prometheus Books, 1991

Kim, Hee-Jin. *Dōgen Kigen: Mystical Realist.* Tucson: University of Arizona Press, 1975 (revised ed. 1987).

———. *Flowers of Emptiness: Selections from Dōgen's Shōbōgenzō.* Lewiston, NY: Edwin Mellen Press, 1985.

King, Ambrose Y. C. "The Individual and Group in Confucianism: A Relational

Perspective." In *Individualism and Holism: Studies in Confucian and Daoist Values,* ed. Donald Munro. Ann Arbor: University of Michigan Press, 1985.

King, Winston L. *Death Was His Kōan: The Samurai-Zen of Suzuki Shōsan.* Berkeley: Asian Humanities Press, 1986.

Kirkland, Russell. "'Responsible Non-Action' in a Natural World: Perspectives from the *Neiye, Zhuangzi, and Daode jing.*" In *Daoism and Ecology: Ways within a Cosmic Landscape,* eds. N. J. Giradot, James Miller, and Liu Xiaogan. Cambridge: Harvard University Press, 2001.

Konstan, David. "Altruism." www.apapclassics.org/Publications/PresTalks/KONSTAN/ html.

———. "Ancient Pity." www.brown.edu/Faculty/Faculty_Governance/facbulletin/98FacBulHtml/konstan.html.

———. *Friendship in the Classical World.* Cambridge, UK: Cambridge University Press, 1997.

———. "Pity and Self-Pity." http://scholar.lib.vt.edu/ejournals/ElAnt/V5N2/konstan.html.

———. *Pity Transformed.* London: Duckworth, 2001.

Kroeger-Mappes, Joy. "The Ethic of Care vis-à-vis the Ethic of Rights: A Problem for Contemporary Moral Theory." *Hypatia* 9, no. 3 (summer 1994): 108–131.

Laozi. *Daodejing: "Making This Life Significant:" A Philosophical Translation.* Trans. Roger T. Ames and David L. Hall. New York: Ballantine Books, 2003.

———(Lao Tzu). *Tao Te Ching.* Trans. D. C. Lau. London: Penguin Books, 1963.

———(Lao-tzu). *Te-Tao Ching.* Trans. Robert G. Henricks. New York: Ballantine Books, 1989.

Lau, D. C. "Theories of Human Nature in Mencius and Shyuntzyy." *Bulletin of the School of Oriental and African Studies* 15 (1953): 541–565.

Legge, James, trans. *The Texts of Taoism: The Tao Te Ching and the Writings of Chuang-tzŭ.* New York: Julian Press, 1959.

Lewis, C. S. *The Four Loves.* London: Geoffrey Bles, 1960.

MacIntyre, Alasdair. *After Virtue.* Notre Dame, IN: University of Notre Dame Press, 1981.

———. *Dependent Rational Animals.* Chicago: Carus Publishing, 1999.

Maezumi Taizan Roshi and Francis Dojun Cook, revisers. *Shōbōgenzō Genjō Kōan.* Los Angeles: Zen Center of Los Angeles, 1977.

Maraldo, John C. "The Practice of Body-Mind: Dōgen's *Shinjingakudō* and Comparative Philosophy." In *Dōgen Studies,* ed. William R. LaFleur. Honolulu: University of Hawai'i Press, 1985.

Markowitz, Sally. "Feminism and Abortion." *Social Theory and Practice* 16 (spring 1990): 1–17.

Masunaga Reihō, trans. *A Primer of Sōtō Zen: A Translation of Dōgen's* Shōbōgenzō Zuimonki. Honolulu: University of Hawai'i Press, 1971.

May, Larry. *Sharing Responsibility.* Chicago: University of Chicago Press, 1992.

McCain, John, with Mark Salter. *Why Courage Matters: The Way to a Braver Life.* New York: Random House, 2004.

McDonald, Julie M. "Diverse Moral Perspectives and Moral Relativism." In *Contemporary Moral Issues in a Diverse Society,* ed. Julie M. McDonald. Belmont, CA: Wadsworth, 1998.

McKeon, Richard, ed. *The Basic Works of Aristotle.* New York: Random House, 1941.

Melzack, Ronald. *The Challenge of Pain.* New York: Basic Books, 1973.

———. *The Puzzle of Pain.* New York: Basic Books, 1973.

Mencius. *Mencius.* Trans. D. C. Lau. New York: Penguin Classics, 1970.

Mercer, Philip. *Sympathy and Ethics: A Study of the Relationship between Sympathy and Morality with Special Reference to Hume's* Treatise. Oxford: Clarendon Press, 1972.

Mikkelson, Douglas K. "Who Is Arguing about the Cat? Moral Action and Enlightenment in Dōgen." *Philosophy East and West* 47 no. 3, University of Hawai'i Press, 1997.

Miller, Mark Crispin. *The Bush Dyslexicon: Observations on a National Disorder.* New York: W. W. Norton & Co., 2001.

Mills, Charles W. *The Racial Contract.* Ithaca, NY: Cornell University Press, 1997.

———. "White Being Black Being: Metaphysics of Race." In Jeff Donaldson et al., *Kerry James Marshall: One True Thing: Meditations on Black Aesthetics.* Chicago: Museum of Contemporary Art, 2003.

Mishima Yukio. "Patriotism." Trans. Geoffrey W. Sargent. In Mishima Yukio, *Death in Midsummer and Other Stories.* New York: New Directions, 1966.

Nāgārjuna. *Mūlamadhyamakakārikā.* Trans. Kenneth K. Inada. Tokyo: Hokuseido Press, 1970.

Nagel, Thomas. "What Is It Like to Be a Bat?" *Philosophical Review* 83, no. 3 (October 1974): 435–450.

Nakamura Hajime. *Jihi.* Kyoto: Heirakuji-shoten, 1956.

Needham, Joseph. *Science and Civilisation in China,* vol. 2. Cambridge, UK: Cambridge University Press, 1954.

Nietzsche, Friedrich. *Thus Spoke Zarathustra.* Trans. Walter Kaufmann. New York: Penguin Books, 1978.

Nivison, David S. "Golden Rule Arguments in Chinese Moral Philosophy." In *The Ways of Confucianism: Investigations in Chinese Philosophy,* ed. David S. Nivison and Bryan W. Van Norden. La Salle, IL: Open Court Press, 1996.

———. "Unweaving the 'One Thread' of *Analects* 4:15." In *The Ways of Confucianism: Investigations in Chinese Philosophy,* ed. David S. Nivison and Bryan W. Van Norden. La Salle, IL: Open Court Press, 1996.

Noddings, Nel. *Caring: A Feminine Approach to Ethics and Moral Education.* Berkeley: University of California Press, 1984.

Nozick, Robert. *Anarchy, State and Utopia.* New York: Basic Books, 1974.

Nussbaum, Martha C. "Compassion and Terror." In *Terrorism and International Justice,* ed. James P. Sterba. Oxford: Oxford University Press, 2003.

———. *Poetic Justice.* Boston: Beacon Press, 1995.

———. *Upheavals of Thought: The Intelligence of Emotions.* Cambridge, UK: Cambridge University Press, 2001.

———. "Virtue Ethics: A Misleading Category?" *Journal of Ethics* 3 (1999): 163–201.

Nygren, Anders. *Agape and Eros.* Philadelphia: Westminster Press, 1953.

Odin, Steve. *The Social Self in Zen and American Pragmatism.* Albany: State University of New York Press, 1996.

O'Neill, Onora. *Towards Justice and Virtue.* New York: Cambridge University Press, 1996.

Parfit, Derek. "Divided Minds and the Nature of Persons." In *Thoughts on Intelligence, Identity, and Consciousness,* eds. Colin Blakemore and Susan Greenfield. Oxford: Basil Blackwell, 1987.

———. "Personal Identity." *Philosophical Review* 80, no. 1 (January 1971): 3–27.

Parkes, Graham. *Composing the Soul: Reaches of Nietzsche's Psychology.* Chicago: University of Chicago Press, 1991.

———. "Death and Detachment: Montaigne, Zen, Heidegger and the Rest." In *Death and Philosophy,* eds. Jeff Malpas and Robert C. Solomon. London: Routledge, 1999.

———. "Voices of Mountains, Trees, and Rivers: Kūkai, Dōgen, and a Deeper Ecology." In *Buddhism and Ecology: The Interconnection of Dharma and Deeds,* eds. Mary Evelyn Tucker and Duncan Ryūken Williams. Cambridge, MA: Harvard University Press, 1997.

Pateman, Carol. *The Sexual Contract.* Stanford, CA: Stanford University Press, 1988.

Plato. "Apology." Trans. G. M. A. Grube. In *Readings in Ancient Greek Philosophy from Thales to Aristotle,* eds. S. Marc Cohen et al. Indianapolis: Hackett Publishing, 1995.

———. *The Symposium.* Trans. Walter Hamilton. Harmondsworth, UK: Penguin Books, 1974.

Post, Stephen G. *A Theory of Agape: On the Meaning of Christian Love*. London: Associated University Presses, 1990.

Prejean, Helen, C.S.J. *Dead Man Walking: An Eyewitness Account of the Death Penalty in the United States*. New York: Fount, 1993.

——. *The Death of Innocents: An Eyewitness Account of Wrongful Executions*. New York: Random House, 2004.

Rachels, James. "Active and Passive Euthanasia." *New England Journal of Medicine* 292: 78–80.

——. *The Elements of Moral Philosophy*. New York: Random House, 1986.

Rahula, Walpola Sri. *What the Buddha Taught*. New York: Grove Press, 1974.

Ramsey, Paul. *The Patient as Person*. New Haven, CT: Yale University Press, 1970.

Ratti, Oscar, and Adele Westbrook. *Secrets of the Samurai: The Martial Arts of Feudal Japan*. Rutland, VT: Charles E. Tuttle, 1973.

Reisert, Joseph R. *Jean-Jacques Rousseau: A Friend of Virtue*. Ithaca, NY: Cornell University Press, 2003.

Rilke, Rainer Maria. *The Selected Poetry of Rainer Maria Rilke*. New York: Vintage, 1984.

Roberts, Rodney C. *Injustice and Rectification*. New York: Peter Lang, 2003.

Rousseau, Jean-Jacques. *Emile*. Trans. Allan Bloom. New York: Basic Books, 1979.

——. *The Social Contract and Discourses*. Trans. G. D. H. Cole. London: J. M. Dent and Sons; New York: E. P. Dutton, 1913.

Śāntideva. *The Bodhicaryāvatāra*. Trans. Kate Crosby and Andrew Skilton. Oxford: Oxford University Press, 1995.

Scheler, Max. *The Nature of Sympathy*. Trans. Peter Heath. Hamden, CT: Archon Books, 1970.

——. *Zur Phänomenologie und Theorie der Sympathiegefühle und von Liebe und Hass, mit einem Anhang über den Grund zur Annahme der Existenz des fremden Ich*. Halle, Germany: Verlag von Max Niemeyer, 1913.

Schroeder, John W. *Skillful Means: The Heart of Buddhist Compassion*. Honolulu: University of Hawaiʻi Press, 2001.

Sevenhuisjen, Selma. *Citizenship and the Ethics of Care: Feminist Considerations on Justice, Morality and Politics*. Trans. Liz Savage. London: Routledge, 1998.

Sidgwick, Henry. *The Methods of Ethics*, 7th ed. Chicago: University of Chicago Press, 1907.

Singer, Peter. *The Expanding Circle: Ethics and Sociobiology*. New York: Farrar, Straus & Giroux, 1981.

——. "Famine, Affluence, and Morality." *Philosophy and Public Affairs* 1, no. 3 (1972): 229–243.

Slote, Michael. "Agent-Based Virtue Ethics." *Midwest Studies in Philosophy* 20 (1995): 83–101.

———. *From Morality to Virtue.* New York: Oxford University Press, 1992.

Snow, Nancy. "Compassion." *American Philosophical Quarterly* 28, no. 3 (July 1991): 195–205.

Solomon, Robert C. *A Passion for Justice.* Reading, MA: Addison-Wesley, 1990.

Spinoza, Baruch. *Ethics.* Trans. G. H. R. Parkinson. Oxford: Oxford University Press, 2000.

Sullivan, Andrew. *Virtually Normal: An Argument about Homosexuality.* New York: Alfred A. Knopf, 1995.

Sullivan, Thomas D. "Active and Passive Euthanasia: An Impertinent Distinction?" *Human Life Review* 3, no. 3 (1977): 40–46.

Suzuki Daisetz T. *Zen and Japanese Culture.* Princeton, NJ: Princeton University Press, 1959.

Suzuki Shōsan. *Warrior of Zen: The Diamond-hard Wisdom Mind of Suzuki Shōsan.* Trans. and ed. Arthur Braverman. New York: Kodansha International, 1994.

Tachibana, S. *The Ethics of Buddhism.* London: Curzon Press, 1975.

Thomas, Laurence Mordekhai. *Vessels of Evil: American Slavery and the Holocaust.* Philadelphia: Temple University Press, 1993.

Trivers, Robert. "The Evolution of Reciprocal Altruism." *Quarterly Review of Biology* 46 (1971): 35–57.

Tronto, Joan C. *Moral Boundaries: A Political Argument for an Ethic of Care.* New York: Routledge, 1993.

Van den Haag, Ernest. "In Defense of the Death Penalty: A Practical and Moral Analysis." *Criminal Law Bulletin* 14, no. 1 (1978): 51–68.

Van Norden, Bryan W., ed. *Confucius and the Analects.* Oxford: Oxford University Press, 2002.

Vonnegut, Kurt. "Who Am I This Time?" In Kurt Vonnegut, *Welcome to the Monkey House.* New York: Delta, 1998: 15–29.

Warren, Karen J. *Ecofeminist Philosophy: A Western Perspective on What It Is and Why It Matters.* Lanham, MD: Rowman & Littlefield, 2000.

Watson, Burton, trans. *Basic Writings of Mo Tzu, Hsün Tzu, and Han Fei Tzu.* New York: Columbia University Press, 1964.

Watsuji Tetsurō. "The Significance of Ethics as the Study of Man." Trans. David A. Dilworth. *Monumenta Nipponica: Studies in Japanese Culture* 26, no. 3–4 (fall 1971): 395–413.

———. *Watsuji Tetsurō's Rinrigaku.* Trans. Seisaku Yamamoto and Robert Carter. Albany: State University of New York Press, 1996.

———. *Watsuji Tetsurō Zenshū*. Tokyo: Iwanami Shoten, 1984.

Welch, Holmes. *Taoism: The Parting of the Way,* 2nd ed. Boston: Beacon Press, 1965.

Wilson, Edward O. *Sociobiology: The New Synthesis.* Cambridge, MA: Belknap Press of Harvard University Press, 2000.

Yamamoto Tsunetomo. *Hagakure: The Book of the Samurai.* Trans. William Scott Wilson. Tokyo: Kodansha International, 1986.

Zagzebski, Linda Trinkhaus. *Virtues of the Mind: An Inquiry into the Nature of Virtue and the Ethical Foundations of Knowledge.* New York: Cambridge University Press, 1996.

Zhu Xi. *Focusing the Familiar: A Translation and Philosophical Translation of the Zhongyong.* Trans. Roger T. Ames and David L. Hall. Honolulu: University of Hawai'i Press, 2001.

Zhuangzi (Chuang-tzŭ). *Chuang-tzŭ: The Inner Chapters.* Trans. A. C. Graham. Indianapolis: Hackett Publishing, 2001.

abortion, xiii–xiv, xvii, 122–123, 126, 152–154, 179, 180
agapē. See divine love
altruism, 15, 21, 28, 57, 71, 75, 91, 97, 139–143
American Medical Association, 168, 177–178
Ames, Roger T., 63–80
anātman. See non-ego
animals, xiv, 7, 9, 74, 105, 116, 171, 196n20, 201n4; compassion for, 47, 100–101, 179; and pity, 12, 30
Anscombe, Elizabeth, 125, 126, 179
applied ethics, xvi–xvii, 152–154, 166, 168, 179–181
Arendt, Hannah, 18, 20
Aristotle, xii–xv, 10–15, 43–44, 47, 82–84, 90, 113–119, 123–124, 130, 132; on friendship (*philia*), 13–15, 47; on justice, 15, 173, 186n56; on pity (*eleos*), xiii, 10–13, 40, 44, 47
attentiveness. *See* moment of attentiveness
authoritative conduct (*ren*), 63–64, 68, 71–73, 84
autocompasión. See compassion: for oneself

Baier, Annette, 23–26
Baron, Marcia, 122–123
Bentham, Jeremy, xii–xiii, 100, 196n20
Bloom, Allan, 27–30
Blum, Lawrence A., 37, 39, 42

Brown, Lee M., 10–11, 37, 41–44
Buddha-nature, 100. *See also* impermanence-Buddha-nature
Buddhism, xii–xvi, 16–17, 50–61, 81–86, 143–150, 165, 181, 196n19; and attentiveness, 90–93; early Indian, xvi, 51–57, 115, 120, 139; Japanese, 51–52, 144; and justice, 38–39; on *karuṇā*, 8–9, 75, 88, 115, 117, 153; Mahāyāna, 50, 52–53, 82, 190n36; on *prajñā*, 8–9, 75, 88, 115, 117, 120–121, 153; on self and no-self, 23, 50–61 *passim*, 75, 83–85, 107–110, 113, 130; Zen, xvi, 57–61, 90, 109, 113, 115, 150
Bush, George W., 163–164

capital punishment, xvi, 154–166, 180
care ethics, xvii, 85, 146–150, 180, 183n1, 194–195n2, 199n2, 202n7; and epistemology, 121–122
ceyin. See compassion: *ceyin*
children, xiv, 13–14, 39, 66, 84, 87, 98–99, 116, 136, 176; and capital punishment, 159–161, 163–164; and compassion, 27, 30–31, 101, 106; and Down syndrome, 169–170; and fairness, 144–145; in the *Mencius*, 62
Code, Lorraine, 120–121
Coleman, Diane, 174–177
commiseration, xi–xii, 5–6, 11, 51, 61, 111
compassion: in Buddhism, xii, xvi, 16–17, 50–61, 75, 81–91, 96, 107–115, 127, 130, 139; *ceyin*, 62–63; and Christian

theology, xii–xiii, 15–17, 30, 39, 49; *ci*,
    73–74, 77; and commiseration, xi, 6,
    11, 61, 111; in Confucianism, xv–xvi,
    61–63, 68, 71–73, 81, 88, 130–131, 180;
    in Daoism, xv–xvi, 61, 73–82, 85–88,
    91, 105, 107, 110, 117, 130–131; Dōgen
    on, 50, 57–61, 83, 110, 113; and impre-
    cision, xiii, xiv, 124–126, 154, 178; *jihi*,
    51–52, 61, 83, 87, 89, 130; Kant on, xii,
    xiii, xv, 111, 112; *karunā*, 8–9, 51–53,
    75, 88–89, 115, 120–121, 127, 130, 153;
    mettā, 51–52, 61, 89, 115, 127, 130;
    Nietzsche on, xiii, 35–36; for oneself
    (*autocompasión*), 98; *pitié*, 26–27,
    31–32, 48; Rousseau on, 26–32, 48,
    116, 151–152; Śāntideva on, 50–57,
    59, 61; Scheler on, 3, 5, 8–9, 39, 47;
    Spinoza on, xiii, xv, 1, 38, 91, 110–112;
    and utilitarianism, xiii, 1, 88–89,
    112–113, 126–129
concentric ring model of self, 97–110
Confucianism, 61–88 *passim*, 94–95,
    102–104, 110, 121–122, 124, 143–150,
    180–181; compassion in, xv–xvi, 50,
    61–73 *passim*, 81–83, 130–131, 180; on
    selfhood, 50, 61, 64–71, 83–85, 148
Cook, Francis H., 59–60, 190n36
courage, 73, 116–117

Dalmiya, Vrinda, 120–121, 183n1
Daoism, xv–xvi, 61, 73–88, 91, 93, 104–
    107, 110, 117–119, 130–131, 145–146
deference (*shu*), 61–73, 83, 145
Descartes, Rene, 23, 85, 152
Dewey, John, 82, 194
disability rights movement, 174–178
divine love (*agapē*), 15–21, 49, 185n46
Dōgen, 50, 57–61, 83, 85, 90, 100, 108–
    110, 113, 146, 149–150
dynamics of *shu*, 61–73

ecosystems, 81, 101, 104–107
egoism, 15, 21, 30, 44, 57, 71, 75, 97,
    139–141
eight conditions of compassion, 49,
    129–130
eleos. See pity: Aristole on
empathy, xi, 1, 3–4, 11, 42, 95
eudaimonia. See living well
euthanasia. *See* physician-assisted
    suicide

fellow-feeling, 3–9, 16, 47, 63, 87
feminism, 85, 92, 120–122, 143–144,
    147, 150, 153–154, 175–176, 178,
    181
Fingarette, Herbert, 69, 191n44
Foot, Philippa, 171–174
four sprouts (*tuan*), 62, 85, 111
friendship (*philia*), 13–15, 47, 117,
    130

Gill, Carol, 174–177
Gilligan, Carol, 82, 201n21
Goleman, Daniel, 92–93
Graham, A.C., 76, 78, 81, 118–119

Hall, David L., 63–65, 67–68, 71,
    73–74, 79–80
Hobbes, Thomas, 27, 39, 41–43
homophobia, 43, 70–71, 97, 99–100,
    144–145, 153
Hume, David, xv, 21–28, 39, 48, 51, 55,
    74, 89, 92
Hursthouse, Rosalind, 123–124, 126,
    197n36

impartiality, xiii, 43, 92, 94–95, 132–139,
    144, 149–150
impermanence-Buddha-nature, 58–60,
    108

jihi. *See* compassion: *jihi*

justice, xiii–xv, xvii, 42–43, 95, 106, 123, 134–139, 144, 164, 199n2; Aristotle on, 15, 173, 186n56; Kant on, 134; Mills on, 138–139; Rawls on, xvii, 138–139, 146, 173; Rousseau on, 31–32, 48, 186n56, 201n4; Solomon on, 37–39, 135

karunā. *See* compassion: *karunā*

Kasulis, Thomas P., 58, 69–70, 189n24

Kevorkian, Jack, 174–176

Kim, Hee-Jin, 58, 197n28

Kirkland, Russell, 74, 76, 80

Laozi, 61, 104, 106

Lau, D. C., 62–64, 73

living well (*eudaimonia*), 13, 83–84

love, 2, 4, 6–10, 16, 62, 72–74, 103, 137, 173. *See also* divine love

Mead, George Herbert, 82, 194n99

Mencius, 50, 61–63, 66, 81, 102, 111

mettā. *See* compassion: *mettā*

Mill, John Stuart, xii–xiii

Mills, Charles W., 138–139, 144, 200n16

misogyny, 97, 99–100, 143–145, 150, 175–176, 178

moment of attentiveness, 16, 88, 90–96, 107, 146–149, 165

moment of will, 88, 95–97, 149, 165

muga. *See* non-ego

Nāgārjuna, 107

Nakamura Hajime, 51–52

Nietzsche, Friedrich, xiii, xv, 2, 15, 27, 32–37, 40, 47–48, 82–83, 89; on compassion, xiii, 35–36; on pity, xiii, 15, 27, 32–35, 40, 47–48

Noddings, Nel, 146–147

noncoercive action (*wu wei*), 76–77, 81, 107

non-ego (*anātman, muga*), 50, 55, 56, 59–61, 75, 108–109, 113, 192n71

no-self. *See* non-ego

Nussbaum, Martha C., xv, 37, 44–46, 49, 122, 132

Nygren, Anders, 17–20

O'Neill, Onora, 106–107

partiality, 43, 94–95, 132, 133–139, 144, 149

perspectivalism, 81, 139, 143

Pettit, Philip, 122–123, 127–128

philia. *See* friendship

physician-assisted suicide, xiv–xv, 154, 166–178, 180

pitié. *See* compassion: *pitié*

pity, xiii, 1, 8–13, 26–49 *passim*, 78, 83, 88, 95–96; Aristotle on, xiii, 10–13, 16, 27, 44, 47; Nietzsche on, xiii, 1, 15, 27, 32–36, 47–48, 78; Rousseau on, 26–31; Scheler on, 3, 5, 8–9

Plato, 82

Prejean, Helen, 154–166

Rachels, James, 76, 122, 167–171, 173–174

racism, 43, 97, 99–100, 102, 132, 138–139, 144–146

Rawls, John, 82, 93–94, 133–136, 138, 144, 199n4; on impartiality, 133–134, 136, 149; on justice, xvii, 138–139, 146, 173

ren. *See* authoritative conduct

Rosemont, Henry, 69, 71, 80

Rousseau, Jean Jacques, xv, 26–32, 48, 89, 116, 151, 152, 197n35, 201n4

Śāntideva, 23, 50–57, 59–61, 85, 154
Scheler, Max, 2–11, 16, 39, 47, 51, 63, 82,
        140–141
Schiavo, Terri, xiv, 176
Schopenhauer 2, 7–9
self-love, 21, 27–29, 35, 49, 151
shu. See deference
Sidgwick, Henry, 87–88, 99, 101
Singer, Peter, 27, 141, 196n26, 199n3
Slote, Michael, 123, 125, 128
Smith, Adam, xiii, 2
Snow, Nancy E., 37, 39–42, 44, 46, 49,
        187n76
Solomon, Robert C., xv, 37–39, 42,
        45–46, 49, 135, 203n20
Sosa, Ernest, 121, 193n97
Spinoza, Baruch, xiii, xv, 1, 38, 91,
        110–112
Sullivan, Thomas D., 168–171, 173, 174,
        178
Suzuki Shunryu, 57–58
sympathy, xiii, 1–10, 37–38, 48, 51, 74,
        83, 87–88, 95; Hume on, xiii, 3, 16,
        21–27, 48, 51, 74; Scheler on, 2–10, 51

Tachibana, S., 51, 183n5
Tronto, Joan, 147
tuan. See four sprouts

utilitarianism, xii, xv, xvii, 21–22,
        48, 84, 122–129, 166, 173, 178; and
        compassion, 1, 38, 88–89, 112–113,
        127–129; and respect for persons, 140,
        142–143

Warren, Karen J., 92–93
Watsuji Tetsurō, 84–85, 104–105, 142–
        143, 147–148, 196n27, 200n15
Welch, Holmes, 76–77
will. *See* moment of will
Wilson, Edwin O., 140–141
wu wei. See noncoercive action

Xunzi, 62

Zagzebski, Linda Trinkhaus, 120–121
Zen Buddhism. *See* Buddhism: Zen
Zhuangzhi, 50, 61, 73–81, 104, 106, 118,
        119, 141

Steve Bein did his graduate studies in comparative philosophy at the University of Hawai'i at Mānoa and at Ōbirin University in Tokyo, receiving his doctorate in 2005. His *Purifying Zen* was the first English translation of Watsuji Tetsurō's landmark study of Dōgen, *Shamon Dōgen*. He teaches courses in ethics, Asian philosophy, and comparative philosophy at Rochester Community and Technical College in Rochester, Minnesota.

SOCIETY FOR ASIAN AND COMPARATIVE PHILOSOPHY
MONOGRAPH SERIES | John W. Schroeder, Editor

No. 1. *The Sage and Society: The Life and Thought of Ho Hsin-Yin,* by Ronald Dimberg, 1974.

No. 2. *Studies in Comparative Aesthetics,* by Eliot Deutsch, 1975.

No. 3. *Centrality and Commonality: An Essay on* Chung-Yung, by Tu Wei-Ming, 1976.

No. 4. *Discourse on the Natural Theology of the Chinese,* by Gottfried W. Leibniz, translated with an introduction, notes, and commentary by Henry Rosemont Jr., and Daniel J. Cook, 1977.

No. 5. *The Logic of Gotama,* by Kisor Kumar Chakrabarti, 1978.

No. 6. *Commentary on the* Lao Tzu *by Wang Pi,* translated by Ariane Rump, introduction by Wing-tsit Chan, 1979.

No. 7. *Han Fei Tzu's Political Theory,* by Wang Hsiao-po and Leo S. Chang, 1986.

No. 8. *The Māṇḍūkya Upaniṣad and the Āgama Śāstra: An Investigation into the Meaning of the Vedanta,* by Thomas E. Wood, 1990.

No. 9. *Mind Only: A Philosophical and Doctrinal Analysis of the Vijñānavāda,* by Thomas E. Wood, 1991.

No. 10. *Accomplishing the Accomplished: The* Vedas *as a Source of Valid Knowledge in Sankara,* by Anantanand Rambachan, 1991.

No. 11. *Nāgārjunian Disputations: A Philosophical Journey through an Indian Looking-Glass,* by Thomas E. Wood, 1994.

No. 12. *Ch'en Liang on Public Interest and the Law,* by Hoyt Cleveland Tillman, 1994.

No. 13. *Definition and Induction: A Historical and Comparative Study,* by Kisor Kumar Chakrabarti, 1995.

No. 14. *Let the Cow Wander: Modeling the Metaphors in Veda and Vedanta,* by Michael W. Meyers, 1995.

No. 15. *The Four Political Treatises of the Yellow Emperor: Original Mawangdui Texts with Complete English Translations and an Introduction,* by Leo S. Chang and Yu Feng, 1998.

No. 16. *Perceptual Error: The Indian Theories,* by Srinivasa Rao, 1998.

No. 17. *Hindu Ethics: A Philosophical Study,* by Roy W. Perrett, 1998.

No. 18. *Skillful Means: The Heart of Buddhist Compassion,* by John W. Schroeder, 2001.

No. 19. *On the Epistemology of the Senses in Early Chinese Thought,* by Jane Geaney, 2002.

No. 20. *A Companion to Angus C. Graham's* Chuang Tzu: *The Inner Chapters,* by Harold D. Roth, 2003.

No. 21. *Contexts and Dialogue: Yogācāra Buddhism and Modern Psychology on the Subliminal Mind,* by Tao Jiang, 2006.

No. 22. *One and Many: A Comparative Study of Plato's Philosophy and Daoism Represented by Ge Hong,* by Ji Zhang, 2012.

No. 23. *Compassion and Moral Guidance,* by Steve Bein, 2013.

Manuscripts should be directed to John W. Schroeder, Department of Philosophy and Religious Studies, St. Mary's College, St. Mary's City, Maryland 20686.

Production Notes for Bein | COMPASSION AND MORAL GUIDANCE
Cover design by Mardee Melton
Interior design by April Leidig
Text in Garamond Premier Pro
Composition by Copperline Book Services, Inc.
Printing and binding by Integrated Book Technology Inc.
Printed on 60 lb. white offset, 435 ppi